Spanish Poetry

Poesía Española

A Dual-Language Anthology
16th–20th Centuries

Edited by
ANGEL FLORES

DOVER PUBLICATIONS, INC.
Mineola, New York

Bibliographical Note

This Dover edition, first published in 1998, is an unabridged but differently formated and slightly corrected republication of the work first published by Doubleday and Company, Inc., 1961, under the title *An Anthology of Spanish Poetry From Garcilaso to García Lorca*. The Editor's Note is new.

Library of Congress Cataloging-in-Publication Data

Spanish poetry = Poesía española : a dual-language anthology / edited by Angel Flores.
    p.   cm.
    Includes bibliographical references.
    ISBN 0-486-40171-5 (pbk.)
    1. Spanish poetry—Translations into English.   2. Spanish American poetry—Translations into English.   3. Spanish poetry.   4. Spanish American poetry.
I. Flores, Angel, 1900–   .
PQ6267.E2   1998
861.008—dc21   97-44224
                                              CIP

Manufactured in the United States of America
Dover Publications, Inc., 31 East 2nd Street, Mineola, N.Y. 11501

Editor's Note

This rich and varied selection of poetry written in the Spanish language during the sixteenth, seventeenth, nineteenth, and twentieth centuries features diverse themes, sensibilities, and styles, from the Golden Age in Spain through the Modernist period in that country and in Latin America. The work of the seventeen poets whose writings are included in this anthology reflects the social and political concerns of their times and places, as well as spiritual and sexual ardor. In the poetry of writers such as Rosalía de Castro, Antonio Machado, and Federico García Lorca, the landscapes, traditions, and people of Spanish regions as diverse as Galicia, Castile, and Andalusia are evoked.

In developing this anthology, the late Professor Angel Flores brought together a range of voices from Latin America with those of poets who lived within the borders of Spain. Miguel de Cuevara, a friar born in Nueva España (now Mexico) learned three Native American languages so he could introduce Christianity to those who did not understand Spanish. Sor Juana Inés de la Cruz escaped the prison of a seventeenth-century female's life by entering a convent, and wrote poetry that resonates with the feminist consciousness of three centuries later. Rubén Darío, revered as the creator of Modernism in Spanish poetry, left rural Nicaragua, the small "nation of poets," for Paris and the world, never finding serenity in his own life, and powerfully condemning in his work the U.S. "Colossus of the North" that subjected Latin America to rule by gunboats and bankers. Manuel González Prada, the social and political activist who for decades spoke and organized against the repressive forces of the clergy and the military in Peru, is represented by a sampling of his multifaceted work. Gabriela Mistral, self-educated provincial schoolteacher from Chile who became a leader in Mexico's education revolution and the idealistic voice of struggles for liberation throughout the world, speaks in her verses of love, pain, and the tenderness she feels for all children.

The translators, who include Samuel Beckett, Kate Flores, Muriel Kittel, Denise Levertov, and M. S. Merwin, have taken widely varying approaches to their art. In some cases the translation is quite literal and thus departs from the rhyme scheme and meter of the original. Other poems are presented in English as new creations in their own right, with an imagery that matches in the English language the beauty and precision of the original Spanish. Denise Levertov's interpretation of Machado's epic *La tierra de Alvargonzález* faithfully translates both the words and the rhythm of his language, as well as the at once peculiarly Spanish and universal realities of the rural family drama it depicts.

Preface to the First Edition

My anthologies devoted to the poetry of France (from Nerval to Valéry) and of Germany (from Hölderlin to Rilke) achieved a certain unity and poignancy by being confined to one century of verse writing. In both cases the emphasis fell upon the nineteenth century. However, in an anthology of Spanish verse this cannot be done, as the lyrical apogee of the Hispanic people is not limited to such a narrow span of time.

Because of factors peculiar to the cultural development of Hispanic civilization, one must look back to the Golden Age (sixteenth and seventeenth centuries) with its turbulent and fertile lyricism and, disregarding the eighteenth century, link it with the nineteenth-century stream, flowing directly into the exciting and varied contemporary scene.

Although the Golden Age of Spain is referred to as the Classical Age, during that period there is little of the rigidity and obedience to rules associated, let us say, with French classicism. Spain's Classical Age was essentially Romantic. It is no wonder that when romanticism blossomed in Germany in the early nineteenth century, writers of the Spanish Golden Age, notably Cervantes, Calderón, and the anonymous ballad writers, were admired and translated, serving as models and inspirers. Similarly, half a century later, during the French Decadence, some French poets applied themselves to the study of Spanish in order to read the works of Góngora. Hence, it may not be too farfetched to claim that the "modern spirit" in poetry, whose inception generally is assigned to nineteenth-century France and Germany, really sprang from the rich soil of the Spanish Golden Age, with its experimentation, symbolism, metaphorizing, and sophistication. The Spanish eighteenth century, concerned as it was with economics, politics, and organizations (academies, dictionaries, museums), expressed itself best in essays and treatises, rather than in verse. Its submerged lyrical afflatus reappeared, with great purity, refinement, and intensity, in the nineteenth century of Gustavo Bécquer, Rosalía de Castro, and Rubén Darío, entering, thereafter, the contemporary age of Juan Ramón Jiménez, Antonio Machado, Federico García Lorca, and Gabriela Mistral.

Viewing in broad perspective the past and present of Hispanic lyricism, one feels that an organic relationship exists between them—in fact, that they are inextricably interwoven. Góngora's baroquism, for instance, is as ubiquitous in contemporary poetry as the hermetic intensity of Saint John of the Cross and the folkloric magic of Lope de Vega.

ANGEL FLORES

Contents

GARCILASO DE LA VEGA
(c. 1501–1536)

This Toledan nobleman served under the imperial banners of Charles V in Germany and Italy, dying in battle while still in his thirties. At the brilliant court of Naples he read and studied assiduously the Italian poets. His works—limited to thirty-eight sonnets, three eclogues, two elegies, an epistle in verse, and five canzones—clearly show the ideological orientation and formalistic concern of the Renaissance. With him, therefore, begins a new chapter in Spanish poetry. Keeping aloof from the dominant folkloric and popular trend, he depicted only a charming, artificial, and stylized world. Yet, despite obvious echoes from Petrarch, Sannazaro, and Tasso, Garcilaso was able to produce works which were unmistakably personal.

BEST EDITIONS: T. Navarro Tomás (ed.): *Obras*, Madrid, 1924 [Clásicos Castellanos, Vol. 3]; H. Keniston (ed.). *Works*, New York, 1925.

ABOUT GARCILASO DE LA VEGA: H. Keniston: *Garcilaso de la Vega, A Critical Study of His Life and Works*, New York, 1922. *Also*: J. Fitzmaurice-Kelly: *Some Masters of Spanish Verse*, Oxford, 1924, pp. 43–72; P. Salinas: *Reality and the Poet in Spanish Poetry*, Johns Hopkins University, 1940, pp. 67–93; L. Spitzer: "Garcilaso's Third Eclogue," lines 265–71, *Hispanic Review* 20 (1952), pp. 243–48.

Égloga I

[líneas 239–407]

Corrientes aguas, puras, cristalinas;
árboles que os estáis mirando en ellas,
verde prado de fresca sombra lleno,
aves que aquí sembráis vuestras querellas,
hiedra que por los árboles caminas,
torciendo el paso por su verde seno;
yo me vi tan ajeno
del grave mal que siento,
que de puro contento
con vuestra soledad me recreaba,
donde con dulce sueño reposaba,
o con el pensamiento discurría
por donde no hallaba
sino memorias llenas de alegría.

Y en este mismo valle, donde agora
me entristezco y me canso, en el reposo
estuve ya contento y descansado.
¡Oh bien caduco, vano y presuroso!
Acuérdome durmiendo aquí algún hora,
que despertando, a Elisa vi a mi lado.
¡Oh miserable hado!
¡Oh tela delicada,
antes de tiempo dada
a los agudos filos de la muerte!
Más convenible fuera aquesta suerte
a los cansados años de mi vida,
que es más que el hierro fuerte,
pues no la ha quebrantado tu partida.

¿Dó están agora aquellos claros ojos
que llevaban tras sí, como colgada,
mi ánima do quier que se volvían?
¿Dó está la blanca mano delicada,
llena de vencimientos y despojos
que de mí mis sentidos le ofrecían?
Los cabellos que vían
con gran desprecio al oro,
como a menor tesoro

Eclogue I

[lines 239–407]

O waters running pure and crystal clear,
Woods that watch your image in the waters,
Green fields harboring delicious shade,
Birds in this air scattering your sorrows,
Ivy advancing to the tops of trees,
Their green hearts shrinking at the turns you make:
I saw myself quite safe
From the deep ill I feel,
And there in utter peace
My soul lay drinking in your solitude,
Lay drowsing in a soft and tranquil mood
Or meditated through a panorama
Of thoughts where I was sure
To find no memory not filled with gladness.

And this is the very valley where I languish
So sadly now: this valley of my ease,
Of my refreshing rest, of my content.
O fragile happiness, fading with such speed!
Once, I recall, I woke where I was lying
Here asleep: by my side Eliza slept.
O fated wretchedness!
O web of subtle work,
So early and so curt
The biting blades of death closed in on you!
Such destiny would have appeared less rude
Falling on the worn years of my own life
Which now shows the strange iron of its root
Unbroken by your unreturning flight.

Where now are those bright-glancing eyes that drove
My soul in their quick traces helplessly,
Bound to the slightest movement that they made?
Where is the fine white hand that once received
The spoils and triumphs of myself, that stole
Away with all the gifts my senses gave?
And the high locks of hair
That looked askance on gold
As less fair than their own—

¿adónde están? ¿Adónde el blanco pecho?
¿Dó la coluna que el dorado techo
con presunción graciosa sostenía?
Aquesto todo agora ya se encierra,
por desventura mía,
en la fría, desierta y dura tierra.

¿Quién me dijera, Elisa, vida mía,
cuando en aqueste valle el fresco viento
andábamos cogiendo tiernas flores,
que había de ver con largo apartamiento
venir el triste y solitario día
que diese amargo fin a mis amores?
El cielo en mis dolores
cargó la mano tanto,
que a sempiterno llanto
y a triste soledad me ha condenado;
y lo que siento más es verme atado
a la pesada vida y enojosa,
solo, desamparado,
ciego sin lumbre en cárcel tenebrosa.

Después que nos dejaste, nunca pace
en hartura el ganado ya, ni acude
el campo al labrador con mano llena.
No hay bien que en mal no se convierta y mude:
la mala yerba al trigo ahoga, y nace
en lugar suyo la infelice avena;
la tierra, que de buena
gana nos producía
flores con que solía
quitar en sólo vellas mil enojos,
produce agora en cambio estos abrojos,
ya de rigor de espinas intratable;
y yo hago con mis ojos
crecer, lloviendo, el fruto miserable.

Como al partir del sol la sombra crece,
y en cayendo su rayo se levanta
la negra escuridad que el mundo cubre,
de do viene el temor que nos espanta,
y la medrosa forma en que se ofrece
aquello que la noche nos encubre,

Where have they gone? Where is that gentle breast?
Where is the column that swayed up to lend
A golden capital its conscious grace?
Everything is buried that was proud;
My joy is in the grave,
My joy lies freezing in the hard blank ground.

Eliza, my life, how could I have believed
—While we were following the valley wind
Which blew a freshness on our sweet picked flowers—
That there would come a separation, a swift
Parting time of loneliness and of grief
To leave my love to sew its bitter shroud?
The hand of heaven is down
So firm upon my pain
That I am made to bear
An unrelieved lament, cast out, alone:
And what is worse, to know that I must grow
Into this dull relentless life, unhelped,
Deserted, left to grope
Round the blind darkness of a lightless cell.

Since you have gone from us, the flocks are loath
To eat their fill, and in the farmer's barns
The fields no longer swell out their glad grain.
There is no good that fails to turn to harm.
Weeds rise up to choke the wheat, wild oats
Brandish their miserable power in its place.
The earth which in its day
Produced unstintedly
Such flowers as even to see
Could sweep a thousand troubles from the heart
Produces now instead these thistles, sharp-
Spined, rooted in intractable plots.
Rain of my tears imparts
A thriving to the wretched thistle crops.

Just as, when the sun sinks and shadows creep,
When the last rays go down before the darkness
That throws its black cloak out across the world,
We feel a shudder, and our pulses startle
At the uneasy phantom shapes we meet
Sheeted in night, until the night has turned

hasta que el sol descubre
su luz pura y hermosa;
tal es la tenebrosa
noche de tu partir, en que he quedado
de sombra y de temor atormentado,
hasta que muerte el tiempo determine
que a ver el deseado
sol de tu clara vista me encamine.

Cual suele el ruiseñor con triste canto
quejarse, entre las hojas escondido,
del duro labrador, que cautamente
le despojó su caro y dulce nido
de los tiernos hijuelos, entre tanto
que del amado ramo estaba ausente,
y aquel dolor que siente
con diferencia tanta
por la dulce garganta
despide, a su canto el aire suena,
y la callada noche no refrena
su lamentable oficio y sus querellas,
trayendo de su pena
al cielo por testigo y las estrellas;
desta manera suelto yo la rienda
a mi dolor, y así me quejo en vano
de la dureza de la muerte airada.
Ella en mi corazón metió la mano,
y de allí me llevó mi dulce prenda;
que aquél era su nido y su morada.
¡Ay muerte arrebatada!
Por ti me estoy quejando
al cielo y enojando
con importuno llanto al mundo todo:
el desigual dolor no sufre modo.
No me podrán quitar el dolorido
sentir, si ya del todo
primero no me quitan el sentido.

Tengo una parte aquí de tus cabellos,
Elisa, envueltos en un blanco paño,
que nunca de mi seno se me apartan;
descójolos, y de un dolor tamaño

Towards the day it shunned—
The pure, fair, naked sun:
So too, where you are gone
I find a night, a blackness, in which I stand
Alone with my dread and vexed by a shadow
Till death decides the time when I must go
Beyond the dark barrier
To feel your wished-for sunlight pierce my soul.

And as the nightingale deep in the brake
Complains, complains in her lamenting song
Against the ruthless farm boy who has seized
So craftily her tender brood, all lost
From the dear sweet nest while she was away
A moment from the branch she loved, and she
Pours out the grief she feels
With what a different note
From her expressive throat
Until the air re-echoes all she sings
And voiceless night encourages her hymns,
Her lamentations and her grievances,
And brings as witnesses
Of this one pain, the very stars and heavens:
So I myself give full vent to the sorrow
That stirs within me, and thus I live bewailing
In vain the punishing harshness of death.
Death slid a hand into my heart, taking
My dearest treasure from me, for my solace
Found in that place its protection and its nest.
Bewildering death! You sent
My cries towards heaven, you made
My lamentable state
Importune every listening worldly ear.
Extravagance in pain has no reprieve.
I cannot lose the sufferings I feel
Unless I am relieved
Of all the feelings I can suffer here.

See how I have kept a curl of your hair
Eliza!—enclosed in a white cloth
Which guards it always safely near my breast.
Here I unwrap it, and I feel my thoughts
Melt in such grief and pity that my gaze

enternecerme siento, que sobre ellos
nunca mis ojos de llorar se hartan.
Sin que de allí se partan,
con sospiros calientes,
más que la llama ardientes,
los enjugo del llanto, y de consuno
casi los paso y cuento uno a uno;
juntándolos, con un cordón los ato:
tras esto el importuno
dolor me deja descansar un rato.

Mas luego a la memoria se me ofrece
aquella noche tenebrosa, escura,
que tanto aflige esta ánima mezquina
con la memoria de mi desventura.
Verte presente agora me parece
en aquel duro trance de Lucina,
y aquella voz divina,
con cuyo son y acentos
a los airados vientos
pudieras amansar, que agora es muda,
me parece que oigo que a la cruda,
inexorable diosa demandabas
en aquel paso ayuda;
y tú, tú, rústica diosa, ¿dónde estabas?

¿Íbate tanto en perseguir las fieras?
¿Íbate tanto en un pastor dormido?
¿Cosa pudo bastar a tal crueza,
que, conmovida a compasión, oído
a los votos y lágrimas no dieras
por no ver hecha tierra tal belleza,
o no ver la tristeza
en que tu Nemoroso
queda, que su reposo
era seguir tu oficio, persiguiendo
las fieras por los montes, y ofreciendo
a tus sagradas aras los despojos?
¿Y tú, ingrata, riendo
dejas morir mi bien ante mis ojos?

Might go on blinding me with tears unshed
For ever. The locks are wet,
I dry them with warm sighs
Hotter than living fires,
And as I dry them, pass them through my fingers
One by one, as if to count them; bringing
Them all at last together in a band.
In this way, in these minutes
My desperate sorrow briefly rests its lance.

But soon my recollection fills again
With images of that dark baffling night
Which batters this unhappy soul so hard
Through memories of my bereaving time.
And now I seem to see you here, your bed
Become a prey to childbirth's wild alarms,
And seeing you, to start
At your voice, whose marvelous tone
And accents might have borne
Stillness to angry winds, but now is silent——
I seem to hear it calling out and crying
To an unmoved, unpitying deity
For help in that great trial.
And you, Diana, where were you that day?

Were you so busy hunting the forest beasts?
Were you so busy with a drowsy shepherd?
Could any reason fire such cruelty
As made you, to the piteous endeavors
Of her who poured her tears and vows, turn ears
Gone deaf, in order not to see such beauty
Become dust, or the melancholy
Descend on your Nemoroso
Who was happy in your glory
And followed the wild beasts about the hills
And saw the sacred ritual fulfilled
With offerings from the kill upon your altars?
And yet you were thankless still——
Before my eyes you let my salvation be squandered?

Divina Elisa, pues agora el cielo
con inmortales pies pisas y mides,
y su mudanza ves, estando queda,
¿por qué de mí te olvidas, y no pides
que se apresure el tiempo en que este velo
rompa del cuerpo, y verme libre pueda,
y en la tercera rueda
contigo mano a mano
busquemos otro llano,
busquemos otros montes y otros ríos,
otros valles floridos y sombríos,
donde descanse, y siempre pueda verte
ante los ojos míos,
sin miedo y sobresalto de perderte?

Canción III

Con un manso ruïdo
de agua corriente y clara,
cerca el Danubio una isla, que pudiera
ser lugar escogido
para que descansara
quien como yo estó agora, no estuviera;
do siempre primavera
parece en la verdura
sembrada de las flores;
hacen los ruiseñores
renovar el placer o la tristura
con sus blandas querellas,
que nunca día ni noche cesan dellas.

Aquí estuve yo puesto,
o por mejor decillo,
preso, forzado y solo en tierra ajena;
bien pueden hacer esto
en quien puede sufrillo
y en quien él a sí mismo se condena.

Divine Eliza, since the sky is now
The floor and path of your undying feet,
And since you see its changes without changing,
Why do you not remember me, not speed
The coming of the time when all this cloud
Of the body will be rent, my soul free-faring——
And hand in hand enlacing
As we pass the third sphere
We'll search for another field,
For other mountains we'll search, and other rivers,
For other valleys, shady, flower-heady,
Where I may rest and have before my eyes
The sight of you for ever,
With no fear that my paradise will die?

—EDWIN MORGAN

Song III

Surrounded by the gentle sound
of clear water in motion,
near the Danube, no island could exist
that might be a spot chosen where
anyone as I am now, could rest;
where eternally spring
appears in its verdure
strewn with flowers;
where nightingales
renew either pleasure or sadness
with their suave plaints,
and never, day or night, desist from them.

Here was I placed,
or, to speak more truly,
prisoned, forced and alone in a foreign land;
they can well do this
to one who can suffer it
and to one who, to himself, condemns himself.

Tengo sólo una pena,
si muero desterrado
y en tanta desventura,
que piensen por ventura
que junto tantos males me han llevado;
y sé yo bien que muero
por sólo aquello que morir espero.

El cuerpo está en poder
y en manos de quien puede
hacer a su placer lo que quisiere;
mas no podrá hacer
que mal librado quede,
mientras de mí otra prenda no tuviere.
Cuando ya el mal viniere
y la postrera suerte,
aquí me ha de hallar,
en el mismo lugar;
que otra cosa más dura que la muerte
me halla y ha hallado;
y esto sabe muy bien quien lo ha probado.

No es necesario agora
hablar más sin provecho,
que es mi necesidad muy apretada;
pues ha sido en un hora
todo aquello deshecho
en que toda mi vida fue gastada.
¿Y al fin de tal jornada
presumen espantarme?
Sepan que ya no puedo
morir sino sin miedo;
que aun nunca qué temer quiso dejarme
la desventura mía,
que el bien y el miedo me quitó en un día.

Danubio, río divino,
que por fieras naciones
vas con tus claras ondas discurriendo,
pues no hay otro camino
por donde mis razones
vayan fuera de aquí, sino corriendo

One anxiety only I have:
should I die exiled
with such misfortune
that they believe it good fortune
so many heaped-up ills have carried me off;
when I know well that I die
simply because I hope to die.

My body is in the power
and in the hands of him who can
do at his pleasure what he pleases;
but he will not be able to do
what may have been evilly done
so long as from me he has no other pledge.
Were evil to come, indeed,
and the ultimate fate,
here am I to be found,
in the same place;
for something harsher than death
finds and has found me;
and this he knows who has put it to test.

There is no necessity now
to speak further to no advantage
than is my most distressed need;
since in one hour
all has been undone
which in my whole life was won.
At the end of a journey like this,
they presume, in me, to strike terror?
Let them know that I cannot now
die otherwise than without fear;
though never did I wish to cease fearing
my misfortune in having to discard
both fortune and fear in a day.

Danube, river divine,
who, with your currents,
go winding through savage nations,
since there is no other course
by way of which my thoughts
may escape from here, if not riding

por tus aguas y siendo
en ellas anegadas;
si en tierra tan ajena
en la desierta arena
fueren de alguno acaso en fin halladas,
entiérralas, siquiera,
porque su error se acabe en tu ribera.

Aunque en el agua mueras,
canción, no has de quejarte;
que yo he mirado bien lo que te toca.
Menos vida tuvieras
si hubieras de igualarte
con otras que se me han muerto en la boca.
Quién tiene culpa desto,
allá lo entenderás de mí muy presto.

Un rato se levanta mi esperanza . . .

Un rato se levanta mi esperanza.
Tan cansada de haberse levantado
torna a caer, que deja, mal mi grado,
libre el lugar a la desconfianza.

¿Quién sufrirá tan áspera mudanza
del bien al mal? ¡Oh, corazón cansado!
esfuerza en la miseria de tu estado,
que tras fortuna suele haber bonanza.

Yo mismo emprenderé a fuerza de brazos
romper un monte, que otro no rompiera,
de mil inconvenientes muy espeso.

Muerte, prisión no pueden, ni embarazos,
quitarme de ir a veros, como quiera,
desnudo espíritu o hombre en carne y hueso.

your waters and in them
being totally submerged;
if in a land so foreign
in a desert so desolate
they should by some chance at last be found—
bury them, if for no other reason than that
their error terminates on your shore.

Although you may die, song,
in the water, you need not complain;
I have carefully studied your situation.
Less life you would find
if you had to contend
with others that have died on my lips.
And who is at fault in this matter,
you will learn from me very soon.
—FRANCES FLETCHER

One Moment My Hope Rises Up On Wings . . .

One moment my hope rises up on wings,
The next, grown weary of its high estate,
It turns and falls, and leaves me, like my fate,
Wide open to the diffidence it brings.

What man would bear such harsh revisitings
Of evil to good? O wearied heart, be great!
Make strength in misery your surrogate;
Wait for the calms that follow buffetings.

And I myself will promise by main force
To break obstructions none have dared to break,
Bristling with thousands of impediments.

No death or stumbling blocks or prison doors
Can keep you from my sight, though they should make
My naked ghost gaze through its fleshly rents.
—EDWIN MORGAN

Escrito está en mi alma vuestro gesto . . .

Escrito está en mi alma vuestro gesto,
y cuanto yo escribir de vos deseo;
vos sola lo escribistes, yo lo leo
tan solo, que aun de vos me guardo en esto.

En esto estoy y estaré siempre puesto;
que aunque no cabe en mí cuanto en vos veo,
de tanto bien lo que no entiendo creo,
tomando ya la fe por presupuesto.

Yo no nací sino para quereros;
mi alma os ha cortado a su medida;
por hábito del alma misma os quiero.

Cuanto tengo confieso yo deberos;
por vos nací, por vos tengo la vida,
por vos he de morir y por vos muero.

Por ásperos caminos . . .

Por ásperos caminos he llegado
a parte que de miedo no me muevo;
y si a mudarme o dar un paso pruebo,
allí por los cabellos soy tornado.

Mas tal estoy, que con la muerte al lado
busco de mi vivir consejo nuevo;
y conozco el mejor y el peor apruebo,
o por costumbre mala o por mi hado.

Por otra parte, el breve tiempo mío,
y el errado proceso de mis años,
en su primer principio y en su medio,

mi inclinación, con quien ya no porfío,
la cierta muerte, fin de tantos daños,
me hacen descuidar de mi remedio.

Your Face Is Written in My Soul . . .

Your face is written in my soul, and when
I want to write about you, you alone
Become the writer, I but read the line;
I watch you where you still watch me, within.

This state I am and always will be in.
For though my soul imprints a half-design
Of what I see in you, the good unknown
Is taken on a trusting regimen.

What was I born for if not to adore you?
My ills have shaped you to the bent they give.
I love you by a daily act of soul.

All that I have I must confess I owe you.
For you I came to life, for you I live,
For you I'd die, and do die, after all.

—EDWIN MORGAN

Rough Are the Roads . . .

Rough are the roads that led me to this place.
I stand here in such fear I cannot stir.
If I should move, or take one step, my hair
Is seized to make all effort powerless.

Yet I must strain, even in death's embrace,
To make my life my latest counselor;
I see the best, but still the worst is dear,
Through fate, or through a sin's deep-rootedness.

This too: the meager time our fates allow,
The years I swung perverse from their supports
At the beginning and in the midst of life,

My inclination, unresisted now,
And death's sure end to such a world of hurts
Make me a laggard in my godly strife.

—EDWIN MORGAN

Oh dulces prendas . . .

¡Oh dulces prendas, por mi mal halladas,
dulces y alegres cuando Dios quería!
Juntas estáis en la memoria mía,
y con ella en mi muerte conjuradas.

¿Quién me dijera, cuando en las pasadas
horas en tanto bien por vos me vía,
que me habíades de ser en algún día
con tan grave dolor representadas?

Pues en una hora junto me llevastes
todo el bien que por términos me distes,
llevame junto el mal que me dejastes.

Si no, sospecharé que me pusistes
en tantos bienes, porque deseastes
verme morir entre memorias tristes.

En tanto que de rosa y azucena . . .

En tanto que de rosa y azucena
se muestra la color en vuestro gesto,
y que vuestro mirar ardiente, honesto,
enciende al corazón y lo refrena;

y en tanto que el cabello, que en la vena
del oro se escogió, con vuelo presto,
por el hermoso cuello blanco, enhiesto,
el viento mueve, esparce y desordena;

coged de vuestra alegre primavera
el dulce fruto, antes que el tiempo airado
cubra de nieve la hermosa cumbre.

Marchitará la rosa el viento helado,
todo lo mudará la edad ligera,
por no hacer mudanza en su costumbre.

Sweet Gifts . . .

Sweet gifts, by me found something less than sweet,
Though joyous gifts enough when God so willed!
You are knit into memory, I am killed
When you and memory conspire to meet.

Who would have told me, when my whole heart beat
With joy for you, that those times would be stilled,
And that your image must one day be filled
With heavy grief such as these words repeat?

Since one hour was enough for you to take
The very gift you gave me for my aim,
Take too the misery you left to break.

If not, I must suspect you made the same
Reward of happiness as you were to make
Of these sad memories I die to name.

—EDWIN MORGAN

While There Is Still the Color of a Rose . . .

While there is still the color of a rose
And of a lily in your countenance,
And you with such an ardent candid glance
Can fire the heart, and check the flames it shows;

And while that golden hair of yours that flows
Into a knot can leap into a dance
As the wind blows with livelier dalliance
Upon the fairest proud white neck it knows:

Gather together from your happy spring
Fruits that are sweet, before time ravages
With angry snow the beauty of your head.

The rose will wither as the cold wind rages,
And age come gently to change everything,
Lest our desire should change old age instead.

—EDWIN MORGAN

A la entrada de un valle, en un desierto . . .

A la entrada de un valle, en un desierto,
do nadie atravesaba ni se vía,
vi que con estrañeza un can hacía
estremos de dolor con desconcierto;

ahora suelta el llanto al cielo abierto,
ora va rastreando por la vía;
camina, vuelve, para, y todavía
quedaba desmayado como muerto.

Y fue que se apartó de su presencia
su amo, y no le hallaba, y esto siente;
mirad hasta dó llega el mal de ausencia.

Movióme a compasión ver su accidente;
díjele lastimado: «Ten paciencia,
que yo alcanzo razón, y estoy ausente.»

I Came to a Valley in the Wilderness . . .

I came to a valley in the wilderness
Where no one walked across the waste but me,
And there I saw a sudden misery,
A dog, distraught, wild with unhappiness.

Its howl would mount into the emptiness,
And then it would go sniffing eagerly
For tracks, run on, turn back, and stop—to be
Fretted again by a desperate distress.

And it was this: the dog had missed the presence
Of its master; could not find him; felt its loss.
See to what straits they drive, the ills of absence!

The dog's bewilderment tore my heart across;
I said to it in pity: "Cling to patience:
I am a man, yet absence is my cross."

—EDWIN MORGAN

GUTIERRE DE CETINA
(1518?–1554?)

Called "the Spanish Anacreon" by his contemporaries, this Sevillian poet is known today only for his ten-line madrigal *Ojos claros, serenos* . . . , although he left hundreds of lyrics of different types, surpassed by few works in the Spanish language in their intrinsic melodic expression and delicacy of feeling. Like Garcilaso, Cetina served under Charles V's banners and was influenced by the Italian poets, especially Petrarch and Ariosto. Invited by his brother, a comrade of Hernán Cortés, he went to Mexico in 1546 and was murdered in Puebla by a jealous rival while praising the eyes of a certain young lady at her window.

BEST EDITION: J. Hazañas y la Rua (ed.): *Obras*, Seville, 1895, 2 vols.

ABOUT GUTIERRE DE CETINA: A. W. Whithers: *The Sources of the Poetry of Cetina*, Philadelphia, 1923. *Also*: A. F. G. Bell: "Gutierre de Cetina," *Modern Language Review* xx (1925), pp. 179–83.

Horas alegres que pasáis volando . . .

Horas alegres que pasáis volando
porque a vueltas del bien, mayor mal sienta;
sabrosa noche que en tan dulce afrenta
el triste despedir me vas mostrando;

importuno reloj que apresurando
tu curso, mi dolor me representa;
estrellas con quien nunca tuve cuenta
que mi partida vais acelerando;

gallo que mi pesar has denunciado,
lucero que mi luz va obscureciendo,
a tú, mal sosegada y moza aurora:

Si en vos cabe dolor de mi cuidado,
id poco a poco el paso deteniendo,
si no puede ser más, siquiera un hora.

Madrigal: Ojos claros, serenos . . .

Ojos claros, serenos,
si de un dulce mirar sois alabados,
¿por qué, si me miráis, miráis airados?
Si cuando más piadosos,
más bellos parecéis a aquel que os mira,
no me miréis con ira,
porque no parezcáis menos hermosos.
¡Ay tormentos rabiosos!
Ojos claros, serenos,
ya que así me miráis, miradme al menos.

Happy Hours That Hurry Away . . .

Happy hours that hurry away
Leaving, in return for bliss, all the greater pain;
Luscious night, that with such sweet affront
Gives me sad departure;

Importunate clock, inexorably
Designating my sorrow;
Stars I never reckoned with
Hastening my farewell;

Rooster heralding my plight,
Morning star come to dim my light,
And you, brash and youthful dawn:

If you have room for my prudence,
Linger a little, stay your step,
If by no more than merely a single hour.

—KATE FLORES

Madrigal: Eyes of Clear Serenity . . .

Eyes of clear serenity,
If your tender gaze endear,
Why for me is your gaze severe?
If the gazer be more beguiled
When you gently stare,
That you may not seem less fair,
Let your gaze be mild.
O torment wild!
Eyes of clear serenity,
Having gazed upon me thus, at least now gaze at me.

—KATE FLORES

¿En cuál región, en cuál parte del suelo . . . ?

¿En cuál región, en cuál parte del suelo,
en cuál bosque, en cuál monte, en cuál poblado,
en cuál lugar remoto y apartado
puede ya mi dolor hallar consuelo?

Cuanto se puede ver debajo el cielo,
todo lo tengo visto y rodeado;
y un medio que a mi mal había hallado,
hace en parte mayor mi desconsuelo.

Para curar el daño de la ausencia
píntoos cual siempre os vi, dura y proterva;
mas Amor os me muestra de otra suerte.

No queráis a mi mal más experiencia,
sino que ya como herida cierva,
do quier que voy, conmigo va mi muerte.

In What Region, in What Part of the World . . . ?

In what region, in what part of the world,
In what forest, in what mountain, in what town,
In what far-off, secluded place
Can my suffering find surcease now?

All that is to be seen beneath the sky,
All I have seen and explored;
And a balm that for my torment I had found
Has but dejected me the more.

The injury of your absence to amend,
I paint you as I always saw you, hard, perverse;
But Love portrays you to me differently, my friend.

Wish me of misery no further experience,
For already like a wounded deer,
Everywhere I go, with me goes my end.

—KATE FLORES

FRAY LUIS DE LEÓN
(c. 1527–91)

In Fray Luis's lyrics the "pagan" aestheticism of the Italians, which permeates the works of Garcilaso and Cetina, is tempered by his religious feeling. Fray Luis profited by the Renaissance's technical discoveries, adding to the Platonic-Horatian ideology his pious fervor, his theological concerns, and his Biblical imagery. At fifteen, Fray Luis joined the Order of Saint Augustine and, after studying philosophy and theology, taught in several Augustinian convents. He completed his graduate studies at the University of Salamanca, where he taught until his death. But this was not, as it may seem, a quiet assignment. At first he had to fight for his appointment against a powerful rival (Garcilaso's son); later he was jailed for a five-year term (1572–76) by the Holy Inquisition for his unorthodox interpretation of the Bible. At his release he had to surrender to the authorities his magnificent translation of the *Song of Songs*. On his return to the classroom after this long period in jail, he began his lectures with that classic understatement: "As we were saying yesterday. . . ."

Two dozen original poems constitute Fray Luis's lyrical output; the rest are translations from the Psalms, from Pindar, Euripides, Virgil, and Horace. In his lyrics he expresses the wish to escape all human bondage, especially the turbulent life of the Spanish Court, and return to rural simplicity—to close contact with a harmonious Nature that reminds him of God and the eternal truths. His mystic adumbrations reflect one of the essential components of sixteenth-century Spanish poetry.

BEST EDITIONS: P. J. Llobera (ed.): *Obras poéticas*, Cuenca, 1931–32, 2 vols.; P. Angel C. Vega (ed.): *Poesías*, Madrid, 1955.

ABOUT FRAY LUIS DE LEÓN: A. F. G. Bell: *Luis de León, A Study of the Spanish Renaissance*, Oxford, 1925. *Also:* A. F. G. Bell: "Notes on

28

Luis de León's Lyrics," *Modern Language Review* XXI (1926), pp. 168–77; and "Notes on the Spanish Renaissance," *Revue Hispanique*, 1930, pp. 319–652; W. J. Entwistle: "Fray Luis de León's Life in His Lyrics," *Revue Hispanique* LXXI (1927), pp. 176–223; J. Fitzmaurice-Kelly: *Fray Luis de León*, Oxford, 1921; E. A. Peers: "Mysticism in the Poetry of Fray Luis de León," *Bulletin of Spanish Studies* XIX (1942), pp. 25–40; P. Salinas: *Reality and the Poet in Spanish Poetry*, Johns Hopkins University, 1940, pp. 97–114; E. J. Schuster: "Fray Luis de León and the Linguistic Approach to Epistemology," *Kentucky Foreign Language Quarterly* 6 (1959), pp. 195–200.

Vida retirada

¡Qué descansada vida
la del que huye el mundanal ruido,
y sigue la escondida
senda por donde han ido
los pocos sabios que en el mundo han sido!

Que no le enturbia el pecho
de los soberbios grandes el estado,
ni del dorado techo
se admira, fabricado
del sabio moro, en jaspes sustentado.

No cura si la fama
canta con voz su nombre pregonera,
ni cura si encarama
la lengua lisonjera
lo que condena la verdad sincera.

¿Qué presta a mi contento
si soy del vano dedo señalado,
si en busca de este viento
ando desalentado
con ansias vivas y mortal cuidado?

¡Oh campo, oh monte, oh río!
¡Oh secreto seguro deleitoso!
roto casi el navío,
a vuestro almo reposo
huyo de aqueste mar tempestuoso.

Un no rompido sueño,
un día puro, alegre, libre quiero;
no quiero ver el ceño
vanamente severo
de quien la sangre ensalza o el dinero.

Despiértenme las aves
con su cantar süave no aprendido,
no los cuidados graves
de que es siempre seguido
quien al ajeno arbitrio está atenido.

The Life Withdrawn

How tranquil is man's life
When he has turned from the world's turbulent roar
To follow the path that lies
Apart, where wise men go—
The hidden way the earth's few sages chose!

For his breast is unperturbed
By vanities, great men, or high estate,
And his wonder is not stirred
By Moorish artistry,
By gilded roof and jasper colonnade.

He is unmoved by the song
Of fame, of voices heralding his name;
When flattering tongues exalt
What open truth disdains
He is unmoved by their misguided praise.

Why should my heart be glad
If thoughtless fingers point out where I go?
If I lose what breath I have
Seeking that windy goal
Where desperate cares and burning longings roam?

O mountain, spring, and stream!
O my delicious refuge! I am safe!
I have fled from storms of the sea,
In a ship half-smashed, to take
My rest in your protecting, holy place.

I want a sleep unbroken,
I want a daytime happy, bright, and free.
I do not want to know the
Emptily severe
Frown that makes money and blue blood revered.

Let the birds waken me
With their delightful and unmannered songs—
Not those anxieties
That always cling and stalk
About the man who scours another's pot.

Vivir quiero conmigo,
gozar quiero del bien que debo al cielo
a solas, sin testigo,
libre de amor, de celo,
de odio, de esperanzas, de recelo.

Del monte en la ladera
por mi mano plantado tengo un huerto,
que con la primavera
de bella flor cubierto,
ya muestra en esperanza el fruto cierto.

Y como codiciosa
de ver y acrecentar su hermosura,
desde la cumbre airosa
una fontana pura
hasta llegar corriendo se apresura.

Y luego sosegada
el paso entre los árboles torciendo,
el suelo de pasada
de verdura vistiendo,
y con diversas flores va esparciendo.

El aire el huerto orea,
y ofrece mil olores al sentido,
los árboles menea
con un manso rüido,
que del oro y del cetro pone olvido.

Ténganse su tesoro
los que de un flaco leño se confían:
no es mío ver el lloro
de los que desconfían
cuando el cierzo y el ábrego porfían.

La combatida antena
cruje, y en ciega noche el claro día
se torna; al cielo suena
confusa vocería,
y la mar enriquecen a porfía.

I want to live by myself,
I want the use of my blessings, lent from heaven;
Alone; no witnesses;
Neither in love, nor jealous;
Neither hating, nor hoping, nor tormented.

A little orchard garden
I have planted with my own hands on the hill slopes;
Already flower starry
With a brave spring show
It promises sure fruit and fulfilled hope.

And as if in diligence
To see and swell the beauty of the place,
A pure stream descends
From the breezy bluff and strains
To meet it with its quickly running waves.

And soon it winds its path
Between the trees in great tranquillity;
Clothing the ground it calms
With green of grass and leaf
And feeding many flowers where it steals.

The cool, refreshing air
Sends up a thousand garden scents to breathe,
And moves the trees to make
That dear murmur which keeps
Gold and the scepter far off and asleep.

Treasure belongs to those
Who trustingly embark a leaky vessel;
I shall not need to deplore
The tears of the adventurers
When their hearts sink at north-and-south cross tempests!

The timber of the spar
Cracks in the gale, bright day becomes blind night,
An indistinct uproar
Rises into the sky,
They glut the sea with wealth they fear to prize.

A mí una pobrecilla
mesa, de amable paz bien abastada
me baste, y la vajilla
de fino oro labrada,
sea de quien la mar no teme airada.

Y mientras miserable-
mente se están los otros abrasando
en sed insacïable
del no durable mando,
tendido yo a la sombra esté cantando.

A la sombra tendido
de yedra y lauro eterno coronado,
puesto el atento oído
al son dulce, acordado,
del plectro sabiamente meneado.

Oda a Francisco Salinas

El aire se serena
y viste de hermosura y luz no usada,
Salinas, cuando suena
la música extremada
por vuestra sabia mano gobernada.

A cuyo son divino
mi alma que en olvido está sumida,
torna a cobrar el tino,
y memoria perdida
de su origen primera esclarecida.

Y como se conoce,
en suerte y pensamientos se mejora,
el oro desconoce
que el vulgo ciego adora,
la belleza caduca, engañadora.

Traspasa el aire todo
hasta llegar a la más alta esfera,
y oye allí otro modo

A little modest table
Well furnished with the peace I love is enough
To please me; let the darer
Of raging seas be the one
To have his exquisite gold plate and cup.

And while the rest are miserably
burning where they stand, with thirst
Unquenchable to win
A transient captaincy,
Let me lie stretched out in the shade, and sing.

Stretched out in the shade,
Crowned with ivy and lasting laurel leaves,
My ear intent and grave
To hear the well-tuned, sweet
Sounds of the plectrum subtly pick and weave. —EDWIN MORGAN

Ode to Francisco Salinas

The air grows calm and clear
And clothes itself in beauty and strange light,
Salinas, when the extreme
Art of your music strikes
Out from that skilled and tempering hand I admire.

It is a heavenly sound
That makes my dull, all-too-forgetful soul
Find its senses and rouse
Its lost recollections of those
First days in its primordial glorious home.

Yes, it goes back, it remembers;
In thoughts, and fate, it grows a better thing;
For gold, it loses fervor:
Let that brittle glint
Trap the adoring slavelike mob, not this

Soul that crosses space,
Climbs till it has reached the highest sphere,
And hears a music there

de no perecedera
música, que es de todas la primera.

Ve como el gran maestro,
a aquesta inmensa cítara aplicado,
con movimiento diestro
produce el son sagrado,
con que este eterno templo es sustentado.

Y como está compuesta
de números concordes, luego envía
consonante respuesta,
y entrambas a porfía
mezclan una dulcísima armonía.

Aquí la alma navega
por un mar de dulzura, y finalmente
en él así se anega,
que ningún accidente
extraño o peregrino oye o siente.

¡Oh desmayo dichoso!
¡oh muerte que das vida, oh dulce olvido!
¡durase en tu reposo,
sin ser restituido
jamás a aqueste bajo y vil sentido!

A este bien os llamo,
gloria del Apolíneo sacro coro,
amigos, a quien amo
sobre todo tesoro,
que todo lo demás es triste lloro.

¡Oh suene de contino,
Salinas, vuestro son en mis oídos!
por quien al bien divino
despiertan los sentidos,
quedando a lo demás amortecidos.

That's made for other ears,
Unfading notes and the first notes to speak.

It sees the master player
With that great cosmic cithern in his arms
Pluck out sure and clear
The sacred chord that guards
This everlasting temple from all harm.

And since it is itself
Composed of many chords, it quickly gives
Its answer in an echo,
And both together mix
Their vying sounds in sweetest harmony.

Now through a sea of sweetness
The soul goes voyaging on, until at last
It plunges drowned so deep there
That neither eye nor heart
Takes notice of what happens above or apart.

O blessed loss of sense!
O life-enhancing death! O sweet forgetting!
If I could enjoy your rest
Without regaining, ever,
This consciousness so earthbound and so wretched!

To this blessing I call you,
Glory of Apollo's holy choir, friends
I love more dearly than all the
Things that are treasured well,
For what is all the rest but a lament?

O play, still play, Salinas,
Still sound the sound of music in my ear;
Let this unblind the feelings
Till the divine good appears
And every other thing stays sunk in sleep.

— EDWIN MORGAN

Noche serena

Cuando contemplo el cielo
de innumerables luces adornado,
y miro hacia el suelo
de noche rodeado,
en sueño y en olvido sepultado,

El amor y la pena
despiertan en mi pecho una ansia ardiente;
despiden larga vena
los ojos hechos fuente;
la lengua dice al fin con voz doliente:

Morada de grandeza,
templo de claridad y hermosura,
mi alma que a tu alteza
nació, ¿qué desventura
la tiene en esta cárcel baja, oscura?

¿Qué mortal desatino
de la verdad aleja así el sentido,
que de tu bien divino
olvidado, perdido
sigue la vana sombra, el bien fingido?

El hombre está entregado
al sueño, de su suerte no cuidando,
y con paso callado
el cielo vueltas dando
las horas del vivir le va hurtando.

¡Ay, despertad, mortales;
mirad con atención en vuestro daño!
las almas inmortales,
hechas a bien tamaño,
¿podrán vivir de sombra, y solo engaño?

¡Ay, levantad los ojos
a aquesta celestial eterna esfera!
Burlaréis los antojos

Tranquil Night

Contemplating the sky
Studded with its innumerable lights
I swing down my eyes
To the ground wrapped round in night,
Buried in sleep, forgetful of past time;

And love and pain together
Wake ardent longings in my breast, Olarte,
And eyes turned into wellsprings
Brim with streams of sadness,
And at the end I speak, I voice my heartache:

Home of all true greatness,
Temple of transparent beauty, why
Should my soul, born to share you,
Be held as if in gyves
In this degraded cell where nothing shines?

Surely some desperate folly
Drives consciousness so far off from the truth,
And makes it all forgotten,
All lost, your divine good:
In favor of a feigned good, a shadow of doom!

Man is delivered to slumber.
What solicitude has he for his fate?
The sky he slumbers under
Turns in noiseless space
And steals his whole life hour by hour away.

O mortal men, awake!
Examine here your perilous estate.
The deathless soul, made
To be so blest, so fair—
How can it live on these delusions and shades?

When will you lift your eyes
To that unchangeable celestial sphere,
And scorn the fantasies

de aquesta lisonjera
vida, con cuanto teme y cuanto espera.

¿Es más que un breve punto
el bajo y torpe suelo, comparado
a aqueste gran trasunto
do vive mejorado
lo que es, lo que será, lo que ha pasado?

Quien mira el gran concierto
de aquestos resplandores eternales,
su movimiento cierto,
sus pasos desiguales,
y en proporción concorde tan iguales:

La luna cómo mueve
la plateada rueda, y va en pos de ella
la luz do el saber llueve,
y la graciosa estrella
de amor le sigue reluciente y bella:

Y cómo otro camino
prosigue el sanguinoso Marte airado,
y el Júpiter benino,
de bienes mil cercado,
serena el cielo con su rayo amado:

Rodéase en el cumbre
Saturno, padre de los siglos de oro,
tras él la muchedumbre
del reluciente coro
su luz va repartiendo y su tesoro:

¿Quién es el que esto mira,
y precia la bajeza de la tierra,
y no gime y suspira
por romper lo que encierra
el alma, y de estos bienes la destierra?

Aquí vive el contento,
aquí reyna la paz; aquí, asentado
en rico y alto asiento,

Of this life, with its fears,
Its hopes, and its engrossing flatteries?

What is the torpid world
That grovels here but a spot, a moment, compared
With its great transcript, where
A better life awaits
All things that are, or will be, or were made?

Let any man look up
At that great deathless ring of brilliances,
Its circuits undisturbed,
Its paces various
Yet making one well-measured even dance;

Up at the moon, moved
On its silver wheel, and at the following light
Where wisdom laves the moon,
And at that later sign,
The star of love—how fair and sweet it shines!

And then at blood-red Mars
Marching upon a different, angry road,
And Jupiter from whose heart
A thousand blessings flow:
His still rays wash the skies till we adore!

And so to the zenith, to Saturn
Revolving, to the father of the Golden Age,
And beyond him the vast masses
Of the starry choruses
Scattering treasure and fire as they go on their way:

O who can see these things
And value his unworthy worldly state
Without groaning and sighing
For his soul to loose the chains
That bind it and deny it all these blessings?

This is the place of contentment,
This is the haunt of peace. This is the rich
Throne of a reverence,

está el amor sagrado,
de honra y de deleites rodeado.

Inmensa hermosura
aquí se muestra toda; y resplandece
clarísima luz pura,
que jamás anochece;
eterna primavera aquí florece.

¡Oh campos verdaderos!
¡Oh prados con verdad frescos y amenos,
riquísimos mineros!
¡Oh deleitosos senos,
repuestos valles de mil bienes llenos!

En la Ascensión

¿Y dejas, Pastor santo,
tu grey en este valle hondo, escuro,
con soledad y llanto;
y tú, rompiendo el puro
aire, te vas al inmortal seguro?

Los antes bienhadados,
y los ahora tristes y afligidos,
a tus pechos criados,
de ti desposeídos,
¿a dó convertirán ya sus sentidos?

¿Qué mirarán los ojos
que vieron de tu rostro la hermosura,
que no les sea enojos?
Quién oyó tu dulzura,
¿qué no tendrá por sordo y desventura?

Aqueste mar turbado,
¿quién le pondrá ya freno? Quién concierto
al viento fiero, airado?
Estando tu encubierto,
¿qué norte guiará la nave al puerto?

Of a holy love, in the midst
Of honor and of joy: this place is his.

This is the only place
That a vast beauty fills; where the clearest light
Throws pure and splendid rays
And there is no twilight.
This is where spring flowers never die.

O fields grown deep in truth!
O meadows fresh and soft and truth-bedewed!
O mines most rich to hew!
O quiet that walks and broods
Through valleys of a thousand gifts of good!   —EDWIN MORGAN

At the Ascension

Good Shepherd, have You skipped away, to leave
Your flock in this deep, hidden vale,
Their lonely legacy to grieve
Their stay, while You, beyond the blue sky's trail,
Attain assuring immortality?

They are now reft of joy who once were filled
From the fond kindness of Your breast;
Where can the leaderless, who willed
To follow, turn? the hungry, lest
They lose their way, seek out Your company?

What vision in this world can satisfy
Those who have gazed upon Your face?
Less beauty but disturbs the eye;
The music in this world is dull, lacks grace,
For those who heard Your words' sweet harmony.

Who is there now to calm the white-foamed lake?
Who now to still the roaring gales?
Now that a cloud has lowered to take
And cover You, how can we set our sails
For port? What north star pilots destiny?

¡Ay! nube envidïosa
aun de este breve gozo, ¿qué te aquejas?
¿Dó vuelas presurosa?
¡Cuán rica tú te alejas!
¡Cuán pobres y cuán ciegos ay, nos dejas!

Al salir de la cárcel

Aquí la envidia y mentira
me tuvieron encerrado.
Dichoso el humilde estado
del sabio que se retira
de aqueste mundo malvado;
y con pobre mesa y casa,
en el campo deleitoso,
con sólo Dios se compasa
y a solas su vida pasa
ni envidiado ni envidioso.

¡Oh cortesía, oh dulce acogimiento . . . !

¡Oh cortesía, oh dulce acogimiento,
oh celestial saber, oh gracia pura,
oh de valor dotado y de dulzura,
pecho real y honesto pensamiento!

¡Oh luces de amor querido asiento,
oh boca donde vive la hermosura,
oh habla suavísima, oh figura
angélica, oh mano, oh sabio acento!

Quien tiene en sólo vos atesorado
su gozo y vida alegre y su consuelo,
su bienaventurada y rica suerte:

cuando de vos se viere desterrado,
¡ay!, ¿qué le quedará si no es recelo,
y noche y amargor y llanto y muerte?

Why do you run so fast, O cloud, as though
You envied us brief happiness?
Why hoard the sun, only to show
How rich you are?—miser without largesse,
Scorning our blindness and our poverty!   —JAMES EDWARD TOBIN

On Leaving Prison

Here envying and lies
Held me shut fast.
Happy his simple state
Who, wise at last,
To this ill-dealing world himself denies,
And with poor board and bed
In the sweet countryside
By only God is tried,
And lives his life alone,
None envying him, and he not anyone.   —BRENDA M. SACKETT

O Courtesy, O Harborage Most Sweet . . . !

O courtesy, O harborage most sweet,
heavenly science, and grace well refined
with valor and with gentleness complete,
O kingly breast and honorable mind!

O eyes of love the dear abiding place,
O mouth where beauty's self has made her dwelling,
O melting language and angelic face,
O hand and voice both of high wisdom telling!

who has in you alone compiled his treasure
of joy, rejoicing hours and consolation,
his life's most prosperous and abounding measure,

banished from you, how much his desolation!
Alas! what's left him but mistrustful breath,
darkness, and bitterness, and tears, and death?
                                    —BRENDA M. SACKETT

SAN JUAN DE LA CRUZ
(1542–91)

Although he wrote only five hundred lines which merit the classification of genuinely lyrical poetry, these remain among the most memorable in the Spanish language and perhaps in world literature. Born the son of a weaver, in a Castilian village near Ávila, he joined the Carmelite Order at the age of twenty-one, studying for four years at the University of Salamanca. There he read Garcilaso and the Bible and probably met Fray Luis, his contemporary. Sick and suffering, pining for a life of greater austerity, he decided to enter a convent. However, in 1567 he met Saint Teresa of Jesus and, under her guidance, devoted himself instead to the task of religious reform. The ensuing struggle was bitter; he was thrown in jail, remaining for eight months in a dark cell where, some claim, he began the composition of his poems. When he succeeded in escaping, he continued, unremittingly, his religious work, founding many monasteries with Saint Teresa for the new Order of Discalced Carmelites. From 1578 to 1588 he held several posts in Andalusia, and there, in touch with luxuriant nature (quite in contrast with his barren Castile), he wrote more verse. However, religious persecution uprooted him once again; he was stripped of all honors and exiled to Sierra Morena until his death.

On a manifest level, San Juan's poems resemble secular love lyrics, heightened by passionate love. Unlike the stylized detachment and intellectual control of his contemporaries, especially those most influenced by the Italians, San Juan's poetry is intensely personal and overflows with imagery, reminiscent of the Arabic poets. However, after more careful consideration, and with the help of San Juan's own explanations, one becomes aware of his essentially religious symbolism. Thus, what appeared at first as secular love referred, after all, to the soul's relationship with God and its struggle to become united with Him.

BEST EDITIONS: Father G. de San Juan (ed.): *Obras*, Toledo, 1912–14, 3 vols.; P. Silverio de Santa Teresa (ed.): *Obras*, Burgos, 1929–31, 5 vols.; J. M. Gallegos Rocafull (ed.): *Obras completas*, Mexico, 1942; P. Salinas (ed.): *Poesías completas*, Santiago de Chile, 1947.

ABOUT SAN JUAN DE LA CRUZ: Father Bruno: *St. John of the Cross*, London & New York, Sheed & Ward, 1958; Father Crisógono de Jesús: *The Life of St. John of the Cross*, London, Longmans; New York, Harper, 1958. *Also*: G. Brenan: "St. John of the Cross," *Horizon* (London), May & June 1947; Bede Frost: *St. John of the Cross*, London, Hodder & Stoughton, 1937; P. Gabriel of St. Mary Magdalen: *St. John of the Cross*, Westminster, 1937; I. I. Macdonald: "The Two Versions of the *Cántico Espiritual*," *Modern Language Notes* xxv (1930), pp. 165–84; E. A. Peers: *Spirit of Flame*, London & New York, 1945; R. Sencourt: *Carmelite and Poet*, London, Hollis & Carter, 1943; L. Forster & A. A. Parker: "Quirinus Kuhlmann and the Poetry of St. John of the Cross," *Bulletin of Spanish Studies* 35 (1958) 1–23; H. Hatzfeld: "*Las profundas cavernas*. The Structure of a Symbol of San Juan de la Cruz," *Quedrni Ibero-Americani* 11 (1952) 171–74; R. M. Icaza: *The Stylistic Relationship Between Poetry and Prose in the* Cántico Espiritual *of Saint John of the Cross*, Catholic University, 1957; L. Spitzer: *A Method of Interpreting Literature*, Smith College, 1949, pp. 21–45 [on *En una noche obscura*]; Jorge Guillén: *Language and Poetry*, Harvard University Press, 1961, pp. 79–121.

En una noche obscura . . .

En una noche obscura
Con ansias en amores inflamada
¡Oh dichosa ventura!
Salí sin ser notada,
Estando ya mi casa sosegada.

A escuras, y segura
Por la secreta escala disfrazada
¡Oh dichosa ventura!
A escuras y en celada
Estando ya mi casa sosegada.

En la noche dichosa
En secreto, que nadie me veía,
Ni yo miraba cosa,
Sin otra luz y guía
Sino la que en el corazón ardía.

Aquesta me guiaba
Más cierto que la luz del mediodía
Adonde me esperaba
Quien yo bien me sabía,
En parte donde nadie parecía.

¡Oh noche que guiaste
Oh noche amable más que el alborada
Oh noche que juntaste
Amado con amada,
Amada en el Amado transformada!

En mi pecho florido
Que entero para él sólo se guardaba
Allí quedó dormido,
Y yo le regalaba
Y el ventalle de cedros aire daba.

El aire de la almena
Cuando yo sus cabellos esparcía
Con su mano serena

One Dismal Night . . .

One dismal night
With the ardors of love aflame
O venture bright!
Unobserved I slipped away
While my dwelling still unstirring lay.

In disguise of night
By the secret stair's security
O venture bright!
Into the dark and stealthily
While my dwelling still unstirring lay.

In the secrecy
Of the glorious night, unseen my face
Nor able any part to see
Having no light to guide my way
Save the one within my heart ablaze.

This more luminously
Led me than the radiance of noon
Thence to where in waiting for me
One to me well known
Kept a place where no one had been drawn.

O that night that guided me
O night lovelier than the dawn
O that night of ecstasy
When Beloved and Lover joined,
Into Lover the Beloved transformed!

On my flowering breast,
Kept for Him alone away,
Him I caressed
And He drowsed and stayed
And the cedars softly zephyrs swayed.

The turreted breeze
In stroking His hair
With fingers serene

En mi cuello hería
Y todos mis sentidos suspendía.

Quedéme y olvidéme
El rostro recliné sobre el Amado
Cesó todo, y dejéme
Dejando mi cuidado
Entre las azucenas olvidado.

Cántico espiritual

Esposa

¿Adónde te escondiste,
Amado, y me dejaste con gemido?
Como el ciervo huiste,
Habiéndome herido;
Salí tras ti clamando, y eras ido.

Pastores, los que fuerdes
Allá por las majadas al otero,
Si por ventura vierdes
Aquel que yo más quiero,
Decidle que adolezco, peno y muero.

Buscando mis amores,
Iré por esos montes y riberas,
Ni cogeré las flores,
Ni temeré las fieras,
Y pasaré los fuertes y fronteras.

Pregunta a las criaturas

O bosques y espesuras,
Plantadas por la mano del Amado,
O prado de verduras,
De flores esmaltado,
Decid si por vosotros ha pasado.

My throat touched near
And all my senses languished there.

    Lingering and forgetting
Face in the Lover reposing fair
All lapsed and I surrendered
Surrendering my care
Amidst the lilies remembering no more.

                    —KATE FLORES

Spiritual Canticle

The bride

    Where have you hidden away?
Never a crumb of comfort day or night,
Dearest? To wound your prey
and off like a stag in flight!
I hurried forth imploring you—out of sight!

    You shepherds, you that rove
up in the ranches on the mountain's brow,
if you should meet my love,
my one love, tell him now
I'm heartsick, fevered, and fast sinking now.

    I'll go myself and scour
highland and lowland over for my dear;
not dawdle for a flower;
no fang of prowler fear;
bursting by each confronter and frontier.

A question to the creatures

    O groves and leafy screen,
foliage planted by a lover's hand,
meadows of bluegreen
with marigolds japanned,
tell me, has he been lately in your land?

Respuesta de las criaturas

Mil gracias derramando,
Pasó por estos sotos con presura,
Y yéndolos mirando,
Con sola su figura
Vestidos los dejó de hermosura.

Esposa

¡Ay, quién podrá sanarme!
Acaba de entregarte ya de vero.
No quieras enviarme
De hoy más ya mensajero,
Que no saben decirme lo que quiero.

Y todos cuantos vagan,
De ti me van mil gracias refiriendo
Y todos más me llagan,
Y déjame muriendo
Un no sé qué que quedan balbuciendo.

Mas, ¿cómo perseveras,
O vida, no viviendo donde vives,
Y haciendo porque mueras,
Las flechas que recibes,
De lo que del Amado en ti concibes?

¿Por qué, pues has llagado
A aqueste corazón, no le sanaste?
Y pues me le has robado,
¿Por qué así le dejaste,
Y no tomas el robo que robaste?

Apaga mis enojos,
Pues que ninguno basta a deshacellos,
Y véante mis ojos,
Pues eres lumbre dellos,
Y sólo para ti quiero tenellos.

Descubre tu presencia,
Y máteme tu vista y hermosura;

Their response

    Lavishing left and right
a world of wonders, he went streaming by
these orchards, meteor-bright:
beneath his brilliant eye
rose many a green pavilion to the sky.

The bride

    What cure for my disease?
Give up, give up in earnest. Make an ending.
These tedious deputies,
I beg of you, stop sending:
what good are these—pretending and pretending?

    Figures that come and go
bring news of you indeed: what jubilant rumor!
I reel as with a blow;
sink stricken at the glimmer
of something heard ecstatic in the stammer.

    Strange! to feel the breath
of life endure, not living where life is.
Brought low and close to death
by those bowmen of his
to each inroad of love sharp witnesses.

    Unready yet to mend
the havoc in this heart—so quick to break it?
Possess and not intend
ever to take it?
Have it by force and forcibly forsake it?

    Oh shorten the long days
of burning thirst—no other love allays them.
Let my eyes see your face,
treasure to daze them.
Except for love, it's labor lost to raise them.

    Appear here at my side,
though I die dazzled in a blaze of grace.

Mira que la dolencia
De amor, que no se cura
Sino con la presencia y la figura.

    ¡Oh cristalina fuente,
Si en esos tus semblantes plateados,
Formases de repente
Los ojos deseados,
Que tengo en mis entrañas dibujados!

    Apártalos, Amado,
Que voy de vuelo.

Esposo

    Vuélvete, paloma,
Que el ciervo vulnerado
Por el otero asoma,
Al aire de tu vuelo, y fresco toma.

Esposa

    Mi Amado, las montañas,
Los valles solitarios nemorosos,
Las ínsulas extrañas,
Los ríos sonorosos,
El silbo de los aires amorosos.

    La noche sosegada
En par de los levantes de la aurora,
La música callada,
La soledad sonora,
La cena, que recrea y enamora.

    Nuestro lecho florido,
De cuevas de leones enlazado,
En púrpura tendido,
De paz edificado,
De mil escudos de oro coronado.

    A zaga de tu huella
Las jóvenes discurren al camino

Look at love's invalid,
heartsick, a failing case—
only one chance of comfort: face to face.

If only, crystal well,
clear in the mirror's silver could arise
suddenly by some spell
the long awaited eyes
the poor heart scrapes in clay to improvise!

Love, cover those bright eyes!
I'm voyaging on air!

The bridegroom

Float downward, dove.
The stag from covert lies
hurt on the hill above,
stirred by your wing he loves the coolness of.

The bride

My love: the mountain's height;
forest ravines and faraway recesses;
torrents' sonorous weight;
isles no explorer guesses;
the affectionate air all whisper and caresses;

the serene flow of night
with dawn a rising twilight in the skies;
music of still delight;
a desert of sweet cries;
a supper of light hearts and lovelit eyes.

Our bed: in roses laid,
patrols of lions ranging all around;
of royal purple made,
pitched on halcyon ground,
with blazonry of golden bucklers crowned.

Breathless, on roads you mark
girls whirl to the four winds; their foreheads shine

Al toque de centella,
Al adobado vino,
Emisiones de bálsamo Divino.

En la interior bodega
De mi Amado bebí, y cuando salía
Por toda aquesta vega,
Ya cosa no sabía,
Y el ganado perdí, que antes seguía.

Allí me dio su pecho,
Allí me enseñó ciencia muy sabrosa,
Y yo le di de hecho
A mí, sin dejar cosa;
Allí le prometí de ser su esposa.

Mi alma sa ha empleado,
Y todo mi caudal en su servicio:
Ya no guardo ganado,
Ni ya tengo otro oficio;
Que ya sólo en amar es mi ejercicio.

Pues ya si en el ejido
De hoy más no fuere vista ni hallada,
Diréis que me he perdido,
Que andando enamorada,
Me hice perdidiza, y fui ganada.

De flores y esmeraldas
En las frescas mañanas escogidas,
haremos las guirnaldas
En tu amor florecidas,
Y en un cabello mío entretejidas.

En sólo aquel cabello,
Que en mi cuello volar consideraste,
Mirástele en mi cuello,
Y en él preso quedaste,
Y en uno de mis ojos te llagaste.

Cuando tú me mirabas,
Tu gracia en mí tus ojos imprimían:

stung by a sudden spark,
flushed with delightful wine.
What swirls of fragrance widening and divine!

Shown deeper than before
in cellars of my love I drank; from there
went wandering on the moor;
knew nothing, felt no care;
the sheep I tended once are who knows where?

There he broke secrecy;
had honey of revelation to confide.
There I gave all of me;
put chariness aside:
there I promised to become his bride.

Forever at his door
I gave my heart and soul. My fortune, too.
I've no flock any more,
no other work in view.
My occupation: love. It's all I do.

If I'm not seen again
in the old places, on the village ground,
say of me: lost to men.
Say I'm adventure-bound
for love's sake. Lost (on purpose) to be found.

In the cool morning hours
we'll gather many a tender wreath to wear,
with emeralds and dayflowers
sprung in love's summer air.
I'll give for their entwining a lock of hair

curling upon my shoulder—
you loved to see it lifted on the air.
You loved it, fond beholder
caught fascinated there—
my glance embedded then the barb you wear.

Your eyes caressing me
fell on their living image in my own

Por eso me adamabas,
Y en eso merecían
Los míos adorar lo que en ti vían.

   No quieras despreciarme,
Que si color moreno en mí hallaste,
Ya bien puedes mirarme,
Después que me miraste,
Que gracia y hermosura en mí dejaste.

   Cogednos las raposas,
Que está ya florecida nuestra viña,
En tanto que de rosas
Hacemos una piña,
Y no parezca nadie en la montiña.

   Detente, Cierzo muerto;
Ven, Austro, que recuerdas las amores,
Aspira por mi huerto,
Y corran sus olores,
Y pacerá el Amado entre las flores.

Esposo

   Entrádose ha la Esposa
En el ameno huerto deseado,
Y a su sabor reposa,
El cuello reclinado
Sobre los dulces brazos del Amado.

   Debajo del manzano,
Allí conmigo fuiste desposada,
Allí te di la mano,
Y fuiste reparada,
Donde tu madre fuera violada.

   A las aves ligeras,
Leones, ciervos, gamos saltadores,
Montes, valles, riberas,
Aguas, aires, ardores,
Y miedos de las noches veladores:

and loved distractedly.
That stirring look alone
gave mettle to return the fervor shown.

Please, no pitying brow
seeing my cheek was dusky in those days.
Only turn this way now
as once before—that gaze
adorned me fresh and lovely in its rays.

Now that the bloom uncloses
catch us the little foxes by the vine,
as we knit cones of roses
cunning as those of pine.
Let no intruder loom on our skyline.

Dwindle, O wind of death.
Come, southern wind, for lovers; come and stir
the garden with your breath.
Make affluent the air.
My love is gladdened among lilies there.

The bridegroom

She enters, the bride! closes,
soft, the enchanting garden dreams foretold her.
Gracefully she reposes;
my arms enfold her,
her throat affectionate upon my shoulder.

Under the apple tree
the words of our betrothal and their spell:
I took you tenderly,
hurt virgin, made you well
where all the scandal on your mother fell.

Wings twinkling here and there,
lion and gamboling antler, shy gazelle,
peak, precipice, and shore,
flame, air, and flooding well,
night-watchman terror, with no good to tell—

Por las amenas liras
Y canto de sirenas os conjuro
Que cesen vuestras iras,
Y no toquéis al muro,
Porque la Esposa duerma más seguro.

Esposa

Oh ninfas de Judea,
En tanto que en las flores y rosales
El ámbar perfumea,
Morá en los arrabales,
Y no queráis tocar nustros umbrales.

Escóndete, Carillo,
Y mira con tu haz a las montañas,
Y no quieras decillo:
Mas mira las compañas
De la que va por ínsulas extrañas.

Esposo

La blanca palomica
Al Arca con el ramo se ha tornado,
Y ya la tortolica
Al socio deseado
En las riberas verdes ha hallado.

En soledad vivía,
Y en soledad ha puesto ya su nido,
Y en soledad la guía
A solas su querido,
También en soledad de amor herido.

Esposa

Gocémonos, Amado,
Y vámonos a ver en tu hermosura
Al monte u al collado,
Do mana el agua pura;
Entremos más adentro en la espesura.

by many a pleasant lyre
and song of sirens I command you all:
bury this wrangling air;
no nuzzling at the wall.
But let the bride in a deep slumber fall.

The bride

Girls of Jerusalem,
now that the breath of roses more and more
eddies on leaf and stem,
be stranger than before.
Stand further. And no darkening our door.

And darling, settle here.
Look to the mountain ranges; turn your face.
Hush! nothing in my ear.
But look what crewmen grace
the passer of fabulous islands in her chase

The bridegroom

The little pearl-white dove
with frond of olive to the Ark returns.
Wedded, the bird of love
no longer yearns,
nestled above still water, among ferns.

She spent most lonely days,
in loneliest of regions kept her nest,
her guide on lonesome ways
her love, who knew them best—
that arrow from the desert in his breast.

The bride

A celebration, love!
Let's revel at both our beauty in your eyes!
To the hill and heights above!
cascades that freshen these!
then further, deep and deeper in the trees.

Y luego a las subidas
Cavernas de la piedra nos iremos,
Que están bien escondidas,
Y allí nos entraremos,
Y el mosto de granadas gustaremos.

Allí me mostrarías
Aquello que mi alma pretendía,
Y luego me darías
Allí tú, vida mía,
Aquello que me diste el otro día:

El aspirar del aire,
El conto de la dulce Filomena,
El soto y su donaire,
En la noche serena
Con llama que consume y no da pena.

Que nadie lo miraba,
Aminadab tampoco parecía,
Y el cerco sosegaba,
Y la caballería
A vista de las aguas descendía.

¡Oh llama de amor viva . . . !

¡Oh llama de amor viva
Que tiernamente hieres
De mi alma en el más profundo centro!
Pues ya no eres esquiva
Acaba ya si quieres
Rompe la tela deste dulce encuentro.

¡Oh cauterio suave!
¡Oh regalada llaga!
¡Oh mano blanda! ¡Oh toque delicado,
Que a vida eterna sabe,
Y a toda deuda paga!
Matando, muerte en vida la has trocado.

And on to the steeple rock
all honeycombed with caverns and with mines
well off the common track.
Safe in those high confines
we'll taste the tingle of pomegranate wines.

There finally you'll show
something my soul long wept and waited for,
and the same moment, O
my dearest life, restore
what once upon a time you gave before:

the breathing of the air,
the nightingale in her affectionate vein,
woods and the freshness there
in night's unruffled reign —
these, and the flames embracing without pain.

None loitering to see:
Aminadab the demon fled affrighted.
The siege sank quietly.
The horsemen sighted
vistas of shining water and alighted.

—JOHN FREDERICK NIMS

O Living Flame of Love . . .

O living flame of love,
How tender is your wound,
Your burning at the center of my soul!
You are no longer shy —
Please finish, know me at the source;
Break the hymen of our sweet intercourse!

O easy cautery!
Oh wound that is really gift!
Oh gentle hand! Oh delicate touch of a knife
That brings eternal life
And pays all petty debts!
Killing, you turn my death into flaming life!

¡Oh lámparas de fuego
En cuyos resplandores
Las profundas cavernas del sentido,
Que estaba obscuro y ciego,
Con extraños primores
Calor y luz dan junto a su querido!

Cuán manso y amoroso
Recuerdas en mi seno
Donde secretamente solo moras
Y en tu aspirar sabroso
De bien y gloria lleno
Cuán delicadamente me enamoras!

Entréme donde no supe . . .

Entréme donde no supe,
Y quedéme no sabiendo,
Toda sciencia trascendiendo.

Yo no supe dónde entraba,
Pero, cuando allí me vi,
Sin saber dónde me estaba,
Grandes cosas entendí;
No diré lo que sentí,
Que me quedé no sabiendo,
Toda sciencia trascendiendo.

De paz y de piedad
Era la sciencia perfecta,
En profunda soledad,
Entendida vía recta;
Era cosa tan secreta,
Que me quedé balbuciendo,
Toda sciencia trascendiendo.

Estaba tan embebido,
Tan absorto y ajenado,
Que se quedó mi sentido
De todo sentir privado;

O lamps of living fire,
In whose renewing splendors
The deep and smoking caverns of the senses,
Which once were black and blind,
Provide amazing delights,
Give heat and light to their awaking lover!

How tender, mild, and blessed
Is your image in my breast,
Where, secretly, you live alone, a king;
And with your soft breathing,
The bliss and glory of the Dove,
How delicately you induce my love!   —STEPHEN STEPANCHEV

I Entered Where I Did Not Know . . .

I entered where I did not know,
And there remained unknowing,
All reason now transcended.

I did not know the door
But when I found the way,
Unknowing where I was,
I learned unheard of things,
But what I heard I cannot say,
For I remained unknowing,
All reason now transcended.

My knowledge was fulfilled
With piety and peace.
In deepest solitude
I found the narrow way:
A secret giving such release
That I was left there stammering,
All reason now transcended.

I was so fully drunk,
So dazed and far away,
My senses were released
From feelings of my own.

Y el espíritu dotado
De un entender no entendiendo,
Toda sciencia trascendiendo.

El que allí llega de vero,
De sí mismo desfallesce;
Cuanto sabía primero
Mucho bajo le paresce;
Y su sciencia tanto cresce,
Que se queda no sabiendo,
Toda sciencia trascendiendo.

Cuanto más alto se sube,
Tanto menos entendía
Qué es la tenebrosa nube
Que a la noche esclarecía;
Por eso quien la sabía
Queda siempre no sabiendo,
Toda sciencia trascendiendo.

Este saber no sabiendo
Es de tan alto poder,
Que los sabios arguyendo
Jamás le pueden vencer;
Que no llega su saber
A no entender entendiendo,
Toda sciencia trascendiendo.

Y es de tan alta excelencia
Aqueste sumo saber,
Que no hay facultad ni sciencia
Que le puedan emprender;
Quien se supiere vencer
Con un no saber sabiendo,
Irá siempre trascendiendo.

Y si lo queréis oír,
Consiste esta suma sciencia
En un subido sentir
De la divinal Esencia;
Es obra de su clemencia
Hacer quedar no entendiendo
Toda sciencia trascendiendo.

My mind had found a surer way:
A knowledge of unknowing,
All reason now transcended.

And he who does arrive,
Collapses as in sleep;
For all he knew before
Now seems of little worth,
    And so his knowledge grows so deep
That he remains unknowing,
All reason now transcended.

The higher he ascends,
The darker is the wood;
It is the shadowy cloud
That clarified the night,
And so the one who understood
Remains at last unknowing,
All reason now transcended.

This knowledge by unknowing
Is such a soaring force
That scholars argue long
But never leave the ground.
Their reason always fails the source:
To understand unknowing,
All reason now transcended.

This knowledge is supreme
And meets a blazing height,
Though formal reason tries,
It crumbles in the dark.
For one who would control the night,
By knowledge of unknowing
He will have all transcended.

This is my final word,
The highest learning lead
To an ecstatic feeling
Of the most holy Being;
And from his mercy comes his deed:
To make one stay unknowing,
All reason now transcended.

—WILLIS BARNSTONE

Vivo sin vivir en mí . . .

Vivo sin vivir en mí,
  y de tal manera espero
  que muero porque no muero.

En mí yo no vivo ya,
  y sin Dios vivir no puedo,
  pues sin Él y sin mí quedo,
  este vivir, ¿qué será?
  Mil muertes se me hará,
  pues mi misma vida espero,
  muriendo porque no muero.

Esta vida que yo vivo,
  es privación de vivir;
  y así, es contino morir
  hasta que vivo contigo.
  Oye, mi Dios, lo que digo,
  que esta vida no la quiero,
  que muero porque no muero.

Estando ausente de Ti,
  ¿Qué vida puedo tener
  sino muerte padecer
  la mayor que nunca vi?
  Lástima tengo de mí,
  pues de suerte persevero,
  que muero porque no muero.

El pez que del agua sale
  aun de alivio no carece,
  que la muerte que padece
  al fin de muerte le vale.
  ¿Qué muerte habrá que se iguale
  a mi vivir lastimero,
  pues si más vivo más muero?

Cuando me empiezo a aliviar
  de verte en el Sacramento,
  háceme más sentimiento
  el no te poder gozar.

I Live and Do Not Live in Myself . . .

I live and do not live in myself,
    And so I strongly hope that I
    May die because I do not die.

I live no longer in myself
    And cannot live without my God,
    And since I live without myself and God,
    My God, what will this living be?
    A thousand deaths will rain on me
    As I wait for life in my foul sty,
    Dying because I do not die.

This black and joyless life I live
    Is really a negation of life
    And a bloody, never-ending dying
    Until I live my life with you.
    Listen, my God, to what I say:
    I do not want this fevered life;
    I die because I do not die.

When I am absent from you, Lord,
    What life can I expect to know
    But needled suffering of a death
    Greater than I knew before?
    I pity my battered, humble self
    Because I live on in this sty.
    I die because I do not die.

The fish that leaps out of the sea
    Is not without its blessed relief,
    For its spasms of death, its agony,
    Serve as real death finally.
    What death is there to equal mine,
    This pitiful living of a lie,
    For the more I live the more I die?

When I begin to feel relief,
    Seeing you in the Sacrament,
    I feel an even greater grief:
    I cannot enjoy your company.

Todo es para más penar
por no verte como quiero
que muero porque no muero.

Y, si me gozo, Señor,
   con esperanza de verte,
   en ver que puedo perderte
   se me dobla mi dolor,
   viviendo en tanto pavor
   y esperando como espero,
   que muero porque no muero.

Sácame de aquesta muerte,
   mi Dios, y dame la vida;
   no me tengas impedida
   en este lazo tan fuerte.
   Mira que muero por verte,
   y mi mal es tan entero
   que muero porque no muero.

Lloraré mi muerte ya,
   y lamentaré mi vida
   en tanto que detenida
   por mis pecados está.
   ¡Oh mi Dios! ¿Cuándo sera?
   cuando yo diga de vero:
   vivo ya porque no muero.

Tras de un amoroso lance . . .

Tras de un amoroso lance,
Y no de esperanza falto,
Volé tan alto, tan alto,
Que le di a la caza alcance.

Para que yo alcance diese
A aqueste lance divino,
Tanto volar me convino,
Que de vista me perdiese;

Everything makes for pain and sighs:
I do not see you as I wish.
I die because I do not die.

And, if I console myself, O lord,
  With hope of seeing you at last,
  I see that I may lose all sight
  Of you and pain redoubles fast.
  Living in such awful fear
  And hoping as I hope to climb,
  I die because I do not die.

Rescue me from this living death,
  My God, and give me deathless life;
  Do not keep me bleeding, bound
  By ropes so strong no man can break them.
  See that I die to see you, God,
  And I am sick, so shattered where I lie
  I die because I do not die.

I shall mourn now for my death,
And I shall sorrow for my life,
Prolonged by painful, fevered breath
I earned with sins, frivolity.
Oh, my God, when will it be
That I can say without a lie:
I live because I do not die?

                          — STEPHEN STEPANCHEV

Not Without Hope Pulsing My Breast . . .

Not without hope pulsing my breast,
Adventuring in love I flew;
So high, so far I soared the blue
That I at last attained my quest.

In order to achieve this aim,
Even pursue this divine end,
I had to fly to heights unkenned
By sharpest eye; but, all the same,

Y con todo, en este trance
En el vuelo quedé falto;
Mas el amor fue tan alto,
Que le di a la caza alcance.

Cuando más alto subía,
Deslumbróseme la vista,
Y la más fuerte conquista
En escuro se hacía;
Mas por ser de amor el lance
Di un ciego y oscuro salto,
Y fui tan alto, tan alto,
Que le di a la caza alcance.

Cuanto más alto llegaba
De este lance tan subido,
Tanto más bajo y rendido
Y abatido me hallaba.
Dije: No habrá quien alcance;
Y abatíme tanto, tanto,
Que fui tan alto, tan alto
Que le di a la caza alcance.

Por una extraña manera
Mil vuelos pasé de un vuelo,
Porque esperanza de cielo
Tanto alcanza cuanto espera;
Esperé sólo este lance,
Y en esperar no fui falto,
Pues fui tan alto, tan alto,
Que le di a la caza alcance.

Un pastorcico solo está penado . . .

Un pastorcico solo está penado,
Ajeno de placer y de contento,
Y en su pastora puesto el pensamiento,
Y el pecho del amor muy lastimado.

My flight fell short and in that test
Almost experienced defeat——
Yet ardent love bade me compete
Till I at last attained my quest.

Confused and dazzled by the light
Blinding my certainty of eye,
As I explored the highest sky
My greatest conquest came by night.
Adventuring in love, I pressed
My reckless flight, so far, so steep,
And dared so dark an eye-shut leap,
That I at last attained my quest.

At that exalted altitude,
The higher that I dared to soar,
Adventuring in love, the more
Depressed I felt, an attitude
Which drew my cry: no one finds rest
In tiredness, or hope in gloom;
Never to reach love seems my doom——
Yet I at last attained my quest.

By a means puzzling and strange
Each single flight was multiplied
A thousandfold, for heavenside
Is only reached by those who range
With hope where hope is; thus, my best
Adventuring in love, despair
Denied, was in love's utmost air——
There I at last attained my quest.

—JAMES EDWARD TOBIN

A Shepherd, Young and Mournful, Grieves Alone . . .

A shepherd, young and mournful, grieves alone,
Alien his pleasure, absent his content;
The shadow-memory of his shepherdess
Strikes at his heart as though love were a stone.

No llora por haberle amor llagado,
Que no le pena verse así afligido,
Aunque en el corazón está herido;
Mas llora por pensar que está olvidado.

Que sólo de pensar que está olvidado
De su bella pastora, con gran pena
Se deja maltratar en tierra ajena,
El pecho del amor muy lastimado.

Y dice el Pastorcico: ¡Ay, desdichado
De aquel que de mi amor ha hecho ausencia,
Y no quiere gozar la mi presencia,
Y el pecho por su amor muy lastimado!

Y a cabo de un gran rato se ha encumbrado
Sobre un árbol do abrió sus brazos bellos,
Y muerto se ha quedado, asido de ellos,
El pecho del amor muy lastimado.

Que bien sé yo la fonte que mana y corre . . .

Que bien sé yo la fonte que mana y corre,
　　Aunque es de noche.

Aquella eterna fonte está escondida,
Que bien sé yo do tiene su manida,
　　Aunque es de noche.

Su origen no lo sé, pues no le tiene,
Mas sé que todo origen de ella viene,
　　Aunque es de noche.

Sé que no puede ser cosa tan bella,
Y que cielos y tierra beben de ella,
　　Aunque es de noche.

Bien sé que suelo en ella no se halla,
Y que ninguno puede vadealla,
　　Aunque es de noche.

Physical pain does not evoke lament,
Such suffering is not what brings the hurt;
Although his heart is battered by the blow,
He weeps to realize neglect is meant.

In realizing thus that he is not
The center of his shepherdess' life
He sadly finds his heart is wounded more;
Alien to joy, he hears love taunt: Forgot.

The shepherd cries: Why does she stand apart?
Ah, woe to him who holds her distantly,
Keeps her in willing absence from my side,
Shutting her eyes to how love tears my heart.

He stretched his lovely, loving arms out wide,
Climbing a tree in time to hold them so;
His heart still deeply wounded by her love,
He clung there, waiting her, until he died.
                                        —JAMES EDWARD TOBIN

I Know Full Well the Water's Flowing Power . . .

I know full well the water's flowing power,
        Though it be dark.

A secret font, an everlasting force—
I know exactly where it has its source,
        Though it be dark.

And yet I do not know; for therein lies
The origin from which origins rise,
        Though it be dark.

I know that nothing can be quite so fair
And that earth drinks from it as well as air,
        Though it be dark.

I know its depth cannot be sounded, know
That none can cross against the eddies' flow,
        Though it be dark.

Su claridad nunca es escurecida,
Y sé que toda luz de ella es venida,
   Aunque es de noche.

Sé ser tan caudalosas sus corrientes,
Que infiernos, cielos riegan, y las gentes,
   Aunque es de noche.

El corriente que nace de esta fuente,
Bien sé que es tan capaz y omnipotente,
   Aunque es de noche.

El corriente que de estas dos procede
Sé que ninguna de ellas le precede,
   Aunque es de noche.

Aquesta eterna fonte está escondida
En este vivo pan por darnos vida,
   Aunque es de noche.

Aquí se está llamando a las criaturas,
Y de esta agua se hartan, aunque a escuras,
   Porque es de noche.

Aquesta viva fuente, que deseo
En este pan de vida yo la veo,
   Aunque es de noche.

Nothing can dim its ever-brilliant gleam,
From which all other light and wisdom stream,
    Though it be dark.

I know its many branches stretch and wind
To reach all heights and depths and all mankind,
    Though it be dark.

I know how well this nourished current laves
Each bank, how very powerful its waves,
    Though it be dark.

Both source and swirling stream are one, I sense——
Their unity permits no precedence——
    Though it be dark.

Its deathless strength, its hidden riverhead,
Are in grace-giving eucharistic Bread,
    Though it be dark.

And all mankind is called and asked to share
The nourishment of hidden mystery there,
    Though it be dark.

Desiring and desired, this mystery
Within the Bread of life I clearly see,
    Though it be dark.

                    —JAMES EDWARD TOBIN

LUIS DE GÓNGORA
(1561–1627)

Soon after the birth of the national literatures of Europe, during the Middle Ages, writers in the vernacular aspired to lift their writings to such formalistic beauty that they would have no reason to envy the literature in classical tongues. During the late sixteenth and early seventeenth centuries they surrendered themselves to the use of exaggerated elegance and super-refinement. They filled their works with mythological allusions, indulged in puns, piled metaphor upon metaphor, accumulated wide varieties of hyperbatons and zeugmas, and propped up their relatively young languages with Latinized syntax, which resulted in a sort of "obscurity" which in the hands of gifted practitioners was as challenging as it was delightfully "brilliant." A few generations back, this trend was blithely dismissed as a literary fashion of slight significance, the ravings of lunatic writers. History has proved this judgment false: the baroque trend, known in Spain as "Gongorism," after its loftiest practitioner, Luis de Góngora, was a necessary stage in the development of poetry—a fundamental phase of liberation which has persisted in most of our contemporary writing, from Eliot, Lorca, and Auden to Neruda and Allen Ginsberg.

Born in Córdoba, Luis de Góngora at the age of fifteen was sent to study law at the University of Salamanca; he had a wild time there, outshining his fellow students both in wickedness and poetical spark. He was especially versed and fluent in the composition of satire and festive poetry. On his return home he took minor orders and became prebendary of the cathedral, but refused to give up either his pranks and practical jokes or his wenching, gambling, and dueling. However, his sins were overlooked because of the successful completion of his duties, especially during his missions to Burgos, Granada, Alcalá, and Madrid. Furthermore, his reputation as a poet grew, his work becoming often deeply patriotic, so that, through the Duke of Lerma's influence, in 1612 he became chaplain to Philip III. Squandering his salary in lavish entertainment, he frequently found himself in financial embarrassment. He returned to Córdoba, suffered paralysis and loss of memory, and died, years later, of apoplexy. Envied and hated by Lope de Vega and Quevedo, loved and imitated by the Count of Villamediana and Sor Juana Inés de la Cruz, Góngora remains today among the most vitally alive of all classic Spanish poets.

BEST EDITIONS: J. & I. Millé y Giménez (eds.): *Obras completas*, Madrid, 1943; D. Alonso (ed.): *Las Soledades*, Madrid, 1956 (3rd ed.); R. Foulché-Delbosc (ed.): *Obras poéticas*, New York, 1921, 3 vols.

ABOUT LUIS DE GÓNGORA: J. Fitzmaurice-Kelly: *Góngora*, London, 1917; E. J. Gates: *The Metaphors of Luis de Góngora*, Philadelphia, 1933; R. Jeffers: *Poetry, Gongorism and a Thousand Years*, Los Angeles, 1949; E. K. Kane: *Gongorism and the Golden Age*, University of North Carolina, 1928; C. L. Penney: *Luis de Góngora*, New York, 1926; P. Salinas: *Reality and the Poet in Spanish Poetry*, Johns Hopkins University, 1940, pp. 131–50; E. J. Gates: "Don Francisco Fernández de Córdoba, Defender of Góngora," *Romanic Review* 42 (1951), pp. 18–26; E. J. Gates: "New Light on the *Antídoto* Against Góngora's 'pestilent' *Soledades*," *PMLA* 56 (1951), p. 746–64; L. Nelson: "Góngora and Milton: Toward a Definition of the Baroque," *Comparative Literature* 6 (1954), pp. 53–63; E. E. Uhrhan: *Linguistic Analysis of Góngora's Baroque Style*, University of Illinois dissertation, 1950, abstracted in H. R. Kahane & A. Pietrangeli: *Descriptive Studies in Spanish Grammar*, University of Illinois, 1954, Jorge Guillén: *Language and Poetry*, Harvard University Press, 1961, pp. 27–75.

Ande yo caliente . . .

Ande yo caliente,
y ríase la gente.

Traten otros del gobierno
del mundo y sus monarquías,
mientras gobiernan mis días
mantequillas y pan tierno,
y las mañanas de invierno
naranjada y aguardiente;
Y ríase la gente.

Coma en dorada vajilla
el príncipe mil cuidados
como píldoras dorados
que yo en mi pobre mesilla
quiero más una morcilla
que en el asador reviente;
Y ríase la gente.

Cuando cubra las montañas
de plata y nieve el enero,
tenga yo lleno el brasero
de bellotas y castañas,
y quien las dulces patrañas
del rey que rabió me cuente;
Y ríase la gente.

Busque muy en hora buena
el mercader nuevos soles;
yo conchas y caracoles
entre la menuda arena,
escuchando a Filomena
sobre el chopo de la fuente;
Y ríase la gente.

Pase a media noche el mar,
y arda en amorosa llama
Leandro por ver su dama;
que yo más quiero pasar

Roistering I'll Chaff . . .

Roistering I'll chaff
So let the people laugh!

Let others cope with governing
The kingdoms of the world,
While I let days be governed
By butter cakes and bread,
And, fresh on winter mornings,
By rum and orangeade,
So let the people laugh!

Let princes eat on golden plate
A thousand cares,
Like gilded pills,
While I, at my poor table,
Make sausages at will,
Waiting for another to burst upon the grill,
So let the people laugh!

When January covers
The peaks with silver snow,
My brazier will be popping
With chestnuts all aglow,
With acorns and old fairy tales
Of never-never kings,
So let the people laugh!

Let the early merchant
Go looking for new suns;*
I'll take snails and cockles
Where quiet tidepools run,
And listen to the nightingale
In poplars by the spring,
So let the people laugh!

Leander swam the Hellespont
At midnight, for his flame,
But I'll just wade the easy stream

---

*suns, i.e., *soles*, also means money, a typical play on words.

de Yepes a Madrigar
la regalada corriente;
Y ríase la gente.

  Pues Amor es tan cruel,
que de Príamo y su amada
hace tálamo una espada,
do se junta ella y él;
sea mi Tisbe un pastel,
y la espada sea mi diente;
Y ríase la gente.

Alegoría de la brevedad de las cosas humanas

Aprended, flores, en mí,
lo que va de ayer a hoy,
que ayer maravilla fui,
y sombra mía aun no soy.

La Aurora ayer me dio cuna,
la noche ataúd me dio;
sin luz muriera, si no
me la prestara la Luna.
Pues de vosotras ninguna
deja de acabar así,

Aprended, flores, en mí,
lo que va de ayer a hoy,
que ayer maravilla fui,
y sombra mía aun no soy.

Consuelo dulce el clavel
es a la breve edad mía,
pues quien me concedió un día,
dos apenas le dio a él.
Efímeras del vergel,
yo cárdena, él carmesí,

From Yepes to Madrigar,
So let the people laugh!

   For Cupid in his cruelty
To Pyramus and bride,
Made their bed a sword;
There, beneath the mulberry tree,
My Thisbe is a pie,
My tooth, the fatal sword,
So let the people laugh!

                             —WILLIAM M. DAVIS

Allegory of the Brevity of Things Human

Learn, flowers, from me, what parts we play
From dawn to dusk. Last noon the boast
And marvel of the fields, today
I am not even my own ghost.

The fresh aurora was my cot,
The night my coffin and my shroud;
I perished with no light, save what
The moon could lend me from a cloud.
And thus, all flowers must die — of whom
Not one of you can cheat the doom.

Learn, flowers, from me, what parts we play
From dawn to dusk. Last noon the boast
And marvel of the fields, today
I am not even my own ghost.

What most consoles me from my fleetness
Is the carnation fresh with dew,
Since that which gave me one day's sweetness
To her conceded scarcely two:
Ephemerids in briefness vie
My scarlet and her crimson die.

Aprended, flores, en mí,
lo que va de ayer a hoy,
que ayer maravilla fui,
y sombra mía aun no soy.

Flor es el jazmín, si bella,
no de las más vividoras,
pues dura pocas más horas
que rayos tiene de estrella;
si el ámbar florece, es ella
la flor que él retiene en sí.

Aprended, flores, en mí,
lo que va de ayer a hoy,
que ayer maravilla fui,
y sombra mía aun no soy.

Aunque el alhelí grosero
en fragancia y en color,
más día ve que otra flor,
pues ve los de un mayo entero,
morir maravilla quiero,
y no vivir alhelí.

Aprended, flores, en mí,
lo que va de ayer a hoy,
que ayer maravilla fui,
y sombra mía aun no soy.

A ninguna al fin mayores
términos concede el Sol
si no es al girasol,
Matusalem de las flores;
ojos son aduladores
cuantas en él hojas vi.

Aprended, flores, en mí,
lo que va de ayer a hoy,
que ayer maravilla fui,
y sombra mía aun no soy.

Learn, flowers, from me, what parts we play
From dawn to dusk. Last noon the boast
And marvel of the fields, today
I am not even my own ghost.

The jasmine, fairest of the flowers,
Is least in size as in longevity.
She forms a star, yet lives less hours
Than it has rays. Her soul is brevity.
If amber could a flower be grown
It would be she, and she alone!

Learn, flowers, from me, what parts we play
From dawn to dusk. Last noon the boast
And marvel of the fields, today
I am not even my own ghost.

The gillyflower, though plain and coarse,
Enjoys on earth a longer stay.
And sees more suns complete their course
—As many as there shine in May.
Yet better far a marvel die
Than live a gillyflower, say I!

Learn, flowers, from me, what parts we play
From dawn to dusk. Last noon the boast
And marvel of the fields, today
I am not even my own ghost.

To no flower blooming in our sphere did
The daystar grant a longer pardon
Than to the Sunflower, golden-bearded
Methusaleh of every garden.
Eying him through as many days
As he shoots petals forth like rays.

Yet learn from me, what parts we play
From dawn to dusk. Last noon the boast
And marvel of the fields, today
I am not even my own ghost.

—ROY CAMPBELL

¡Oh claro honor del líquido elemento . . . !

¡Oh claro honor del líquido elemento,
dulce arroyuelo de luciente plata!
cuya agua entre la yerba se dilata
con regalado son, con paso lento.

Pues la por quien helar y arder me siento
mientras en ti se mira, Amor retrata
de su rostro la nieve y escarlata
en tu tranquilo y blando movimiento,

vete como te vas, no dejes floja
la undosa rienda al cristiano freno
con que gobiernas tu procaz corriente:

que no es bien que confusamente acoja
tanta belleza en su profundo seno
el gran señor del húmedo tridente.

Ilustre y hermosísima María . . .

Ilustre y hermosísima María,
mientras se dejan ver a cualquier hora
en tus mejillas la rosada aurora,
Febo en tus ojos, y en tu frente el día;

y mientras con gentil descortesía
mueve el viento la hebra voladora,
que la Arabia en sus venas atesora,
y el rico Tajo en sus arenas cría;

antes que de la edad Febo eclipsado,
el claro día vuelva en noche obscura,
huya la aurora del mortal nublado;

antes que lo que hoy es rubio tesoro,
venza a la blanca nieve su blancura,
goza, goza el color, la luz, el oro.

Pride of the Fourth and Liquid Element . . .

Pride of the fourth and liquid element,
Sweet brook whose waters with soft music pass,
Stretching, pellucid and pre-eminent,
Their ribbon of bright silver through the grass,

Since Cupid on your smooth and quiet stream,
As she looks into it, portrays the snow
And scarlet of her face, for whom I seem
At times to freeze, at other times to glow,

Watch how you move; be careful to keep taut
The crystal bridle's wavy rein with which
You curb your current's striving to run faster.

It would be wrong if beauty should be caught,
Confused, in that deep breast, beauty so rich,
Caught by the watery trident's mighty master.

—J. M. COHEN

O Noble and Most High in Beauty, Thou . . .

O noble and most high in beauty, thou,
Maria, while every hour there royally grows
Rosial Aurora on thy cheek's pale rose,
And Phoebus beaks through those eyes, the contour of thy brow;

While in insolent lenity Zephyrus' hands
The gold of that glib-hanging hair profanes,
Arabia's avarice hides in her veins,
Or opulent Tagus filters through his sands.

Ere Phoebus shall be all eclipsed by time,
Ere day be lost and night be all thy prime,
To fly that unhued and last dawn, O be bold!

Ere that which burns, precarious rubies now,
Be stifled by the long hands of the snow,
Enjoy, enjoy the gusts of color, light, and gold!

—IAIN FLETCHER

De la armada que fue a Ingalaterra

Levanta, España, tu famosa diestra
desde el francés Pirenne al moro Atlante,
y al ronco son de las trompas belicosas
haz, envuelta en durísimo diamante,
de tus valientes hijos feroz muestra
debajo de tus señas victoriosas;
tal, que las flacamente poderosas
fieras naciones contra tu fe armadas,
al claro resplandor de tus espadas
y a la de tus arneses fiera lumbre,
    con mortal pesadumbre
    ojos y espaldas vuelvan,
y como al Sol las nieblas, se resuelvan;
o cual la blanda cera desatados
a los dorados luminosos fuegos
    de los yelmos grabados,
queden, como de fe, de vista ciegos.

Tú, que con celo pío y noble saña
el seno undoso al húmido Neptuno
de selvas inquïetas has poblado,
y cuantos en tus reinos uno a uno
empuñan lanza contra la Bretaña,
sin perdonar al tiempo, has enviado
en número de todo tan sobrado,
que a tanto leño el húmido elemento
y a tanta vela es poco todo el viento,
fía que en sangre del inglés pirata
    teñirá de escarlata
    su color verde y cano
el rico de ruinas Ocëano;
y aunque de lejos con rigor traídas,
ilustrará tus playas y tus puertos
    de banderas rompidas,
de naves destrozadas, de hombres muertos.

Oh ya isla católica, y potente
templo de fe, ya templo de herejía,
campo de Marte, escuela de Minerva,
digna de que las sienes que algún día

On the Armada That Battled Against England

Raise up your valorous right arm, O Spain,
From the Pyrenees to the dark Atlantic wave!
Answer the trumpet burst in martial manner
And make your adamantine shield, the brave
Assembly of your sons, show forth again
The intent of war beneath a conquering banner;
That the presuming foe with shrill Hosanna,
Heading the nations armed against God's word
Shall view the wounding glitter of your sword
And your proud armor lucid on the air;
And shall, in mortal fear,
Avert their eyes and run
Like clouds before the frenzy of the sun;
Or whom, like dwindling wax, shall overwhelm
The sharp effulgence of that golden fire
From each incised, cold helm,
When blind in eye and faith they shall expire.

You who in noble anger, zeal of right,
Upon the uneasy ledges of the sea
Have crammed the wave-flung hull and restless mast
As many in your realm as be
Acute to combat with the English might
These have you sent to battle to the last
So many, nay, in numbers unsurpassed
That this steep element may scarce avail
To rear their keels nor wind assumpt their sail;
Then make the island pirates' raddled blood
Glower crimson on the flood
And wax the greens and grays
Of Ocean, rich with wrecks of other days;
Though from beyond they fought to bring their flags,
Your shores, your harbors will have only found
A standard rived to rags,
Their vessels foundered and their warriors drowned.

O, Mary's Dowry and you brave stronghold
Of earnest faith, now shrine of heresy;
Home of the arts and of a soldier breed,
Which has dishonored every sanctuary,

ornó corona real de oro luciente
ciña guirnalda vil de estéril hierba,
madre dichosa y obediente sierva
de Arturos, de Eduardos y de Enricos,
ricos de fortaleza, y de fe ricos;
ahora condenada a infamia eterna
    por la que te gobierna
    con la mano ocupada
del huso en vez de sceptro y de la espada;
mujer de muchos, y de muchos nuera,
¡oh reina torpe, reina no, mas loba
    libidinosa y fiera,
fiamma dal ciel su le tue trezze piova!

Tú, en tanto, mira allá los otomanos,
las Jonias aguas que el Sicano bebe,
sembrar de armados árboles y entenas,
y con tirano orgullo en tiempo breve,
domando cuellos y ligando manos,
y sus remos hiriendo las arenas,
despoblar islas y poblar cadenas.
Mas cuando su arrogancia y nuestro ultraje
no encienda en ti un católico coraje,
mira (si con la vista tanto vuelas),
    entre hinchadas velas
    el soberbio estandarte
que a los cristianos ojos (no sin arte),
como en desprecio de la Cruz sagrada,
mas desenvuelve, mientras más tremola,
    entre lunas bordada
del caballo feroz la crespa cola.

Fija los ojos en las blancas lunas,
y advierte bien, en tanto que tú esperas
gloria naval de las britanas lides,
no se calen rayendo tus riberas,
y pierdan el respeto a las colunas
llaves tuyas y término de Alcides;
mas si con la importancia el tiempo mides,
enarbola, oh gran madre, tus banderas,
arma tus hijos, vara tus galeras,

Once clothed in royalty of florid gold,
With the low tribute of a crown of weed;
Fortunate mother, as prompt to serve the need
Of Arthurs, Edwards, Henrys whom you bore
In courage rich, and rich in faith the more,
Now shadowed by unending infamy
In that your polity
Corrupts in hands assured
That loom and distaff may control the sword!
Many have made you kin and many bride
O evil Queen, no queen, but beast of prey
Engorged with lust and pride!
God's purging fire be all your crown today!

Meantime regard the sea-borne Turk advance
On Grecian waters where his pennons spoke;
And with full bloom of sail and rigging manned,
Threaten to bring the tyrant's hornèd yoke
That bends the neck and cows the rebel glance
And, as his long oars grate upon the sand,
To brim his galleys from the outraged land.
But should that insolence and our rank shame
No more enkindle you to Catholic flame,
If to such distance your eye avails,
Among the haughty sails
Observe that surging banner
That to our Christian eyes in impious manner
As though the Cross itself were dealt that scorn
Its insolent and brute device unfurls
Around the crescent horn
A stallion's ramping tail superbly curls.

Fix on those gleaming crescents now your eyes
And keep stark vigil, lest although you seek
Glory by sea upon the English wars,
The foe edge stealthily up every creek
To tame the spirit of those companies
That are the stronghold of your further shores.
But if your counsel such defeat abhors,
Then heave the flag upon your garrisons,
O Motherland, launch ships and arm your sons;

y sobre los castillos y leones
    que ilustran tus pendones,
    levanta aquel león fiero
del tribu de Judá, que honró el madero;
que él hará que tus brazos esforzados
llenen el mar de bárbaros nadantes,
    que entreguen anegados
al fondo el cuerpo, al agua los turbantes.

Canción, pues que ya aspira
a trompa militar mi tosca lira,
después me oirán (si Febo no me engaña)
el carro helado y la abrasada zona
    cantar de nuestra España
las armas, los triunfos, la corona.

De la toma de Larache

En roscas de cristal serpiente breve,
por la arena desnuda de Luco yerra,
el Luco, que con lengua al fin vibrante,
si no niega el tributo, intima guerra
al mar, que el nombre con razón le bebe,
y las faldas besar le hace de Atlante.
Desta, pues, siempre abierta, siempre hiante
    y siempre armada boca,
cual dos colmillos, de una y otra roca,
Africa (o ya sean cuernos de su Luna,
o ya de su elefante sean colmillos)
ofrece al gran Filipo los castillos,
carga hasta aquí, de hoy más militar pompa;
y del fiero animal hecha la trompa
clarín ya de la Fama, oye la cuna,
la tumba ve del Sol, señas de España,
los muros coronar que el Luco baña.

Las garras, pues, las presas españolas
del rey de fieras no, de nuevos mundos,
ostenta el río, y gloriosamente
arrogándose márgenes segundos,

And on the Lions and Castles superpose
(Since both your arms compose)
Erect, that fiercer Lion,
Which on the ships of Judah honored Zion;
And may we bolt such strength to your right arm
That it may fang the seas with Pagan foe
Surprised in desperate harm:
Turbans afloat and corpses thick below.

Therefore, O Verse, since you aspire
To rouse a martial sound from my crass lyre,
(Or else Apollo has deceived the strain)
Both northern pinewoods and the Carib palms
Shall hear me yield to Spain
The laureled orbit for a victor's arms!
                        —BRIAN SOPER & IAIN FLETCHER

The Capture of Larache

   Abbreviated serpent among crystal rocks,
the Luco undulates over naked sand,
the Luco, which at length with hissing tongue,
though it denies not tribute, announces war
against the sea that drinks by right its numbers,
and makes it kiss Atlantic's hem.
Now from this mouth, ever yawning, ever fierce-breathing,
      ever armed
with its two great fangs, and both of rock,
Africa (whether of newmoon horns
or whether of elephant tusks)
promises great Philip her guarded stores,
yesterday his charge, today new pomp of arms;
and the home country hears that clarion fame
for which, so soon, the bestial trumpet serves;
it sees the sun's sepulchre, Spain's emblem,
diademing the walls that Luco bathes.

   It is the talons, then, the Spanish booty
of the king of beasts, not newfound worlds,
that the river celebrates; and, resplendent
as it takes for heritage these wider shores,

en vez de escamas de cristal, sus olas
guedejas visten ya de oro luciente.
Brama, y menospreciándole serpiente,
  león ya no pagano
le admira reverente el Ocëano.
Brama, y cuantas la Libia engendra fieras,
que le escuchaban elefante apenas,
surcando ahora piélagos de arenas
lo distante interponen, lo escondido,
al imperio feroz de su bramido.
Responden las confusas, las postreras
cavernas del Atlante, a cuyos ecos
si Fez se estremeció, tembló Marruecos.

  Gloriosa y del suceso agradecida,
dirige al cielo España en dulce coro
de sacros cisnes cánticos süaves,
a la alta de Dios sí, no a la de un moro
bárbara Majestad, reconocida
por las fuerzas que le ha entregado: llaves
de las mazmorras de Africa más graves,
  forjadas, no ya donde
de las fraguas que ardiente el Etna esconde
llamas vomita, y sobre el yunque duro
gime Bronte, y Stérope no huelga,
sino en las oficinas donde el belga
rebelde anhela, el berberisco suda,
el brazo aquél, la espalda éste desnuda,
forjando las que un muro y otro muro
por guardas tiene, llaves ya maestras
de nuestros mares, de las flotas nuestras.

  Al viento más opuesto abeto alado
sus vagas plumas crea, rico el seno
de cuanta Potosí tributa hoy plata.
Leño frágil de hoy más al sereno,
copos fíe de cáñamo anudado,
seguro ya sus remos de piratas.
Piloto el interés sus cables ata,
  cuando ya en el puerto
del soplo occidental, de el golfo incierto,
pescadora la industria, flacas redes,

its waves put on, instead of crystal scales,
manes of lucent gold.
The lion roars, and serpent scorns him; yet
    (he is lion, not pagan)
the ocean, reverent, admires.
He roars: and whatever Libya-engendered beasts
have heard his voice—save only the elephant—
now furrow archipelagoes of sand,
interposing distance, secrecy between themselves
and the savage dominion of his roar.
Ambiguous, his answer comes from ultimate
caves of the Atlantic, at whose echoes,
if Fez shuddered, Morocco would quake.

Renowned, and for the outcome grateful,
Spain, in sweet chorus of sacred swans,
sends toward heaven her gentle hymns
to the grandeur of God, not to the majesty
of Moor, barbarian; yet a majesty acclaimed
by his newly abrogated powers, keys
to the most substantial of Africa's dungeons
    and forged not there
where from furnaces that burning Aetna hides.
Bronte casts up flame and Sterope has no rest:
but in workshops where the rebel Belgian
gasps for breath, the Berber sweats; where
brute strength strips the one, sword the other,
even as they fashion the custodian keys
for both our walls—in these days master keys,
the master keys of our oceans, our fleets.

Its mast flying before contrariest wind,
and henceforth increasingly serene, the fragile bark,
with its lowered plumes, embellishes the breast
of every Potosí that offers silver tribute;
it may trust to its meshes of knotted hemp;
safe, new (with its pirate ears;
its pilot, interest; its cables, the same)
    when in port
the fishing industry recalls to the ample shore,
from western blasts of the uncertain gulf,

que dio a la playa desde su barquilla,
graves revoca a la espaciosa orilla.
La libertad al fin que saltëada,
señas, o de cautiva, o despojada
dio un tiempo de Neptuno a las paredes,
hoy bálsamo espirantes cuelga ciento
faroles de oro al agradecimiento.

    Vuestra, oh Filipo, es la fortuna, y vuestra
de Africa será la monarquía.
Vuestras banderas nos lo dicen, puesto
duro yugo a los términos del día
en los mundos que abrevia tanta diestra;
que si a las armas no, si no al funesto
son de las trompas, que no aguardo a esto
    Abíla su coluna
a vuestros pies rindió, a vuestra fortuna;
Calpe desde su opuesta cumbre espera,
aunque lo ha dividido el mar en vano,
el término segundo del Tebano
complicado al primero, y penetrada
la ardiente Libia vuestra ardiente espada,
que el Nigris no en su bárbara ribera,
el Nilo sí con militar decoro,
la sed os temple ya en celada de oro.

    Verás, canción, del César africano
al nieto augusto, armada un día la mano,
hacer de Atlante en la silvosa cumbre,
a las purpúreas cruces de sus señas,
nuevos calvarios sus antiguas peñas.

Fábula de Polifemo y Galatea

Al Conde de Niebla [líneas 1–24]

    Estas que me dictó, rimas sonoras,
culta sí, aunque bucólica Talía
—¡oh excelso Conde!—, en las purpúreas horas
que es rosas la alba y rosicler el día,

heavily laden nets which, flaccid,
its small craft gave to the deep.
Liberty, in short, which, pirated,
shows marks of the captive, the ravished,
has given a new balsam weather to Neptune's
walls, and now suspends, in thanksgiving,
a hundred soft-exhaling lanterns of gold.

Yours, O Philip! are the riches, yours
will be Africa's monarchy;
your banners tell us the cruel yoke
has been placed on the very limits of day,
on worlds so much labor irrigates;
and that (if not to your arms nor the awful
sound of your trumpets) Abdullah, surprised by attack,
    surrendered his column
at your feet indeed, to your propitious chance.
Isolated, though in vain, by the sea,
Calpe, on his opposing heights, hopes now
for the second phase of this Thebaid,
involved with the first: hopes—once your sword,
flaming, has penetrated flaming Libya—
that not Niger between barbarous shores,
but Nile with its military decorum,
will temper your thirst in a casque of gold.

You will see, song, one day, the august heir
of Africa's Caesar, sword in hand,
make on the forest heights of Atlantic,
for his blood-red emblematic crosses,
new Calvaries from his ancient rocks.
                                —FRANCES FLETCHER

Fable of Polyphemus and Galatea

Dedication: to the Count of Niebla [lines 1-24]

Now that your nebula, O noble Count, sheds
a golden light, listen to the sonorous verse
I heard from Thalia (civilized, though bucolic)
in the imperial hour when dawn is

ahora que de luz tu Niebla doras,
escucha, al son de la zampoña mía,
si ya los muros no te ven de Huelva
peinar el viento, fatigar la selva.

Templado pula en la maestra mano
el generoso pájaro su pluma,
o tan mudo en la alcándara, que en vano
aun desmentir al cascabel presuma:
tascando haga el freno de oro cano
del caballo andaluz la ociosa espuma;
gima al lebrel en el cordón de seda,
y al cuerno al fin la cítara suceda.

Treguas al ejercicio sean robusto,
ocio atento, silencio dulce, en cuanto
debajo escuchas de dosel augusto
del músico jayán el fiero canto.
Alterna con las Musas hoy el gusto,
que si la mía puede ofrecer tanto
clarín—y de la Fama no segundo—,
tu nombre oirán los términos del mundo.

Canción de amor de Polifemo [líneas 361–464]

"¡Oh bella Galatea, más süave
que los claveles que tronchó la Aurora;
blanca más que las plumas de aquel ave
que dulce muere y en las aguas mora;
igual en pompa al pájaro que, grave,
su manto azul de tantos ojos dora
cuantas el celestial zafiro estrellas!
¡Oh tú que en dos incluyes las más bellas!

"Deja las ondas, deja el rubio coro
de las hijas de Tetis, y el mar vea,
cuando niega la luz un carro de oro,
que en dos la restituye Galatea.
Pisa la arena, que en la arena adoro
cuantas al blanco pie conchas platea,
cuyo bello contacto puede hacerlas,
sin concebir rocío, parir perlas.

roses, and day reflects their color:
listen—if, to the sound of my rustic flute,
the Huelvan walls do not longer see you
combing the wind, fatiguing the forest.

In the master hand let the generous bird,
tempered, put a polish on his feather—
or, so silent in the falcon perch, let him
presume in vain to refute the cajoling bell;
let the bright gold bit of the champing
Andalusian horse exude the froth of idleness;
and the whippet groan in his silken cord,.
and the cithara, at last, replace the horn.

Let there be a truce with robust exercise—
an attentive leisure, a delicious silence, while,
beneath the august canopy, you listen to
the wild song of the music-loving monster.
Taste today favors now one Muse, now another,
and if my own Muse can send forth such resounding
tones, not second, in fame, to others, then
the ends of the earth shall hear your name.

Polyphemus' Love Song [lines 361–464]

O lovely Galatea, sweeter than
the pinks Aurora gathered;
whiter than the feathers of that swan
who lives and gently dies upon the waters;
like, in splendor, to the solemn bird
that gilds his azure mantle with as many eyes
as heaven, with stars, its sapphire!
O Galatea, your eyes hold the brightest stars!

Leave the foam, leave the bright-haired chorus
of Thetis' daughters, let the ocean see
that when a golden chariot refuses light,
the eyes of Galatea can restore it.
Step forth, upon the sand; the conches there
that your white foot makes silver, I adore,
for your light touch, without creating dew,
has power to make them glow like pearls.

"Sorda hija del mar, cuyas orejas
a mis gemidos son rocas al viento;
o dormida te hurten a mis quejas
purpúreos troncos de corales ciento,
o al disonante número de almejas
—marino, si agradable no, instrumento—,
coros tejiendo estés, escucha un día
mi voz, por dulce, cuando no por mía.

"Pastor soy, mas tan rico de ganados,
que los valles impido más vacíos,
los cerros desaparezco levantados,
y los caudales seco de los ríos:
no los que, de sus ubres desatados
o derribados de los ojos míos,
leche corren y lágrimas; que iguales
en número a mis bienes son mis males.

"Sudando néctar, lambicando olores,
senos que ignora aún la golosa cabra,
corchos me guardan, más que abeja flores
liba inquieta, ingeniosa labra;
troncos me ofrecen árboles mayores,
cuyos enjambres, o el abril los abra
o los desate el mayo, ámbar destilan,
y en ruecas de oro rayos de el Sol hilan.

"De el Júpiter, soy hijo de las ondas,
aunque pastor; si tu desdén no espera
a que el Monarca de esas grutas hondas
en trono de cristal te abrace nuera;
Polifemo te llama, no te escondas,
que tanto esposo admira la ribera,
cual otro no vio Febo más robusto,
del perezoso Volga al Indo adusto.

"Sentado, a la alta palma no perdona
su dulce fruto mi robusta mano;
en pie, sombra capaz es mi persona
de innumerables cabras el verano.
¿Qué mucho si de nubes se corona
por igualarme la montaña en vano,
y en los cielos, desde esta roca, puedo
escribir mis desdichas con el dedo?

Unheeding daughter of the sea, whose ears
to my laments are as rocks to wind;
whether, as you sleep, a hundred deep red
coral trees now cheat you of my call,
or whether you are weaving choruses
for the dissonant mollusc-music, ocean's
medium, though harsh—hear, soon, my voice
because it is sweet, if not because it is mine.

Shepherd I am; but so rich in flocks
I change to superflux the emptiest valleys;
I cause the highest hills to disappear
and, of rivers, make the wealth run dry—
not of streams flowing as milk from heavy udders,
nor those, of tears, having for source my eyes:
for like my wealth, in plenty, are my sorrows.

Sweating nectar, dripping odors, trees
of cork keep secret for me nooks which not
the gourmand goat knows of—more numerous than
flowers the bee sips restlessly (ingenious piety).
The larger trees supply these trunks where swarms
(whether April discovers or May torments them)
produce an amber distillation, and spin
the sunshine into honeycombs of gold.

Though shepherd, I am son to Jupiter
of the waves; surely your aspiration scorns
that the deep caves' monarch should embrace you,
his son's wife, on a glass throne!
Polyphemus calls you; don't hide away,
for the shore marvels at so splendid a husband,
never from the lazy Volga to the sullen Indus,
has Phoebus looked on one more lusty.

When I am seated, my hand, powerful, concedes
not to the highest palm its own sweet fruit;
when I stand, my person makes, in summer,
a capacious shade for innumerable goats.
Is it not much that the mountain (in vain)
wears a cloud-coronet to equal me?
And that, from the rock, I can write,
with my finger, my unhappiness in the skies?

"Marítimo Alcïón, roca eminente
sobre sus huevos coronaba, el día
que espejo de zafiro fue luciente
la plaza azul de la persona mía;
míreme, y lucir vi un sol en mi frente,
cuando en el cielo un ojo se veía:
neutra el agua dudaba a cuál fe preste:
o al cielo humano o al Cíclope celeste.

"Registra en otras puertas el venado
sus años, su cabeza colmilluda
la fiera, cuyo cerro levantado
de Helvecias picas es muralla aguda;
la humana suya el caminante errado
dio ya a mi cueva, de piedad desnuda,
albergue hoy por tu causa al peregrino,
do halló reparo, si perdió camino.

"En tablas dividida, rica nave
besó la playa miserablemente,
de cuantas vomitó riquezas graves,
por las bocas de el Nilo el Orïente.
Yugo aquel día, y yugo bien süave,
de el fiero mar a la sañuda frente,
imponiéndole estaba, si no al viento,
dulcísimas coyundas mi instrumento.

"Cuando, entre globos de agua, entregar veo,
a las arenas ligurina haya,
en cajas los aromas de el Sabeo,
en cofres las riquezas de Cambaya:
delicias de aquel mundo, ya trofeo
de Scila que, ostentando en nuestra playa,
lastimoso despojo fue dos días
a las que esta montaña engendra harpías.

"Segunda tabla a un Ginovés mi gruta
de su persona fue, de su hacienda:
la una reparada, la otra enjuta.
Relación de el naufragio hizo horrenda.
Luciente paga de la mejor fruta
que en yerbas se recline, en hilos penda,

I crowned with my person (on a day
when the ocean, blue, made a mirror of
brilliant sapphire) that eminent rock,
maritime Alcion, on his ovoid bases. I looked
at myself and I saw, glowing on my front
a sun, while the sky showed only an eye:
the water, neutral, knew not which to trust—
the human firmament, or Cyclops, celestial.

In other shelters the deer registers
its years, that beast with well-toothed head
whose neck, upraised, presents
a spiked wall of Helvetian lances; and, formerly,
the strayed traveler left his human head
in my pitiless cave, though now, for your sake,
Galatea, I would show a host's consideration
to any stranger who had lost his way.

Its planks divided, a wealth-laden ship
miserably kissed this shore; it discharged
treasure, as much as the fabulous East discharges
through the delta of the Nile.
On that day my instrument was placing,
if not on the wind, at least on the wild sea's
enraged crest, a yoke (a very sweet
yoke), with the most harmonious halters.

When, between spheres of water, I saw
Ligurian offerings washed to the sand:
perfumes of Sheba, in cases;
riches of Cambay in coffers;
luxuries of that world (now Scylla's
trophy) which, deployed on our shores,
was for two days the pitiful spoil
of Harpies born to these mountains.

My cave served a Genoese as second ship,
for both person and possessions—the former
made healthy thereby; the latter, emaciate.
His tale of the shipwreck was frightful.
But a shining wage of the finest fruit
that rests on bushes or hangs on vines

colmillo fue de el animal que el Ganges
sufrir muros le vio, romper falanges.
"Arco, digo, gentil, bruñida aljaba,
obras ambas de artífice prolijo,
y de malaco rey a deidad java
alto don, según ya mi huésped dijo,
de aquél la mano, de ésta el hombro agrava:
convencida la madre, imita al hijo:
serán a un tiempo, en estos horizontes,
Venus de el mar, Cupido de los montes."

Las Soledades

[líneas 1–130]

Era del año la estación florida
en que el mentido robador de Europa
—media luna las armas de su frente,
y el Sol todos los rayos de su pelo—,
luciente honor del cielo,
en campos de zafiro pace estrellas;
cuando el que ministrar podía la copa
a Júpiter mejor que el garzón de Ida,
—náufrago y desdeñado, sobre ausente—
lagrimosas de amor dulces querellas
da al mar; que condolido,
fue a las ondas, fue al viento
el mísero gemido,
segundo de Arión dulce instrumento.

Del siempre en la montaña opuesto pino
al enemigo Noto,
piadoso miembro roto
—breve tabla—delfín no fue pequeño
al inconsiderado peregrino
que a una Libia de ondas su camino
fio, y su vida a un leño.

put tooth in that creature whose walls
the Ganges saw suffer, whose phalanxes it saw break.
See here: a fine bow, a burnished quiver,
both are works of intricate artifice——
an imperial gift (so my guest said)
of a Malaccan king to some goddess of Java.
One is a weight in the hand; the other, on shoulder.
Prevail over the mother, then follow the son; you
will be at once, on these horizons,
Venus of the sea, Cupid of the high places. —FRANCES FLETCHER

The Solitudes

[lines 1–130]

It was the flowery season of the year
In which Europe's perjured robber strays
   Whose brow the arms of the half-moon adorn,
The sun the shining armor of his hide—
Through sapphire fields to feast on stellar corn,
When, fitter cupbearer than Ganymede
For Jupiter, the lovesick boy gave tears
(Absent, disdained, and shipwrecked) to the tide
And winds, which moved by his complaining lays
As to a second Arion's harp gave heed.

A pitying limb from mountain pine, opposed,
The constant enemy to Notus' strife,
Became no puny dolphin on that day
To the unthinking traveler who reposed,
Trusting to miserable boards his life,
And to an Ocean's Lybia his way.

Del Océano pues antes sorbido,
y luego vomitado
no lejos de un escollo coronado
de secos juncos, de calientes plumas,
—alga todo y espumas—,
halló hospitalidad donde halló nido
de Júpiter el ave.

Besa la arena, y de la rota nave
aquella parte poca
que le expuso en la playa dio a la roca:
que aun se dejan las peñas
lisonjear de agradecidas señas.

Desnudo el joven, cuanto ya el vestido
Océano ha bebido,
restituirle hace a las arenas;
y al sol lo extiende luego,
que, lamiéndole apenas
su dulce lengua de templado fuego,
lento le embiste, y con süave estilo
la menor onda chupa al menor hilo.

No bien, pues, de su luz los horizontes
—que hacían desigual, confusamente
montes de agua y piélagos de montes—,
desdorados los siente,
cuando—entregado el mísero extranjero
en lo que ya de el mar redimió fiero—
entre espinas crepúsculos pisando,
riscos que aun igualara mal, volando,
veloz, intrépida ala,
—menos cansado que confuso—escala.

Vencida al fin la cumbre
—del mar siempre sonante,
de la muda campaña
árbitro igual e inexpugnable muro—,
con pie ya más seguro
declina al vacilante
breve esplendor de mal distinta lumbre:

Close by a headland, crowned
With sheltering feathers and dry rushes, he,
Engulfed before, then spewed up by the sea,
(Covered with foam, with seaweed girded) found
A hospitable rest,
Where built the bird of Jupiter his nest.

And, having kissed the sand,
The fragment from the shivered hull he gave
As offering to the rocks, now from the wave
Safe, and restored to land;
For even boulders rude
Are flattered by marks of gratitude.

Naked the youth, that ocean which before
His raiment drank, he gave back to the shore;
And then the garments to the sun he spread,
Which, with its gentle tongue of temperate fire,
Slowly attacked, but with no fierce desire,
The least wave sipping from the smallest thread.

Then the horizon from the evening light
—Which made unequal and confusedly
Mountains of water, oceans of the height—
Not well distinguishing,
And clad the youth forlorn
In what he had redeemed from the wild sea,
He trod the twilight down 'mid many a thorn;
Rocks, which to equal hardly had availed
A swift intrepid wing,
He—more confused than he was weary—scaled.

The summit crowned at last
—Of the resounding sea
And of the silent land
A rampart strong and equal arbiter—
With safer foot he passed
Toward where, tremblingly,
Light indistinct and of brief splendor there

farol de una cabaña
que sobre el ferro está, en aquel incierto
golfo de sombras, anunciando el puerto.
"Rayos—les dice—ya que no de Leda
trémulos hijos, sed de mi fortuna
término luminoso." Y—recelando
de invidïosa bárbara arboleda
interposición, cuando
de vientos no conjuración alguna—
cual, haciendo el villano
la fragosa montaña fácil llano,
atento sigue aquella
—aun a pesar de las tinieblas bella,
aun a pesar de las estrellas clara—
piedra, indigna tiara
—si tradición apócrifa no miente—
de animal tenebroso, cuya frente
carro es brillante de nocturno día:
tal, diligente, el paso
el joven apresura,
midiendo la espesura
con igual pie que el raso,
fijo—a despecho de la niebla fría—
en el carbunclo, norte de su aguja,
o el Austro brame o la arboleda cruja.

El can ya, vigilante,
convoca, despidiendo al caminante;
y la que desviada
luz poca pareció, tanta es vecina,
que yace en ella la robusta encina,
mariposa en cenizas desatada.

Llegó, pues, el mancebo, y saludado,
sin ambición, sin pompa de palabras,
de los conducidores fue de cabras,
que a Vulcano tenían coronado.

"¡Oh bienaventurado
albergue a cualquier hora,

The lantern of a cottage, stood displayed,
At anchor in the uncertain gulf of shade,
Showing the port at hand.

"Oh rays—if not the wavering sons," he said
"Of Leda—then of my misfortune be
The shining boundary."
And—of the barbarous, envying grove in dread
Lest it an obstacle should interpose,
Lest too the winds should make conspiracy
'Gainst him he feared—thus, as the peasant goes
Who makes the rugged mountain plain be
Following always near
—Despite the darkness all its beauty glows,
Even compared to stars it still is clear—
The stone, unworthily
—If apocryphal tradition does not lie—
The crown of a dark animal, whose brow
Is the bright carriage of nocturnal day:
So diligently now
he hastened on his way,
With equal foot to rove
O'er thicket and smooth ground,
Fixed, notwithstanding the cold mist around,
Toward that jewel, his magnetic North,
Despite the whistling grove
And Auster roaring forth.

The watchdog was his guide,
Even though it bayed to affright the wanderer;
And that which far off seemed
A little light, was now much greater deemed,
The holm-oak, sturdy, bare,
Huge butterfly in cinders lay untied.

The youth arrived to be saluted there
Without ambition or the pomp of words
By leaders of the herds
Now holding Vulcan crowned.

"Oh hermitage well found
Whatever hour it be,

templo de Pales, alquería de Flora!
No moderno artificio
borró designios, bosquejó modelos,
al cóncavo ajustando de los cielos
el sublime edificio;
retamas sobre roble,
tu fábrica son pobre,
do guarda, en vez de acero,
la inocencia al cabrero
mas que el silbo al ganado.
¡Oh bienaventurado
albergue a cualquier hora!

No en ti la ambición mora
hidrópica de viento,
ni la que su alimento
el áspid es gitano;
no la que, en vulto comenzando humano,
acaba en mortal fiera,
esfinge bachillera,
que hace hoy a Narciso
ecos solicitar, desdeñar fuentes;
ni la que en salvas gasta impertinentes
la pólvora del tiempo más preciso:
ceremonia profana
que la sinceridad burla villana
sobre el corvo cayado.
¡Oh bienaventurado
albergue a cualquier hora!

Tus umbrales ignora
la adulación, sirena
de reales palacios, cuya arena
besó ya tanto leño:
trofeos dulces de un canoro sueño.
No a la soberbia está aquí la mentira
dorándole los pies, en cuanto gira
la esfera de sus plumas,

Temple of Pales, Flora's granary!
No artificer new
Models designed for thee, or sketches drew,
Adjusting to the skies' concavity
An edifice sublime; for here reveal
The woods of oak and broom
Thy poor and modest room,
In which, instead of steel,
Pure Innocence can keep
The goatherd safe and sound—
More than his pipe, the sheep.
O hermitage well found
Whatever hour it be!

"Ambition not to thee
Do we expect to find,
Hydroptic of the wind;
Nor Envy with her food,
The Egyptian serpent brood;
Nor she, who, though a human face surmounts,
Is a wild beast below,
A Sphinx persuasive, who
Makes the Narcissus new
Solicit echoes and disdain the founts;
Nor she who wastes, impertinent, in show
All the essential powder of our age,
Oh foolish Courtesy!
At whom the villagers sincere may laugh
Over their crooked staff.
O well found hermitage
Whatever hour it be!

"Nor does thy threshold know
Of Adulation bland,
Siren of royal palaces, whose sand
So many vessels greet;
Of a canorous dream the trophies sweet.
Nor turning now her feathered sphere around
Is Pride seen here, while Flattery guides her feet;

ni de los rayos baja a las espumas
favor de cera alado.
¡Oh bienaventurado
albergue a cualquier hora!"

Himno de bodas [líneas 767–844]

Coro I
Ven, Himeneo, ven donde te espera
con ojos y sin alas un Cupido,
cuyo cabello intonso dulcemente
niega el vello que el vulto ha colorido:
el vello, flores de su primavera,
y rayos el cabello de su frente.
Niño amó la que adora adolescente,
villana Psiques, ninfa labradora
de la tostada Ceres. Esta, ahora,
en los inciertos de su edad segunda
crepúsculos, vincule tu coyunda
          a su ardiente deseo.
Ven, Himeneo, ven; ven, Himeneo.

Coro II
Ven, Himeneo, donde, entre arreboles
de honesto rosicler, previene el día
—aurora de sus ojos soberanos—
virgen tan bella, que hacer podría
tórrida la Noruega con dos soles,
y blanca la Etiopia con dos manos.
Claveles de abril, rubíes tempranos,
cuantos engasta el oro del cabello,
cuantas—del uno ya y del otro cuello
cadenas—la concordia engarza rosas,
de sus mejillas, siempre vergonzosas,
          purpúreo son trofeo.
Ven, Himeneo, ven; ven, Himeneo.

Coro I
Ven, Himeneo, y plumas no vulgares
al aire los hijuelos den alados
de las que el bosque bellas ninfas cela;
de sus carcajes, éstos, argentados,
flechen mosquetas, nieven azahares;

And Favor falls not to the foam below
On wings of wax from false security.
O hermitage well found
Whatever hour it be!"

Wedding Hymn [lines 767–844]

Semichorus I
Come Hymen come, for here to thee we bring
With eyes but without wings a god of love,
Whose unshorn locks that sweetly hang above
Conceal the down upon his visage fair;
His down the flowers of a youthful spring,
And sunbeams from his forehead are his hair.
A boy he loved her, but adores today
This Psyche of the village, nymph to wage
For parchèd Ceres. Join her now, we pray,
Who in the twilight of her second age
Uncertain is, join in thy yoke to stay
        At his desire sincere,
Come Hymen, Hymen here.

Semichorus II
Come Hymen come, where in the morning skies
Of candid roses, day is now foretold
By such a beautiful young virgin, she
—Herself the Aurora of her sovereign eyes—
Could warm with her two suns Norwegian lands,
And whiten Ethiopia with two hands.
April carnations, early rubies, see
As many as are set in hair of gold,
With flowers that chain the lovers' necks—behold
The links of concord in the chain of rose—
These to her cheeks, that modesty disclose,
        The purple spoil appear,
Come Hymen, Hymen here.

Semichorus I
Come Hymen come, and may each wingèd son
Of every lovely nymph the woods can show
Render no common feathers to the air;
Some, from the silvered quivers that they bear,

vigilantes aquéllos, la aldehuela
rediman del que más o tardo vuela,
o infausto gime pájaro nocturno;
mudos coronen otros por su turno
el dulce lecho conyugal, en cuanto
lasciva abeja al virginal acanto
          néctar le chupa hibleo.
Ven, Himeneo, ven; ven, Himeneo.

Coro II
Ven, Himeneo, y las volantes pías
que azules ojos con pestañas de oro
sus plumas son, conduzgan alta diosa,
gloria mayor de el soberano coro.
Fíe tus nudos ella, que los días
disuelvan tarde en senectud dichosa;
y la que Juno es hoy a nuestra esposa,
casta Lucina—en lunas desiguales—
tantas veces repita sus umbrales,
que Níobe inmortal la admire el mundo,
no en blanco mármol, por su mal fecundo,
          escollo hoy del Leteo.
Ven, Himeneo, ven; ven, Himeneo.

Coro I
Ven, Himeneo, y nuestra agricultura
de copia tal a estrellas deba amigas
progenie tan robusta, que su mano
toros dome, y de un rubio mar de espigas
inunde liberal la tierra dura;
y al verde, joven, floreciente llano
blancas ovejas suyas hagan, cano,
en breves horas caducar la hierba;
oro le expriman líquido a Minerva,
y—los olmos casando con las vides—
mientras coronan pámpanos a Alcides
          clava empuñe Lïeo.
Ven, Himeneo, ven; ven, Himeneo.

Coro II
Ven, Himeneo, y tantas le dé a Pales
cuantas a Palas dulces prendas esta
apenas hija hoy, madre mañana.

Shoot musket roses, orange blossom snow;
Let others keep the hamlet safe from one,
The most unlucky of nocturnal fowls,
That flies too slowly and ill-boding howls;
And in their flight let some crown silently
The marriage bed, while the lascivious bee
From virginal acanthus sips the rare
       Hyblaean nectar there,
Come Hymen, Hymen here.

Semichorus II
Come Hymen come, the flying steeds and pied
(For azure eyes with lashes of fine gold
Compose their plumes)—the goddess high shall lead,
The greatest glory of the sovereign choir;
And let her guarantee the bonds indeed
Only to be dissolved when they grow old;
She who is Juno now unto our bride
In varying months shall chaste Lucina be,
To greet their threshold so repeatedly
That the world shall her, new Niobe, admire,
But no white marble's ill fecundity
       And cliff to Lethe near,
Come Hymen, Hymen here.

Semichorus I
Come Hymen come, our agriculture heap
With plenty that from friendly stars is due,
A progeny robust, so that their hand
Shall tame wild bulls, and a red sea of grain
Shall liberally flood the stubborn land;
Let too the young and flowery green plain
Be hoary turned by many flocks of sheep,
And all the pasture worn in hours few;
They to Minerva liquid gold shall strain,
And, wedding elms unto the vineyard trees,
Bacchus, with vine shoots crowning Hercules,
       Even the club shall rear,
Come Hymen, Hymen here.

Semichorus II
Come Hymen come, and may she also pay
To Pales as to Pallas pledges sweet,
A mother then, hardly a girl today.

De errantes lilios unas la floresta
cubran: corderos mil, que los cristales
vistan del río en breve undosa lana;
de Aracnes otras la arrogancia vana
modestas acusando en blancas telas,
no los hurtos de amor, no las cautelas
de Júpiter compulsen: que, aun en lino,
ni a la pluvia luciente de oro fino,
      ni al blanco cisne creo.
Ven, Himeneo, ven; ven, Himeneo.

De la brevedad engañosa de la vida

Menos solicitó veloz saeta
destinada señal, que mordió aguda;
agonal carro por la arena muda
no coronó con más silencio meta,

que presurosa corre, que secreta,
a su fin nuestra edad. A quien lo duda,
fiera que sea de razón desnuda,
cada Sol repetido es un cometa.

¿Confiésalo Cartago, y tú lo ignoras?
Peligro corres, Licio, si porfías
en seguir sombras y abrazar engaños.

Mal te perdonarán a ti las horas;
las horas que limando están los días,
los días que royendo están los años.

With wandering lilies some the forest greet;
A thousand lambs whose wavy wool shall dress
The shining crystals of the streamlet slow;
Others Arachne, arrogant and vain,
Shall modestly, accusingly, display
On their white stuff, but never to express
The thefts and amorous wiles of Jove below;
Oh let them hold the shining golden rain
        And the white swan in fear,
Come Hymen, Hymen here.
                                        —EDWARD MYRON WILSON

Deceiver Time

The flying arrow hardly was aware
It left the fateful bow, but cleft its mark;
The death cart ran its journey in the dark
Over mute sand, leaving its burden where

The trail ends: with such speed and soundlessness
Do our days race. He who would cling to doubt
Must see his blind, unreasoning reason's rout,
And meteor pace of every sun confess.

Carthage no longer stands assured, why you?
You walk in peril, Licio, who chase
The shadows and accept the shams, pursue

Time stubbornly. For time is seldom kind:
Eroding hours day and night erase,
And hungry months gnaw seasons to the rind.
                                        —JAMES EDWARD TOBIN

LOPE DE VEGA
(1562–1635)

"The Monster of Nature," as Cervantes called Lope in awe and perhaps in envy, is credited with having composed over two thousand plays, of which about five hundred survive, as well as much work in other genres, his lyrics surpassing those of many of his contemporaries.

Born in Madrid, the son of a poor weaver, after a few years at a Jesuit school he went to serve the Bishop of Ávila who sent him to the University of Alcalá. Thenceforth his life became increasingly adventurous and Don Juanesque: after participating in an expedition to the Azores (1583), he became involved in a scandalous affair with Elena Osorio, an actor's daughter, and was banished to Valencia (1588). A few days later he returned to Madrid incognito and eloped with Isabel de Urbina, the daughter of a court official, whom he married and left, ten days later, to join the Invincible Armada.

After the defeat of the Armada he settled with his wife in Valencia. In 1595, at her death and upon completion of his period of exile, he returned to Madrid, fell madly in love with Micaela Luján, the wife of an actor, and took her away to Toledo and later Seville. There he divided his time between Micaela and Juana de Guardo, whom he had married in 1598. Throughout the years his liaisons kept changing, even after he had been ordained a priest. Despite his fantastically active life he found time to write millions of words, leaving behind, when he died at seventy-three, a solidly established national theater.

BEST EDITIONS: J. F. Montesinos (ed.): *Poesías líricas*, Madrid, 1925, 2 vols.; L. Guerner (ed.): *La lírica de Lope de Vega*, Madrid, 1935, 2 vols.

ABOUT LOPE DE VEGA: A. Flores: *Lope de Vega, Monster of Nature*, New York, Brentano's, 1930, and *Masterpieces of the Spanish Golden Age*, New York, Rinehart, 1957. *Also:* L. K. Delano: "The Relation of

Lope de Vega's Sonnets to Those in His Comedies," *Hispania* XX (1937), pp. 307–20; W. J. Entwistle: "Lope de Vega As a Lyric Poet," *Bulletin of Spanish Studies* XII (1935), pp. 237–39; J. G. Fucilla: "Concerning the Poetry of Lope de Vega," *Hispania* XV (1932), pp. 223–42.

No sabe qué es amor quien no te ama . . .

No sabe qué es amor quien no te ama,
celestial hermosura, esposo bello;
tu cabeza es de oro, y tu cabello
como el cogollo que la palma enrama;

tu boca como lirio, que derrama
licor al alba; de marfil tu cuello;
tu mano el torno, y en su palma el sello,
que el alma por disfraz jacintos llama.

¡Ay Dios!, ¿en qué pensé cuando, dejando
tanta belleza, y las mortales viendo,
perdí lo que pudiera estar gozando?

Mas si del tiempo que perdí me ofendo,
tal prisa me daré, que un hora amando
venza los años que pasé fingiendo.

Suelta mi manso, mayoral extraño . . .

Suelta mi manso, mayoral extraño,
pues otro tienes de tu igual decoro;
deja la prenda que en el alma adoro,
perdida por tu bien y por mi daño.

Ponle su esquila de labrado estaño
y no le engañen tus collares de oro;
toma en albricias este blanco toro
que a las primeras yerbas cumple un año.

Si pides señas, tiene el vellocino
pardo, encrespado, y los ojuelos tiene
como durmiendo en regalado sueño.

Si piensas que no soy su dueño, Alcino,
suelta y verásle si a mi choza viene,
que aún tienen sal las manos de su dueño.

Stranger to Love, Whoever Loves Not Thee . . .

Stranger to love, whoever loves not Thee,
Thou Holy Beauty, Friend and my fair Spouse,
Whose head drops gold, whose radiant hair shades me
As the young leaves, down of the palm's boughs.

Like lily-flowering fountains, thy lips distil
Rich torrents to the dawn; thy neck, a white-sided plinth,
Thy hand the lathe, and in its palm that seal
My soul dissembling sensed as hyacinth.

Ah, God, how much deluded I, in leaving
So just a Beauty, and mortal loves befriending,
Losing that Beauty ever wide in flower:

But if for time lost I linger grieving,
I'll make such haste that by one loving hour
I will root out the years I lived pretending.
— IAIN FLETCHER

Strange Shepherd, Set My Bellwether Free . . .

Strange shepherd, set my bellwether free,
Since you have another worthy of your station,
Send back that pledge that is my soul's passion,
Whose loss will be your gain and grieve me only.

Upon him hang his shaped tin sheep bell,
Do not ensnare him with your golden collars;
Take in gratulation this white bull
Who will be a year old when the first grass appears.

If you want proofs, Alcino, his fleece
Is a cloudy brown, curling; his eyes seem
As though in sleep which a sweet dream tends.

If you will not believe I am his mistress,
Turn him loose and see if he does not come
To his hut where I wait still with salt in my hands.
— W. S. MERWIN

Al triunfo de Judit

Cuelga sangriento de la cama al suelo
el hombro diestro del feroz tirano
que opuesto al muro de Betulia en vano,
despidió contra sí rayos al cielo.

Revuelto con el ansia el rojo velo
del pabellón a la siniestra mano,
descubre el espectáculo inhumano
del tronco horrible, convertido en hielo.

Vertido Baco, el fuerte arnés afea;
los vasos y la mesa derribada,
duermen las guardas, que tan mal emplea;

y sobre la muralla, coronada
del pueblo de Israel, la casta hebrea
con la cabeza resplandece armada.

¿Qué tengo yo, que mi amistad procuras?

¿Qué tengo yo, que mi amistad procuras?
¿Qué interés se te sigue, Jesús mío,
que a mi puerta, cubierto de rocío
pasas las noches del invierno escuras?

¡Oh, cuánto fueron mis entrañas duras
pues no te abrí! ¡Qué extraño desvarío
si de mi ingratitud el yelo frío
secó las llagas de tus plantas puras!

¡Cuántas veces el ángel me decía:
Alma, asómate agora a la ventana,
verás con cuanto amor llamar porfía!

¡Y cuántas, hermosura soberana,
"Mañana le abriremos" respondía,
para lo mismo responder mañana!

On the Triumph of Judith

Blood from the shoulder drips from couch to floor,
Blood from the savage tyrant who in vain
Besieged Bethulia's wall, and caused a rain
Of bolts from Heaven to strike him down in war.

The left hand's anguished rigor, like a claw,
Grips back the scarlet curtain, and again
Horror reveals itself: the attitude of pain,
The hideous torso, one blind mass of gore.

Wine's spilt; the heavy mail has disarrayed
The ornaments; the table's overturned;
The guards asleep forget their vicious lord;

And on the rampart the chaste Hebrew maid,
To Israel's people splendidly returned,
Holds up the armored head as a reward.

—BRIAN SOPER

What Do I Have, That You Seek Out My Friendship? . . .

What do I have, that you seek out my friendship?
What can there be leading you, my Jesus,
Through the wintry nights of darkness,
Drenched with dew, here beside my door?

O what hardness must I have within,
Not to let you in! What strange perversity,
If with the icy cold of my ingratitude
The open wounds of your pure feet were dried!

How many times have I heard the angel tell me:
"Soul, glimpse now at the window;
See with how much love he insistent calls!"

And how many times, sweet Sovereign,
Have I answered, "Tomorrow we shall let him in . . ."
Merely upon the morrow to answer thus again!

—KATE FLORES

Pastor que con tus silbos amorosos . . .

Pastor que con tus silbos amorosos
me despertaste del profundo sueño;
tú, que hiciste cayado de ese leño
en que tiendes los brazos poderosos,

vuelve los ojos a mi fe piadosos
pues te confieso por mi amor y dueño
y la palabra de seguirte empeño
tus dulces silbos y tus pies hermosos.

Oye, pastor, que por amores mueres,
no te espante el rigor de mis pecados
pues tan amigo de rendidos eres.

Espera, pues, y escucha mis cuidados . . .
Pero ¿cómo te digo que me esperes
si estás para esperar los pies clavados?

Nace el Alba María . . .

Nace el Alba María
y el sol tras ella
desterrando la noche
de nuestras penas.
Nace el Alba clara,
la noche pisa,
del cielo la risa
su paz declara:
el tiempo se para
por sólo vella,
desterrando la noche
de nuestras penas.

Para ser Señora
del cielo, levanta
esta niña santa
su luz como Aurora:

Shepherd Who With Your Tender Calls . . .

Shepherd who with your tender calls
From deep slumber has wakened me,
You who made of this log the staff
On which your powerful arms are held,

Upon my faith turn your pitying eyes,
For I confess you my love and lord,
And to follow you pledge my word,
Your beauteous feet and calls so mild.

Here me, Shepherd who dies for love,
Flinch not at my frightful sins,
You to the humbled so much a friend,

Stay, and let my cares be heard . . .
Though why do I ask that you stay for me,
When to make you stay your feet are nailed?

       — KATE FLORES

At Dawn the Virgin Is Born . . .

At dawn the Virgin is born
And with her the sun,
Banishing the night
Of our griefs.
The bright dawn
Tramples down the night;
Heaven's smile
Tells of her peace
And time stands still
To gaze upon her
Banishing the night
Of our griefs.

That she may be
Mistress of heaven, this holy
Child lifts up
Her light, which is the dawn;

él canta, ella llora
divinas perlas,
desterrando la noche
de nuestras penas.

Aquella luz pura
del sol procede,
porque cuanto puede
le da hermosura:
el Alba asegura
que viene cerca,
desterrando la noche
de nuestras penas.

A mi niño combaten fuegos y hielos . . .

A mi niño combaten
    fuegos y hielos,
    sólo amor padeciera
    tan gran tormento.

Del amor el fuego,
    y del tiempo el frío
    al dulce amor mío
    quitan el sosiego:
    digo, cuando llego
    a verle riendo,
    sólo amor padeciera
    tan gran tormento.

Helarse algun pecho,
    y el alma abrasarse,
    sólo puede hallarse
    que amor lo haya hecho:
    niño satisfecho
    de fuego y hielo,
    sólo amor padeciera
    tan gran tormento.

And the light sings while she weeps
Divine pearls,
Banishing the night
Of our griefs.

That pure light
From the sun proceeds,
For all beauty which is
His to give he gives her:
The dawn, whose promise is
That he follows after,
Banishing the night
Of our griefs.

—W. S. MERWIN

Ice and Fires Contend With My Child . . .

Ice and fires
    Contend with my child;
    Only love
    Would suffer such torment.

The fire of love
    And the cold of time
    Rob my sweet love
    Of his peace.
    So that I say
    When I find him smiling:
    Only love
    Would suffer such torment.

Whatever breast freeze
    Or soul blaze
    It will be seen that love
    Alone could have wrought it.
    Child contented
    With ice and fire,
    Only love
    Would suffer such torment.

—W. S. MERWIN

¿Dónde vais, zagala . . . ?

¿Dónde vais, zagala,
sola en el monte?
Mas quien lleva el sol
no teme la noche.

¿Dónde vais, María,
divina esposa,
madre gloriosa
de quien os cría?
¿Qué haréis si el día
se va al Ocaso
y en el monte acaso
la noche os coge?
Mas quien lleva el sol
no teme la noche.

El ver las estrellas
me causa enojos,
pero vuestros ojos
más lucen que ellas.
Ya sale con ellas
la noche oscura;
a vuestra hermosura
la luz se esconde;
Mas quien lleva el sol
no teme la noche.

Cantarcillo de la Virgen

Pues andáis en las palmas,
ángeles santos,
que se duerme mi niño,
tened los ramos.

Palmas de Belén
que mueven airados
los furiosos vientos
que suenan tanto:

Where Are You Going, Maiden . . . ?

Where are you going, maiden,
Alone on the mountain?
But who bears the sun
Does not fear the night.

Where are you going, Mary,
Divine bride,
Glorious mother
Of him who made us?
What would you do if the day
Should sink in the west
And night overtake you
On the mountain?
But who bears the sun
Does not fear the night.

The sight of the stars
Troubles me,
But your eyes
Are brighter than they.
Now with the stars
The dark night comes,
And the light of your beauty
Is hidden away,
But who bears the sun
Does not fear the night.

—W. S. MERWIN

A Little Carol of the Virgin

Angels walking under the palm trees,
holy angels,
let my child sleep,
hold back the branches.

Palms of Bethlehem,
tossing in angry wind,
rustling so loud:

no le hagáis ruido,
corred más paso,
que se duerme mi niño,
tened los ramos.

El niño divino,
que está cansado
de llorar en la tierra
por su descanso,
sosegar quiere un poco
del tierno llanto.
Que se duerme mi niño,
tened los ramos.

Rigurosos yelos
le están cercando;
ya veis que no tengo
con qué guardarlo.
Ángeles divinos
que vais volando,
que se duerme mi niño,
tened los ramos.

Hoy la nave del deleite

Hoy la Nave del deleite
se quiere hacer a la mar;—
¿hay quien se quiere embarcar?

Hoy la Nave del contento
con viento en popa de gusto,
donde jamás hay disgusto,
penitencia, ni tormento,
viendo que hay próspero viento,
se quiere hacer a la mar.
¿Hay quien se quiere embarcar?

for his sake quieten, sway gently——
let my child sleep,
hold back the branches.

The holy child
is tired
of crying for his rest
on earth;
he craves a little respite
from his pathetic plaint.
Let my child sleep,
hold back the branches.

All about him
the bitter frost;
see, I have nothing
with which to shelter him.
Blessed angels,
flying past,
let my child sleep,
hold back the branches.

—DENISE LEVERTOV

Today Delight's Fair Ship . . .

   Today delight's fair ship
Longs to sail the sea;
Does someone long to go?

   Today content's fair ship
With pleasure's wind alee
Where never fares displeasure
Nor penitence or woe
Seeing winds are fair
Longs to sail the sea.
Does someone long to go?

—WILLIAM M. DAVIS

Maya

[*de la pieza de teatro* El robo de Dina]

En las mañanicas
del mes de mayo
cantan los ruiseñores,
retumba el campo.

En las mañanicas
como son frescas,
cubren ruiseñores
las alamedas.

Ríense las fuentes
tomando perlas
a las florecillas
que están más cerca.

Vístense las plantas
de varias sedas
que sacar colores
poco les cuesta.

Los campos alegran
tapetes varios,
cantan los ruiseñores,
retumba el campo.

Blanca me era yo . . .

Blanca me era yo
cuando entré en la siega;
diome el sol y ya soy morena.

May Song

[*from the play* El robo de Dina]

In the early mornings
Of the month of May
The nightingales sing,
The countryside replies.

In the early mornings
When they waken gay,
The poplar groves are covered
With the nightingales.

The little brooks laugh
Scattering their pearls
To the little flowers
Growing nearest by.

The bushes are bedecked
With varieties of silks,
To be arrayed in color
Now is no expense.

With varieties of carpets
The countryside is spread,
The nightingales sing,
The countryside responds.

—KATE FLORES

White Was I . . .

White was I
When I went to harvest;
The sun, though, touched me and now I am dark.

Blanca solía yo ser
antes que a segar viniese,
mas no quiso el sol que fuese
blanco el fuego en mi poder.
Mi edad al amanecer
era lustrosa azucena;
diome el sol y ya soy morena.

Si os partiéredes al alba . . .

Si os partiéredes al alba
quedito, pasito, amor,
no espantéis al ruiseñor.

Si os levántais de mañana
de los brazos que os desean,
porque en los brazos no os vean
de alguna envidia liviana,
pisad con planta de lana,
quedito, pasito, amor,
no espantéis al ruiseñor.

Seguidillas del Guadalquivir

Río de Sevilla,
¡cuán bien pareces,
con galeras blancas
y ramos verdes!

Vienen de Sanlúcar,
moviendo el agua,
a la torre de oro
barcos de plata.

Barcos enramados
van a Triana,
el primero de todos
me lleva el alma.

Pure white I used to be
Before I came a-reaping;
But the power of my flame
The sun would not let pure remain.
A lustrous lily
At dawn I was;
The sun, though, touched me and now I am dark. —KATE FLORES

If You Leave at Daybreak . . .

If you leave at daybreak,
Silently, lightly, love,
Do not alarm the nightingale.

If you part at dawning
From these arms that hold you dear,
That you not be seen in the arms
Of an enviable affair,
Go on woolen tiptoe,
Silently, lightly, love,
Do not alarm the nightingale.

—KATE FLORES

Seguidillas of the Guadalquivir River

River of Seville,
how fair you are
with white barges
and green branches!

Coming from Sanlúcar
churning up the water,
ships of silver
to the tower of gold.

Many-oared, the boats
set off for Triana.
The first of them
bears my heart away.

—DENISE LEVERTOV

Soneto de repente

[*de la pieza de teatro* La niña de plata]

Un soneto me manda hacer Violante,
que en mi vida me he visto en tanto aprieto;
catorce versos dicen, que es soneto;
burla burlando van los tres delante.

Yo pensé que no hallara consonante,
y estoy a la mitad de otro cuarteto,
mas si me veo en el primer terceto,
no hay cosa en los cuartetos que me espante.

Por el primer terceto voy entrando,
y parece que entré con pie derecho,
pues fin con este verso le voy dando.

Ya estoy en el segundo, y aun sospecho
que voy los trece versos acabando;
contad si son catorce, y está hecho.

A Sonnet All of a Sudden

[*from the play* La niña de plata]

Violante has commanded me to write
A sonnet. Oh! what trouble I am in!
Though here go three lines, eager to begin,
A sonnet's lines must number fourteen, quite!

I never thought that I should find a rhyme,
And look! the second quatrain is begun:
But nothing in the quatrains would I shun
If I reach the first tercet in good time.

I enter the first tercet in effect,
And I came in on the right foot, it seems,
Because the end of this verse is in sight.

Already in the second, I suspect
That I am finishing just thirteen lines:
Count them! If there are fourteen, it is right.

—DOREEN BELL

FRANCISCO DE QUEVEDO
(1580–1645)

As versatile as Lope, Quevedo cultivated many genres and is noted for such masterpieces as the picaresque *Vida del Buscón* and the prose allegories and satires *Los Sueños*. Born in Madrid of a good family, Quevedo studied at the University of Alcalá, where he won notoriety for his pamphleteering and lampoons. He was forced to leave the country after a duel and served the Duke of Osuña in Sicily and later in Naples. Involved in the Venetian conspiracy (1618), he fell into disgrace and had to retire to his estates in La Mancha (1621). Years later he obtained a post at the court of Philip IV but, failing to win the good graces of Olivares, the king's favorite, he slandered him and was imprisoned for four years in an underground cell; his health undermined, he died two years later.

A deformed, shortsighted scarecrow forced to wear glasses (in Spanish *quevedos*, named after him), Quevedo was as conscious of the social and political corruption of his age as of his own personal handicaps, and his signal writings were above all satires and vitriolic exposés. Deeply patriotic, he often risked his life in defense of the fatherland, but failed utterly as a courtier because of his lashing and undiplomatic frankness. Most of his occasional verse reflects the popular vein: witty, epigrammatic, coarse, or sparkling, at times obscene; but when he is in a serious vein one feels the presence of a cynical, disillusioned man, obsessed by death. He ridiculed Góngora's baroquism but, like Lope and other notable contemporaries, he too succumbed to it and delighted in distorted conceits, punning, and the clustering of images and metaphors.

BEST EDITION: L. Astrana Marín (ed.): *Obras completas*, Madrid, 1932, 2 vols.

ABOUT FRANCISCO DE QUEVEDO: O. H. Green: "Courtly Love in Quevedo," University of Colorado Studies #30; C. B. Morris: "Parallel Imagery in Quevedo and Alberti," *Bulletin of Spanish Studies* 36 (1959), pp. 135–45.

A Roma sepultada en sus ruinas

Buscas en Roma a Roma, ¡oh peregrino!,
y en Roma misma a Roma no la hallas:
cadáver son las que ostentó murallas,
y tumba de sí propio el Aventino.

Yace donde reinaba el Palatino
y, limadas del tiempo las medallas,
más se muestran destrozo a las batallas
de las edades que blasón latino.

Sólo el Tibre quedó, cuya corriente,
si ciudad la regó, ya sepultura
la llora con funesto son doliente.

¡Oh Roma! En tu grandeza, en tu hermosura,
huyó la que era firme, y solamente
lo fugitivo permanece y dura.

Dichoso tú, que alegre en tu cabaña . . .

Dichoso tú, que alegre en tu cabaña,
mozo y viejo aspiraste la aura pura,
y te sirven de cuna y sepultura
de paja el techo, el suelo de espadaña.

En esa soledad, que, libre, baña
callado sol con lumbre más segura,
la vida al día más espacio dura,
y la hora, sin voz te desengaña.

No cuentes por los cónsules los años;
hacen tu calendario tus cosechas;
pisas todo tu mundo sin engaños.

De todo lo que ignoras te aprovechas;
ni anhelas premios, ni padeces daños,
y te dilatas cuanto más te estrechas.

To Rome Entombed in Her Ruins

You look for Rome in Rome, O traveler!
And in very Rome you find not Rome:
A cadaver now what were her vaunted walls,
And the Aventine the graveyard of itself.

Here lies, where once it reigned, the Palatine;
And the medallions, sanded by time,
Seem rather than Latin emblazonments
The rubble of battles of long ago.

Only the Tiber remains; whose tide,
Having as a city watered her, now as a sepulchre
Mourns her with grievous sound of weeping.

O Rome! Of your grandeur, of your beauty
All that was solid has fled, and only
The fugitive stays and endures.

— KATE FLORES

Happy and Contented in Your Hut . . .

Happy and contented in your hut
In youth and age you drew the pure sweet air
And now you find the cradle and the grave
A roof of straw, and reeds upon the ground.

In solitude thus freely bathed
By silent sun in surer light
Daily life grows slow apace
And quiet hours undeceive you.

Count not the years by consulships
But measure by the harvests;
You tread a world without deceits.

You profit by all you do not know
And seek no prize, nor suffer pain,
But are prolonged with each constraint.

—WILLIAM M. DAVIS

¡Ah de la vida! ¿Nadie me responde? . . .

¡Ah de la vida! ¿Nadie me responde?
Aquí de los antaños que he vivido;
la Fortuna mis tiempos ha mordido,
las Horas mi locura las esconde.

¡Que, sin poder saber cómo ni adónde,
la salud y la edad se hayan huido!
Falta la vida, asiste lo vivido,
y no hay calamidad que no me ronde.

Ayer se fue; Mañana no ha llegado;
Hoy se está yendo sin parar un punto:
soy un Fue y un Será y un Es cansado.

En el hoy y mañana y ayer, junto
pañales y mortaja, y he quedado
presentes sucesiones de difunto.

Todo tras sí lo lleva el año breve . . .

Todo tras sí lo lleva el año breve
de la vida mortal, burlando el brío,
al acero valiente, al mármol frío
que contra el tiempo su dureza atreve.

Antes que sepa andar el pie, se mueve
camino de la muerte, donde envío
mi vida oscura: pobre y turbio río,
que negro mar con altas ondas bebe.

Todo corto momento es paso largo
que doy, a mi pesar, en tal jornada,
pues, parado y durmiendo, siempre aguijo.

Breve suspiro, y último, y amargo,
es la muerte, forzosa y heredada;
mas si es ley y no pena, ¿qué me aflijo?

Ah, What of Life! Does No One Answer Me? . . .

Ah, what of life! Does no one answer me?
Here are the yesteryears I lived:
My times take Fortune's bite,
The Hours, my madness hides.

What, I know not how nor where
My health and years have fled.
Life fails, what has been lived attends
And all calamities pursue me.

Yesterday was, Tomorrow is not come,
Today goes on without a pause,
And wearily I Was, Will Be, and Am.

In today, tomorrow, yesterday, conjoined,
Diapers and shroud, I have remained
A drear succession to the grave.
                                            —WILLIAM M. DAVIS

Everything Is Swept Away by the Brief Year . . .

Everything is swept away by the brief year
Of mortal life, mocking the verve
Of the brave steel, the cold marble
Taunting time with its hardness.

Before the foot yet learns to walk, it starts
Down the road of death, whither I am taking
My dismal life: poor muddy river
Swallowed up by the high waves of a black sea.

Every short moment is a long stride
Which I take, unwilling, along such a journey,
Since always, asleep and unstirring, I spur ever on.

A little sigh, and a final, and a bitter one
Is death, ineluctable and innate;
But if it is law and not retribution, why then should I suffer?
                                            —KATE FLORES

Ya formidable y espantoso suena . . .

Ya formidable y espantoso suena
dentro del corazón el postrer día,
y la última hora, negra y fría,
se acerca, de temor y sombras llena.

Si agradable descanso, paz serena,
la muerte en traje de dolor envía,
señas de su desdén de cortesía;
más tiene de caricia que de pena.

¿Qué pretende el temor desacordado
de la que a rescatar piadosa viene
espíritu en miserias añudado?

Llegue rogada, pues mi bien previene;
hálleme agradecido, no asustado;
mi vida acabe y mi vivir ordene.

Miré los muros de la patria mía . . .

Miré los muros de la patria mía,
si un tiempo fuertes, ya desmoronados,
de la carrera de la edad cansados,
por quien caduca ya su valentía.

Salíme al campo, vi que el Sol bebía
los arroyos del yelo destados,
y del monte quejosos los ganados,
que con sombras hurtó su luz al día.

Entré en mi casa; vi que, amancillada,
de anciana habitación era despojos;
mi báculo, más corvo y menos fuerte.

Vencida de la edad sentí mi espada,
y no hallé cosa en que poner los ojos
que no fuese recuerdo de la muerte.

Now Great and Awesome in My Heart . . .

Now great and awesome in my heart
That final day resounds
And that last hour, black and cold,
In fear and shade draws near.

If pleasant rest, and peace serene
Death sends, in guise of pain,
Her scorn shows signs of courtesy
Less sorrow than caress.

What can discordant fear expect
From her, the pious rescuer
Of spirits wracked with grief?

I summon her, good prophetess,
Grateful, unafraid;
My life may end, my living be ordained.   —WILLIAM M. DAVIS

I Gazed Upon My Country's Walls . . .

I gazed upon my country's walls,
So powerful once, now a withered ruin,
Weary with the passage of the years,
Their valor now by age outworn.

I went into the fields, to see the sun
Had drunk of the streams relinquished by the ice,
And across the querulous cows the hill
Cast shade that robbed their day of light.

I went into my house, to see, decrepit,
It was an aged dwelling's mere remains,
My staff less strong now, and more bent.

Vanquished by the years I felt my sword,
And found no thing on which to rest my eyes
That was not a reminder now of death.   —KATE FLORES

Epístola satírica y censoria

contra las costumbres presentes de los castellanos, escrita a
don Gaspar de Guzmán, conde de Olivares, en su valimiento [líneas 1–48]

No he de callar, por más que con el dedo,
ya tocando la boca y ya la frente,
silencio avises o amenaces miedo.

¿No ha de haber un espíritu valiente?
¿Siempre se ha de sentir lo que se dice?
¿Nunca se ha de decir lo que se siente?

Hoy, sin miedo que libre escandalice,
puede hablar el ingenio, asegurado
de que mayor poder le atemorice.

En otros siglos pudo ser pecado
severo estudio, y la verdad desnuda,
y romper el silencio el bien hablado.

Pues sepa, quien lo niega y quien lo duda,
que es lengua la verdad de Dios severo,
y la lengua de Dios nunca fue muda.

Son, la verdad y Dios, Dios verdadero:
ni eternidad divina los separa,
ni de los dos alguna fue primero.

Si Dios a la verdad se adelantara,
siendo verdad, implicación hubiera
en ser, y en que verdad de ser dejara.

La justicia de Dios es verdadera,
ya la misericordia todo cuanto
es Dios, todo ha de ser verdad entera.

Señor excelentísimo: mi llanto
ya no consiente márgenes ni orillas:
inundación será la de mi canto.

Ya sumergirse miro mis mejillas,
la vista por dos urnas derramada
sobre las aras de las dos Castillas.

Satiric and Censorious Epistle

against current manners in Spain, addressed to don Gaspar de Guzmán,
Count of Olivares, for his edification [lines 1–48]

I'll not be silent, though you put your finger
to lip and then to forehead, counseling
silence first, then threatening fear.

May one not have valiant spirit? Must one
pick one's words? And never
speak from the heart's depth?

Surely today an intelligent man may speak
without thereby endangering his freedom
or being bullied by the powers that be?

In times gone by, deep study and the naked truth
were counted sinful, and the poet's
shattering of silence.

But now, let who denies or doubts it know
that Truth's the tongue of God, of God our judge,
and that the tongue of God was never mute.

They, Truth and God together, are truly God:
divine eternity does not sunder them
nor was the one anterior to the other.

If God had been before the truth,
He, being Truth, truth would be mocked
in his existing without truth.

God's justice is the truth,
His mercy, all the qualities
of God, all must be wholly Truth.

Excellent Sire, my lamentation
now breaks its bounding shores:
my song will be a flood,

my cheeks are wet, my eyes
are urns that overflow and drench
the altars of the two Castiles;

Yace aquella virtud desaliñada
que fue, si rica menos, más temida,
en vanidad y en sueño sepultada.

Y aquella libertad esclarecida
que, en donde supo hallar honrada muerte,
nunca quiso tener más larga vida.

Y, pródiga del alma, nación fuerte,
contaba por afrenta de los años
envejecer en brazos de la suerte.

Del tiempo el ocio torpe, y los engaños
del paso de las horas y del día,
reputaban los nuestros por extraños.

Nadie contaba cuánta edad vivía,
sino de qué manera; ni aun un hora
lograba sin afán su valentía.

La robusta virtud era señora,
y sola dominaba al pueblo rudo:
edad, si mal hablada, vencedora . . .

Está la ave en el aire con sosiego . . .

Está la ave en el aire con sosiego,
en la agua el pez, la salamandra en fuego,
y el hombre, en cuyo ser todo se encierra,
está en sola la tierra.
Yo sólo, que nací para tormentos,
estoy en todos estos elementos:
la boca tengo en aire suspirando,
el cuerpo en tierra está peregrinando,
los ojos tengo en agua noche y día,
y en fuego el corazón y la alma mía.

for Virtue lies in disarray
who, though not rich, was proud;
she sleeps, buried in vanity,

and with her lies illustrious Liberty
who, when she knew where death and honor were,
used never to seek longer life.

Once, the strong nation, prodigal of soul,
was used to think growing old in fortune's arms
was an affront the passing years contrived.

To wile away the time in idleness
and torpor—that was something alien
to Spaniards, in the past.

No one would count the years, but how he lived them,
and not an hour went by that was not marked
by eager striving after valiant deeds.

Robust Virtue was the mistress then,
ruling the simple people in an age
ineloquent yet loud with victories . . .

—DENISE LEVERTOV

Birds Are in the Air at Ease . . .

    Birds are in the air at ease,
Fish at sea, the salamander in fire,
And man, whose being holds all things,
Is on the earth alone.
And I, alone for torments born,
Am in all elements:
My mouth with sighing rends the air,
My body on earth, a pilgrim, fares,
My eyes with sea fill day and night,
My heart and soul with fire.

—WILLIAM M. DAVIS

En crespa tempestad del oro undoso . . .

En crespa tempestad del oro undoso
nada golfos de luz ardiente y pura
mi corazón, sediento de hermosura,
si el cabello deslazas generoso.

Leandro en mar de fuego proceloso
su amor ostenta, su vivir apura;
Ícaro en senda de oro mal segura
arde sus alas por morir glorioso.

Con pretensión de fénix, encendidas
sus esperanzas, que difuntas lloro,
intenta que su muerte engendre vidas.

Avaro y rico, y pobre en el tesoro,
el castigo y la hambre imita a Midas,
Tántalo en fugitiva fuente de oro.

Cerrar podrá mis ojos la postrera . . .

Cerrar podrá mis ojos la postrera
sombra, que me llevaré el blanco día:
y podrá desatar esta alma mía
hora, a su afán ansioso lisonjera;

mas no de esotra parte en la ribera
dejará la memoria en donde ardía;
nadar sabe mi llama la agua fría
y perder el respeto a ley severa.

Alma a quien todo un dios prisión ha sido,
venas que humor a tanto fuego han dado,
médulas que han gloriosamente ardido,

su cuerpo dejarán, no su cuidado:
serán ceniza, mas tendrá sentido,
polvo serán, mas polvo enamorado.

When You Shake Loose Your Hair . . .

When you shake loose your hair from all controlling,
Such thirst of beauty quickens my desire
Over its surge in red tornadoes rolling
My heart goes surfing on the waves of fire.

Leander who for love the tempest dares,
It lets a sea of flames its life consume:
Icarus, from a sun whose rays are hairs,
Ignites its wings and glories in its doom.

Charring its hopes (whose deaths I mourn) it strives
Out of their ash to fan new phoenix-lives
That, dying of delight, new hopes embolden.

Miser, yet poor, the crime and fate it measures
Of Midas, starved and mocked with stacks of treasures,
Or Tantalus, with streams that shone as golden.
— ROY CAMPBELL

From the White Day to Take Me . . .

From the white day to take me, the ultimate
Shade will be able to close my eyes:
And this soul of mine from its raging
Ardor then will be pleasingly parted;

But it will not leave on the farther shore
The memory of where it burned;
My flame to swim the frigid water has learned,
And to lose respect for the rigor of the law.

Soul to whom all love a prison has been,
Veins which have given fuel to so much fire,
Marrow consumed in such a glorious blaze,

Will leave their body, but not their care:
Ashes will be, but ashes aware,
Dust, but enamored dust.
— KATE FLORES

Poderoso caballero es don Dinero . . .

Poderoso caballero
es don Dinero.

Madre, yo al oro me humillo;
él es mi amante y mi amado,
pues de puro enamorado,
de contino anda amarillo;
que pues, doblón o sencillo,
hace todo cuanto quiero,
poderoso caballero
es don Dinero.

Nace en las Indias honrado,
donde el mundo lo acompaña;
viene a morir en España,
y es en Génova enterrado.
Y pues quien le trae al lado
es hermoso, aunque sea fiero,
poderoso caballero
es don Dinero.

Es galán y es como un oro,
tiene quebrado el color,
persona de gran valor,
tan cristiano como moro.
Pues que da quita el decoro
y quebranta cualquier fuero,
poderoso caballero
es don Dinero.

Son sus padres principales,
y es de nobles descendiente,
porque en las venas de Oriente
todas las sangres son reales;
y pues es quien hace iguales
al rico y al pordiosero,
poderoso caballero
es don Dinero.

A Mighty Lord Is Money . . .

A mighty lord
Is Money.

Mother, I bow to gold;
He's my lover and beloved,
For out of pure affection
He always turns more yellow,
And, whether much or little,
He gets me all I want,
A mighty lord
Is Money.

Born in the Indies, honored,
Where all make sure to follow,
He comes to die in Spain
And in Genoa he's buried.
And since, when he's along,
Though ugly, beauty's prized,
A mighty lord
Is Money.

He's gallant as a goldpiece
Whose coloring's corrupt,
A person of great valor,
As Christian as a Moor.
Since he acquits decorum
And breaks all statute law,
A mighty lord
Is Money.

His parentage is princely
And noble his descent
Because in Oriental veins
Every blood is royal
And since he makes an equal
Of paupers and the rich,
A mighty lord
Is Money.

¿A quién no le maravilla
ver en su gloria sin tasa
que es lo más ruin de su casa
doña Blanca de Castilla?
Mas pues que su fuerza humilla
al cobarde y al guerrero,
poderoso caballero
es don Dinero.

Sus escudos de armas nobles
son siempre tan principales,
que sin sus escudos reales
no hay escudos de armas dobles;
y pues a los mismos nobles
da codicia su minero,
poderoso caballero
es don Dinero.

Por importar en los tratos
y dar tan buenos consejos,
en las casas de los viejos
gatos le guardan de gatos.
Y pues él rompe recatos
y ablanda al juez más severo,
poderoso caballero
es don Dinero.

Es tanta su majestad
(aunque son sus duelos hartos),
que aun con estar hecho cuartos,
no pierde su calidad;
pero pues da autoridad
al gañán y al jornalero,
poderoso caballero
es don Dinero.

Who cannot but wonder
At his glory unrestrained
When the lowest in his house
Is Lady Blanca of Castile?
But since his power humbles
The coward and the sword,
A *mighty lord*
Is Money.

His scutcheons'* noble bearings
Grow ever princelier
For without his hard cash scutcheons
Dual scutcheons aren't known.
And since the very nobles
Envy him his source,
A *mighty lord*
Is Money.

To matter in agreements
And gives such good advice
In venerable houses
His sharks** keep sharks away
And since he breaks with prudence
And melts the firmest judge,
A *mighty lord*
Is Money.

His majesty is such
(Though mourners aren't few)
That even when he's quartered
His quality's not lost,
For then he gives authority
To journeymen or farmers,
A *mighty lord*
Is Money.

---

*scutcheons: both *coats of arms* and *escudos* (gold coins).

**sharks: literally *gatos*, meaning cats, but here it means both *cats* and *creditors*, i.e., sharks and *loansharks*.

Nunca vi damas ingratas
a su gusto y afición;
que a las caras de un doblón
hacen sus caras baratas;
y pues las hace bravatas
desde una bolsa de cuero,
poderoso caballero
es don Dinero.

Más valen en qualquier tierra
(¡mirad si es harto sagaz!)
sus escudos en la paz
que rodelas en la guerra.
Pues al natural destierra
y hace propio al forastero,
poderoso caballero
es don Dinero.

Rosal, menos presunción . . .

Rosal, menos presunción,
donde están las clavellinas,
pues serán mañana espinas
las que agora rosas son.

¿De qué sirve presumir,
rosal, de buen parecer,
si aun no acabas de nacer
cuando empiezas a morir?
Hace llorar y reír
vivo y muerto tu arrebol,
en un día o en un sol;
desde el oriente al ocaso
va tu hermosura en un paso,
y en menos tu perfección.

Rosal, menos presunción,
donde están las clavellinas,
pues serán mañana espinas
las que agora rosas son.

I've never seen ladies scornful
To his pleasure or his taste;
For to faces on a goldpiece
They make their faces cheap
And then they find bravado
Inside a leather purse,
A *mighty lord*
Is Money.

More worthy in any land
(Just see if it's not wise!)
Are scutcheons in time of peace
Than bucklers in time of war
And making natives exiles
And foreigners his own,
A *mighty lord*
Is Money.
                                        —WILLIAM M. DAVIS

Rosebush, Less Presumption . . .

Rosebush, less presumption,
Where pink carnations are,
For what today are roses
Tomorrow will be thorns.

What good is it presuming,
Rosebush, on good looks,
If, when your birth's not over,
Your death is soon in store?
Full of tears or laughter
Your live or deathly red
Makes one day or sun.
Your beauty sets and rises
Within a single step,
Your perfectness, in less.

Rosebush, less presumption,
Where pink carnations are,
For what today are roses
Tomorrow will be thorns.

No es muy grande la ventaja
que tu calidad mejora:
si es tu mantilla la aurora,
es la noche tu mortaja:
no hay florecilla tan baja
que no te alcance de días,
y de tus caballerías
por descendiente del alba,
se está riyendo la malva,
caballera de un terrón.

Rosal, menos presunción,
donde están las clavellinas,
pues serán mañana espinas
las que agora rosas son.

A una nariz

Érase un hombre a una nariz pegado,
érase una nariz superlativa,
érase una nariz sayón y escriba,
érase un peje espada muy barbado,

Era un reloj de sol mal encarado,
érase una alquitara pensativa,
érase un elefante boca arriba,
era Ovidio Nasón más narizado,

Érase un espolón de una galera,
érase una pirámide de Egito:
las doce tribus de narices era,

Érase un naricísimo infinito,
muchísimo nariz, nariz tan fiera,
que en la cara de Anás fuera delito.

Not very great's the vantage
Your quality procures
If dawn is your mantilla
And darkest night your shroud.
No flowerlet's so lowly
It cannot match your days
And as for stirring exploits
Descending from the dawn,
The mallow rocks with laughter
Atop its steed of earth!

Rosebush, less presumption,
Where pink carnations are,
For what today are roses
Tomorrow will be thorns.
                                        —WILLIAM M. DAVIS

To a Nose

There was a man suspended from a nose,
Something for all to talk about,
A headsman's pointed blade, a scribe's fat pen,
A shark's sharp and most hairy snout,

A twisted and off-center sundial,
A laboratory beaker bent in thought,
An elephant's high-lifted trunk,
The nose that Ovid Naso never sought,

A floating galley's boastful, pushing prow,
Egypt's enshading pyramid:
One whose nasality was infinite,

So fierce, so swollen, it could not be hid;
A dozen nations lie around its base,
It would have been a crime on Annas' face.
                                        —JAMES EDWARD TOBIN

MIGUEL DE GUEVARA
(c. 1585–c. 1646)

This famous sonnet, judged by Ludwig Pfandl and other distinguished critics to be one of the outstanding poems in the Spanish language, has hitherto been considered of anonymous origin or attributed variously to Saint Teresa, Saint Ignatius, Saint Francis Xavier, and Fray Pedro de los Reyes. However, it has now been proven beyond any doubt to be the work of the Mexican *criollo*, Miguel de Guevara, a gifted friar who learned Aztec, Tarascan, and Matlalzingo in order to indoctrinate the Indians of Charo (1620), Pátzcuaro (1640), and other areas. This sonnet, as well as a few others, followed his "Doctrinal Art and Method for Learning Matlalzingo in order to Administer the Holy Sacrament," a manuscript dated 1634, now in the Mexican Society of Geography and Statistics.

ABOUT MIGUEL DE GUEVARA: A. M. Carreño: *Joyas literarias del siglo XVII*, Mexico, 1915; A. M. Carreño: *Fray Miguel de Guevara*, Mexico, 1921; A. Méndez Plancarte: *Poetas novohispanos*, Vol. I, Mexico, 1942.

A Cristo crucificado

No me mueve, mi Dios, para quererte,
el cielo que me tienes prometido,
ni me mueve el infierno tan temido
para dejar por eso de ofenderte.

Tú me mueves, Señor; muéveme el verte
clavado en esa cruz, y escarnecido;
muéveme el ver tu cuerpo tan herido;
muévenme tus afrentas, y tu muerte.

Muévesme al tu amor en tal manera,
que aunque no hubiera cielo, yo te amara;
y aunque no hubiera infierno, te temiera.

No me tienes que dar, porque te quiera;
que aunque cuanto espero no esperara,
lo mismo que te quiero te quisiera.

To Christ Crucified

I am not moved (O Thou my God!) to love Thee
By Heaven which is Thy promise and my rest.
Hell moves not me, where fear is fearfulest,
To offend no more by mine iniquity.

Thou mov'st me (Lord), it moveth me to see
Even Thee Thyself mocked at, nailed on the Cross;
It moveth me to see Thy wounded Body's loss;
Thy death, their insult, much this moveth me.

Thou mov'st me to Thy love with so much skill,
Were there not Heaven, needs must I love Thee still,
Were there not even Hell, then still must I abhor;

Thou need'st give nothing, I'll love though Thou refrain;
Even if I could not hope, all that I hope being vain,
Even as I love Thee should I love Thee more.　IAIN FLETCHER

SOR JUANA INÉS DE LA CRUZ
(1648–95)

The first great poet to come out of the New World was a woman who lived and died in Mexico during the second half of the seventeenth century, Juana de Asbaje, "The Tenth Muse," better known as Sor Juana Inés de la Cruz. Born in a village near Mexico City, an illegitimate child, she was extremely precocious, reading and writing at the age of three. She learned so much so rapidly that at thirteen she was exhibited at the viceroy's court as a child prodigy, holding forth with leading professors and authorities on physics, musicology, philosophy, and mathematics. She became attached to the viceroy's wife and, either because of this entanglement, which some critics suspected of being inordinately passionate, or because of some other frustrated love affair, she entered a convent of Discalced Carmelites (1667) which she abandoned after three months because of its austere practices, joining, in 1669, the Order of St. Jerome. Criticized by the Bishop of Puebla for her interest in literature and the sciences, she answered him in a memorable letter *(Respuesta a Sor Filotea)* which revealed, to a large extent, her innermost conflict: the force of her literary vocation, her overwhelming need for self-expression, and, also, her sincere devotion. Ever involved in charity work and the organization of church festivities, to which she contributed religious plays, she was twice elected prioress but did not accept. Her presence was felt during the droughts, fires, and epidemics which relentlessly visited Mexico during the years 1691–95. To help the poor she sold her scientific equipment and her library (some 4,000 volumes). While nursing the sick, she fell victim to the epidemic.

Her *opera omnia* consists of plays, theological, philosophical, and scientific treatises, and poetry. Her lyrics register, in simple language, her daily experiences and her philosophy (the rights of women, the vagaries and perversities of males); her baroque language mirrors the much admired Spanish master Góngora, revealing the dreams, shadows, and death that dominated her state of mind.

BEST EDITION: Alfonso Méndez Plancarte (ed.): *Obras completas*, Mexico, 1951–55, 4 vols.

ABOUT SOR JUANA INÉS DE LA CRUZ: E. J. Gates: "Reminiscences of Góngora in the Works of Sor Juana," *MLA* 54 (1933), pp. 1041–58; D. Schons: "The Influence of Góngora on Mexican Literature During the Seventeenth Century," *Hispanic Review* VII (1939), pp. 22–34; D. Schons: "Some Obscure Points in the Life of Sor Juana," *Modern Philology*, November 1926.

SOME COLLECTIONS AND CRITICISM PUBLISHED SINCE 1958: Octavio Paz: *Sor Juana Inés de la Cruz, o, Las trampas de la fe*, 3. ed., Mexico, D.F., Fondo de Cultura Económica, 1995. Francisco García Chávez: *Poesías de Sor Juana Inés de la Cruz, vida y obra*, Mexico, Editores Mexicanos Unidos, 1975 (includes Antología Poética). Clara Campoamor: *Sor Juana Inés de la Cruz*, Madrid, Jucar, 1984. Stephanie Merrim, ed.: *Feminist Perspectives on Sor Juana Inés de la Cruz*, Detroit, Wayne State University Press, 1991. Georgina Sabat de Rivers: *Estudios de literatura hispanoamericana: Sor Juana Inés de la Cruz y otros poetas barrocos de la colonia*, Barcelona, PPU, 1992.

A su retrato

Este que ves, engaño colorido,
que, del arte ostentando los primores,
con falsos silogismos de colores
es cauteloso engaño del sentido;

éste, en quien la lisonja ha pretendido
excusar de los años los horrores,
y venciendo del tiempo los rigores
triunfar de la vejez y del olvido,

es un vano artificio del cuidado,
es una flor al viento delicada,
es un resguardo inútil para el hado:

es una necia diligencia errada,
es un afán caduco y, bien mirado,
es cadáver, es polvo, es sombra, es nada.

En perseguirme, Mundo, ¿qué interesas? . . .

En perseguirme, Mundo, ¿qué interesas?
¿En qué te ofendo, cuando sólo intento
poner bellezas en mi entendimiento
y no mi entendimiento en las bellezas?

Yo no estimo tesoros ni riquezas;
y así, siempre me causa más contento
poner riquezas en mi pensamiento
que no mi pensamiento en las riquezas.

Y no estimo hermosura que, vencida,
es despojo civil de las edades,
ni riqueza me agrada fementida,

teniendo por mejor, en mis verdades,
consumir vanidades de la vida
que consumir la vida en vanidades.

On Her Portrait

What here you see in deceiving tints,
Vaunting its crafty artistry
In specious syllogisms of color,
Is a discreet delusion of the sense;

This which flattery would fain pretend
Could expiate the horrors of the years,
The cruelties of time obliterate,
And triumph over age and nothingness,

'Tis but of apprehensiveness a futile artifice,
'Tis but a brittle blossom in the wind,
'Tis against fate an unavailing wall,

'Tis merely a folly diligently mistaken,
'Tis merely a senile ardor, and truly seen
'Tis a corpse, dust, shadow, nothing at all.

—KATE FLORES

Oh World, Why Do You Thus Pursue Me? . . .

Oh world, why do you thus pursue me?
Wherein do I offend you, if my intent
Is but to bring more beauty to my mind
And not to keep my mind on beauty?

I do not value wealth or riches,
Wherefore I shall be ever more content
To bring more richness to my mind
And not to keep my mind on riches.

To me, constrained beauty is no treasure,
For it becomes the lawful spoil of time;
And wealth is false and brings no pleasure.

In my opinion, better far it be
To destroy vanity within my life
Than to destroy my life in vanity.

—MURIEL KITTEL

Diuturna enfermedad de la Esperanza . . .

Diuturna enfermedad de la Esperanza
que así entretienes mis cansados años
y en el fiel de los bienes y los daños
tienes en equilibrio la balanza;

   que siempre suspendida en la tardanza
de inclinarse, no dejan tus engaños
que lleguen a excederse en los tamaños
la desesperación o la confianza:

   ¿quién te ha quitado el nombre de homicida?
Pues lo eres más severa, si se advierte
que suspendes el alma entretenida;

   y entre la infausta o la felice suerte,
no lo haces tú por conservar la vida
sino por dar más dilatada muerte.

Esperanza

   Verde embeleso de la vida humana,
loca Esperanza, frenesí dorado,
sueño de los despiertos intrincado,
como de sueños, de tesoros vana;

   alma del mundo, senectud lozana,
decrépito verdor imaginado;
el hoy de los dichosos esperado
y de los desdichados el mañana:

   sigan tu sombra en busca de tu día
los que, con verdes vidrios por anteojos,
todo lo ven pintado a su deseo;

   que yo, más cuerda en la fortuna mía,
tengo en entrambas manos ambos ojos
y solamente lo que toco veo.

Perpetual Infirmity of Hope . . .

Perpetual infirmity of hope,
Entertaining thus my failing years,
Holding to the last the equal scale
That balances profit against the loss;

By your tardiness, ever in suspense,
To give your favor, your deceits allow
Success in weighting down the scale
Neither to despair nor confidence:

Who has cleared you of a murderer's name?
When you deserve it far more grievously
For holding back the soul that you sustain;

Hovering between ill luck and happiness,
To keep me in life is not your aim
But to make death come more tardily.

—MURIEL KITTEL

Hope

Green embellishment of human life,
Fatuous hope, gilded bauble,
Dream of the unsleeping, and as bedecked
As dreams with treasures vain;

Lure of the world, senescent lushness,
Imagination's decrepit verdure,
Today expected by the happy,
And by the hapless not before tomorrow:

Those who in quest of your day pursue your shade,
With green-tinted glasses before their eyes,
May see everything painted as they wish;

More frugal of my fortune, I
Keep both my eyes in my two hands,
And see no more than I can touch.

—KATE FLORES

Esta tarde, mi bien, cuando te hablaba . . .

Esta tarde, mi bien, cuando te hablaba,
como en tu rostro y tus acciones vía
que con palabras no te persuadía,
que el corazón me vieses deseaba;

y Amor, que mis intentos ayudaba,
venció lo que imposible parecía:
pues entre el llanto que el dolor vertía,
el corazón deshecho destilaba.

Baste ya de rigores, mi bien, baste;
no te atormenten más celos tiranos,
ni el vil recelo tu quietud contraste

con sombras necias, con indicios vanos,
pues ya en líquido humor viste y tocaste
mi corazón deshecho entre tus manos.

Deténte, sombra de mi bien esquivo . . .

Deténte, sombra de mi bien esquivo,
imagen del hechizo que más quiero,
bella ilusión por quien alegre muero,
dulce ficción por quien penosa vivo.

Si al imán de tus gracias atractivo
sirve mi pecho de obediente acero
¿para qué me enamoras lisonjero,
si has de burlarme luego fugitivo?

Mas blasonar no puedes satisfecho
de que triunfa de mí tu tiranía;
que aunque dejas burlado el lazo estrecho

que tu forma fantástica ceñía,
poco importa burlar brazos y pecho
si te labra prisión mi fantasía.

This Evening When I Spoke to You . . .

This evening when I spoke to you, my dear,
When in your face and gestures I perceived
That I could not persuade you with my words,
Then I desired that you should see my heart.

And love, that came to help my purposes,
Accomplished that which seemed impossible,
For there among the tears that sorrow spilled
Was drop by drop my wasting heart distilled.

Enough of harshness now, my dear, enough;
Nor let cruel jealousy torment you more,
Nor base suspicion attack your virtue now

With foolish shadows, empty evidence,
Since here in watery medium you have seen
And felt within your hands my wasted heart.

—MURIEL KITTEL

Elusive Shadow of My Substance, Stay . . .

Elusive shadow of my substance, stay,
Bewitching image that I want too well,
Illusion fair for whom in joy I die,
Fiction sweet for whom in pain I dwell.

If to the magnet of your gracious charms
My breast obedient as steel is drawn,
Why do you entice my enamored arms
If you would but escape me then in scorn?

Yet you must not think in your tyranny
That you quite succeed in vanquishing me:
For although you mock the tenuous ties

That ever will your phantom form despise,
What matter if my arms and breast you flee
If I keep you prisoner in my fantasy?

—KATE FLORES

Yo no puedo tenerte ni dejarte . . .

Yo no puedo tenerte ni dejarte,
ni sé por qué, al dejarte o al tenerte,
se encuentra un no sé qué para quererte
y muchos sí sé qué para olvidarte.

Pues ni quieres dejarme ni enmendarte,
yo templaré mi corazón de suerte
que la mitad se incline a aborrecerte
aunque la otra mitad se incline a amarte.

Si ello es fuerza querernos, haya modo,
que es morir el estar siempre riñendo:
no se hable más en celo y en sospecha,

y quien da la mitad, no quiera el todo;
y cuando me la estas allá haciendo,
sabe que estoy haciendo la deshecha.

Arguye de inconsecuentes el gusto y la censura de los hombres

Hombres necios que acusáis
a la mujer sin razón,
sin ver que sois la ocasión
de lo mismo que culpáis:

si con ansia sin igual
solicitáis su desdén,
¿por qué queréis que obren bien
si las incitáis al mal?

Combatís su resistencia
y luego, con gravedad,
decís que fue liviandad
lo que hizo la diligencia.

I Can Neither Hold You Nor Let You Go

I can neither hold you nor let you go,
I know not why, to let you go or hold you
Causes me, I know not why, to want you,
Or to find you wanting for what I do not know.

Since you will neither go away nor mend your ways,
I propose in this way to amend my heart:
In only half will love for you be kept apart,
While all the other half will hate you always.

Thus let it be if have each other we must:
Leaving off endless quarrels that rend the soul,
And not suspect, in jealousy and mistrust.

Nor giving half may one expect the whole;
Hence away while making sure that you deceive,
Be sure that here I stay and make believe.

— KATE FLORES

Verses Against the Inconsequence of Men's Taste and Strictures

You stupid men, who do accuse
Women without good reason,
You are the cause of what you blame,
Yet this inference you refuse.

If you seek women's favor to win
With ardor beyond compare,
Why require them to be good,
When 'tis you who urge their sin?

You break down their resistance,
Then say quite seriously
That their lightness has achieved
What you won by your persistence.

Parecer quiere el denuedo
de vuestro parecer loco,
al niño que pone el coco
y luego le tiene miedo.

Queréis con presunción necia,
hallar a la que buscáis,
para pretendida, Thais,
y en posesión, Lucrecia.

¿Qué humor puede ser más raro
que el que, falto de consejo,
él mismo empaña el espejo,
y siente que no esté claro?

Con el favor y el desdén
tenéis condición igual,
quejándoos, si os tratan mal,
burlándoos, si os quieren bien.

Opinión, ninguna gana;
pues la que más se recata,
si no os admite, es ingrata,
y si os admite, es liviana.

Siempre tan necios andáis
que, con desigual nivel,
a una culpáis por crüel
y a otra por fácil culpáis.

¿Pues cómo ha de estar templada
la que vuestro amor pretende,
si la que es ingrata, ofende,
y la que es fácil, enfada?

Mas, entre el enfado y pena
que vuestro gusto refiere,
bien haya la que no os quiere
y quejaos enhorabuena.

Dan vuestras amantes penas
a sus libertades alas,
y después de hacerlas malas
las queréis hallar muy buenas.

You claim to have dared
With your insane point of view,
Like the child who makes faces
And then finds he is scared.

You seek with stupid presumption
To find her whom you pursue
To be Thais when you woo her,
And Lucretia in your possession.

What a strange disposition
Has he who, lacking counsel,
Himself beclouds the mirror
Then deplores its murky reflection.

No woman can your favor win
Since even the most discreet
Is ungrateful if she keeps you out
And loose if she lets you in.

By your good opinion none is graced;
As she who is most reserved,
Is disliked if she doesn't admit you,
And she who admits you is debased.

You are always so obtuse
That, in unequal degrees,
You blame one for being cruel
And the other for being loose.

So how could she be born
Who would gain your love,
If an ungrateful woman displeases
And a complaisant one you scorn?

But amid the anger and pain
Of which it pleases you to speak,
Cheers for she who doesn't love you
And you are welcome to complain.

Your amorous labors give
Wings to their indiscretions,
When you have made women wicked
You wish them virtuously to live.

¿Cuál mayor culpa ha tenido
en una pasión errada:
la que cae de rogada,
o el que ruega de caído?

¿O cuál es más de culpar,
aunque cualquiera mal haga:
la que peca por la paga,
o el que paga por pecar?

Pues ¿para qué os espantais
de la culpa que tenéis?
Queredlas cual las hacéis
o hacedlas cual las buscáis.

Dejad de solicitar,
y después, con más razón,
acusaréis la afición
de la que os fuere a rogar.

Bien con muchas armas fundo
que lidia vuestra arrogancia,
pues en promesa e instancia
juntáis diablo, carne y mundo.

Que expresan sentimientos de ausente

Amado dueño mío,
escucha un rato mis cansadas quejas,
pues del viento las fío,
que breve las conduzca a tus orejas,
si no se desvanece el triste acento
como mis esperanzas en el viento.

Óyeme con los ojos,
ya que están tan distantes los oídos,
y de ausentes enojos
en ecos, de mi pluma mis gemidos;
y ya que a ti no llega mi voz ruda,
óyeme sordo, pues me quejo muda.

In a passion that is guilty
Who bears the greater blame:
She who falls on being entreated
Or he who falls to make entreaty?

When each is guilty of sin,
Which is the most to blame:
She who sins for payment,
Or he who pays for the sin?

Why are you so surprised
At the fault that is your own?
Either prize women as you make them,
Or make them to be prized.

To them no longer urge your suit,
And then with much more reason
Can you blame their affection
When they are in pursuit.

To assert this I have every right;
Your pride has many weapons,
Your persistence and your promises
Devil, world, and flesh unite.

—MURIEL KITTEL*

Verses Expressing the Feelings of a Lover

My love, my lord,
hearken to my weary plaints awhile
as on the wind I cast them,
that it may wing them to thine ears,
so be it scatter not,
even as my hopes, the grievous voice.

With thine eyes hear me,
thou whose ears are so removed
from my pen murmuring
the groaning woes of absence;
and since my rude voice cannot come to thee,
deafly hear me, who mutely mourn.

*Editor's note: A complete translation by Muriel Kittel of this poem was not published.
Thus, some stanzas were newly translated for the 1998 edition.

Si del campo te agradas,
goza de sus frescuras venturosas,
sin que aquestas cansadas
lágrimas te detengan, enfadosas;
que en él verás, si atento te entretienes,
ejemplos de mis males y mis bienes.

Si al arroyo parlero
ves, galán de las flores en el prado,
que, amante y lisonjero,
a cuantas mira intima su cuidado,
en su corriente mi dolor te avisa
que a costa de mi llanto tienes risa.

Si ves que triste llora
su esperanza marchita, en ramo verde,
tórtola gemidora,
en él y en ella mi dolor te acuerde,
que imitan, con verdor y con lamento,
él mi esperanza y ella mi tormento.

Si la flor delicada,
si la peña, que altiva no consiente
del tiempo ser hollada,
ambas me imitan, aunque variamente,
ya con fragilidad, ya con dureza,
mi dicha aquélla y ésta mi firmeza.

Si ves el ciervo herido
que baja por el monte, acelerado,
buscando, dolorido,
alivio al mal en un arroyo helado,
y sediento al cristal se precipita,
no en el alivio, en el dolor me imita.

Si la liebre encogida
huye medrosa de los galgos fieros,
y por salvar la vida
no deja estampa de los pies ligeros,
tal mi esperanza, en dudas y recelos
se ve acosada de villanos celos.

If the fields are pleasant to thee,
joy in their happy verdancy,
untroubled by these faint
vexatious tears;
for there, attentive, thou wilt see
ensample of my woes and weal.

If thou seest the prattling stream,
lover of the meadow flowers,
impart with amorous flattery
to all it looks on its desire,
there flow my tears that thou mayst know
its laughter at my sorrow's cost.

If thou seest the turtledove
plaintive on a green bough mourning
its withered hope,
let bough and dove remind thee of my grief,
for they set forth, in greenness and lament,
my hope and pain.

If thou seest the fragile flower,
the crag that proudly scorns
the spurning tread of time,
both image me, albeit differently,
that my contentment, this my obduracy.

If thou seest the wounded stag
that hastens down the mountainside,
seeking, stricken, in icy stream
ease for its hurt,
and thirsting plunges in the crystal waters,
not in ease, in pain it mirrors me.

If from the savage hounds
the timorous hare in terror flies
and leaves no trace, that it may live,
of its light feet,
so my hope, in doubting and misgiving,
is close pursued by cruel jealousies.

Si ves el cielo claro,
tal es la sencillez del alma mía;
y si, de luz avaro,
de tinieblas se emboza el claro día,
es con su oscuridad y su inclemencia,
imagen de mi vida en esta ausencia.

Así que, Fabio amado,
saber puedes mis males sin costarte
la noticia cuidado,
pues puedes de los campos informarte;
y pues yo a todo mi dolor ajusto,
saber mi pena sin dejar tu gusto.

Mas ¿cuándo, ¡ay, gloria mía!,
mereceré gozar tu luz serena?
¿Cuándo llegará el día
que pongas dulce fin a tanta pena?
¿Cuándo veré tus ojos, dulce encanto,
y de los míos quitarás el llanto?

¿Cuándo tu voz sonora
herirá mis oídos, delicada,
y el alma que te adora,
de inundación de gozos anegada,
a recibirte con amante prisa
saldrá a los ojos desatada en risa?

¿Cuándo tu luz hermosa
revestirá de glorias mis sentidos?
¿Y cuándo yo, dichosa,
mis suspiros daré por bien perdidos,
teniendo en poco el precio de mi llanto,
que tanto ha de penar quien goza tanto?

¿Cuándo de tu apacible
rostro alegre veré el semblante afable,
y aquel bien indecible
a toda humana pluma inexplicable,
que mal se ceñirá a lo definido
lo que no cabe en todo lo sentido?

If thou seest the bright sky,
even such is my soul's purity;
and if the day, niggard of light,
wraps its radiancy in gloom,
its darkness and inclemency
image my life since thou art gone.

Thus, sweet Fabio,
thou mayst with tranquil mind
have tidings of my woes,
perusing nature's face,
and as to every thing I fit my grief,
know my pain and still thy pleasure take.

But when alas! my glory, shall I have
my meed of joyance in thy tranquil light?
When will it be, the day
when thou shall put sweet end to so much pain?
When, dear enchantment, shall I see thine eyes
And tears desist from mine?

When will thy sounding voice
strike softly on mine ear,
and the soul that adores thee,
flooded with spate of joy,
to welcome thee with loving haste
shine forth dissolved in gladness?

When will thy fair light bathe
my sense in splendor?
And I, for happiness,
and soon to hold the guerdon of my tears,
count my vain sighs for nought?
—For such is joy and such the price of pain.

When shall I see the pleasant aspect
of thy gentle joyous face
and that unspeakable boon
no human pen can tell?
—For how should that which overflows the whole
of sense within the finite be contained?

Ven, pues, mi prenda amada:
que ya fallece mi cansada vida
de esta ausencia pesada;
ven, pues: que mientras tarda tu venida,
aunque me cueste su verdor enojos,
regaré mi esperanza con mis ojos.

En que se describe racionalmente los effectos irracionales del amor

Este amoroso tormento
que en mi corazón se ve,
sé que lo siento, y no sé
la causa por que lo siento.

Siento una grave agonía
por lograr un devaneo,
que empieza como deseo
y pára en melancolía.

Y cuando con más terneza
mi infeliz estado lloro,
sé que estoy triste e ignoro
la causa de mi tristeza.

Siento un anhelo tirano
por la ocasión a que aspiro,
y cuando cerca la miro
yo misma aparto la mano.

Porque, si acaso se ofrece,
después de tanto desvelo,
la desazona el recelo
o el susto la desvanece.

Ya sufrida, ya irritada,
con contrarias penas lucho:
que por él sufriré mucho,
y con él sufriré nada.

Come then, beloved treasure,
For already my weary life is dying
Of this sore absence;
Come then, for while thou tarriest thy coming,
My hope, although its greenness cost me dear,
Is watered by mine eyes.

—SAMUEL BECKETT

Describes Rationally the Irrational Effects of Love

This torment of love
That is in my heart,
I know I feel it
And know not why.

I feel the keen pangs
Of a frenzy desired
Whose beginning is longing
And end melancholy.

And when I my sorrow
More softly bewail,
I know I am sad
and know not why.

I feel for the juncture
I crave a fierce panting,
and when I come nigh it
withhold mine own hand.

For if haply it offers
after much weary vigil,
mistrust spoils its savor
and terror dispels it.

Now patient, now fretful,
by conflicting griefs torn,
who for him much shall suffer,
and with him suffer nought.

Sin bastantes fundamentos
forman mis tristes cuidados,
de conceptos engañados,
un monte de sentimientos;

y en aquel fiero conjunto
hallo, cuando se derriba,
que aquella máquina altiva
sólo estribaba en un punto.

Tal vez el dolor me engaña,
y presumo, sin razón,
que no habrá satisfacción
que pueda templar mi saña;

Y aunque el desengaño toco,
con la misma pena lucho,
de ver que padezco mucho
padeciendo por tan poco.

A vengarse se abalanza
tal vez el alma ofendida;
y después, arrepentida,
toma de mí otra venganza.

En mi ciego devaneo,
bien hallada con mi engaño,
solicito el desengaño
y no encontrarlo deseo.

Si alguno mis quejas oye,
más a decirlas me obliga
por que me las contradiga,
que no porque las apoye.

Porque si con la pasión
algo contra mi amor digo,
es mi mayor enemigo
quien me concede razón.

On scant foundations
my sad cares raise
with delusive conceits
a mountain of feeling.

And when that proud mass
falls asunder I find
that the arrogant fabric
was poised on a pin.

Beguiled perhaps by grief
I presume without reason
no fulfillment can ever
my passion assuage.

And though nigh disabused,
still the same grief assails me,
that I suffer so sore
for so little a cause.

Perhaps the wounded soul sweeping
to take its revenge
repents it and wreaks
other vengeance on me.

In my blindness and folly
I, gladly deceived,
beseech disenchantment
and desire it not.

If anyone is hearing my complaints,
I am obliged to recite them
more so that I may be contradicted
than so that I may be supported.

Because if, in passion,
I say something against my love,
whoever says I am right
is my worst enemy.

Y si acaso en mi provecho
hallo la razón propicia,
me embaraza la injusticia
y ando cediendo el derecho.

Nunca hallo gusto cumplido,
porque, entre alivio y dolor,
hallo culpa en el amor
y disculpa en el olvido.

Esto de mi pena dura
es algo del dolor fiero;
y much más no refiero
porque pasa de locura.

Si acaso me contradigo
en este confuso error,
aquel que tuviese amor
entenderá lo que digo.

En reconocimiento a las inimitables Plumas de la Europa

¿Cuándo, Númenes divinos,
dulcísimos Cisnes, cuándo
merecieron mis descuidos
ocupar vuestros cuidados?

¿De dónde a mí tanto elogio?
¿De dónde a mí encomio tanto?
¿Tánto pudo la distancia
añadir a mi retrato?

¿De qué estatura me hacéis?
¿Qué Coloso habéis labrado,
que desconoce la altura
del original lo bajo?

And if by chance I am favored
finding the propitious reason,
the injustice of it impedes me
and I relinquish my rights.

I never find full satisfaction
because, between relief and pain,
I find fault in love
and forgiveness in forgetting.

This harsh grief of mine
consists of savage pain
and I won't say much more,
because it goes beyond insanity.

If by chance I contradict myself
in this confused erring,
one who has been in love
will understand what I say.

—SAMUEL BECKETT*

In Acknowledgment of the Praises of European Writers

Divine Oracles, tell me when,
when, most melodious of Swans,
when did my careless scrawls deserve
to occupy your thoughtful care?

And from what place does so much praise,
so many commendations, come?
Can it be distance that alone
added so much to my portrait?

What stature have you given me?
What great Colossus have you wrought,
entirely ignorant of height,
from this lowly original?

---

*Editor's note: No published translation by Samuel Beckett of the last seven stanzas of this poem was found. Thus, those seven stanzas were newly translated for the 1998 edition.

No soy yo la que pensáis,
sino es que allá me habéis dado
otro sér en vuestras plumas
y otro aliento en vuestros labios,

y diversa de mí misma
entre vuestras plumas ando,
no como soy, sino como
quisisteis imaginarlo.

A regiros por informes,
no me hiciera asombro tanto,
que ya sé cuánto el afecto
sabe agrandar los tamaños.

Pero si de mis borrones
visteis los humildes rasgos,
que del tiempo más perdido
fueron ocios descuidados,

¿qué os pudo mover a aquellos
mal merecidos aplausos?
¿Así puede a la verdad
arrastrar lo cortesano?

¿A una ignorante mujer,
cuyo estudio no ha pasado
de ratos, a la precisa
ocupación mal hurtados;

a un casi rústico aborto
de unos estériles campos,
que el nacer en ellos yo,
los hace más agostados;

a una educación inculta,
en cuya infancia ocuparon
las mismas cogitaciones
el oficio de los ayos,

se dirigen los elogios
de los Ingenios más claros
que en Púlpitos y en Escuelas
el Mundo venera sabios?

I am not what you think I am;
but over there you've given me
another being in your pens,
and other breath upon your lips,

and, different from what I am,
I walk beneath your pens, and am
not what I truly am, but what
you'd prefer to imagine me.

To rule by reputation would
not startle me so very much,
since I already have observed
affection magnifying sizes.

But if you actually saw
the humble features of my scrawls,
which in long-ago squandered time
formed careless recreations, then

what could have prompted you to this
poorly deserved applause? Is it
possible for the truth to be
so far dragged down by courtliness?

Is it to such an ignorant
woman, whose tutelage for the
exacting occupation never
passed beyond poorly chosen snatches;

to a base-born abortion of
some barren fields, that I have made,
by being born among them, more
burned out and barren than before;

to an uncultured education
which in its infancy took up
with these same cogitations all
the tutors' offices; is it

to this, that praises of the most
illustrious, venerated in
pulpits and schools by all the world
as sages, now direct themselves?

¿Cuál fue la ascendente Estrella
que, dominando los Astros,
a mí os ha inclinado, haciendo
lo violento voluntario?

¿Qué mágicas infusiones
de los Indios herbolarios
de mi Patria, entre mis letras
el hechizo derramaron?

¿Qué proporción de distancia,
el sonido modulando
de mis hechos, hacer hizo
cónsono lo destemplado?

¿Qué siniestras perspectivas
dieron aparente ornato
al cuerpo compuesto sólo
de unos mal distintos trazos?

¡Oh cuántas veces, oh cuántas,
entre las ondas de tantos
no merecidos loores,
elogios mal empleados;

¡oh cuántas, encandilada
en tanto golfo de rayos,
o hubiera muerto Faetonte
o Narciso peligrado,

a no tener en mí misma
remedio tan a la mano,
como conocerme, siendo
lo que los pies para el pavo!

Vergüenza me ocasionáis
con haberme celebrado,
porque sacan vuestras luces
mis faltas más a lo claro.

Which was the ascendant star
dominating the planets, that
made you incline toward me, and made
the foreordained voluntary?

What magical infusions, brewed
from herbals of the Indians
of my own country, spilled their old
enchantment over all my lines?

And how much distance is required
to modulate the sound of all
my doings, till it seemed to make
their dissonances harmonize?

What sinister perspectives give
apparent form and ornament
to a vague body outlined by
rough, ill-done sketches, nothing more?

How many times, how many times,
among the waves of so much praise,
none of it merited, and waves
of misdirected compliments;

how many times, dazzled and blind
in such tremendous seas of light,
would not Phaeton have died, or would
Narcissus have been endangered, had

I not possessed within myself
some homely antidote to hand,
like knowledge of myself, being
what ugly feet are to the peacock!

You have brought disgrace on me
in making me so famous, for
the light you shed reveals my faults
more clearly, making them stand out.

Cuando penetrar el Sol
intenta cuerpos opacos,
el que piensa beneficio
suele resultar agravio:

porque densos y groseros,
resistiendo en lo apretado
de sus tortüosos poros
la intermisión de los rayos,

y admitiendo solamente
el superficial contacto,
sólo de ocasionar sombras
les sirve lo iluminado.

Bien así, a la luz de vuestros
panegíricos gallardos,
de mis obscuros borrones
quedan los disformes rasgos.

Honoríficos sepulcros
de cadáveres helados,
a mis conceptos sin alma
son vuestros encomios altos:

elegantes Panteones,
en quienes el jaspe y mármol
Regia superflua custodia
son de polvo inanimado.

Todo lo que se recibe,
no se mensura al tamaño
que en sí tiene, sino al modo
que es del recipiente vaso.

Vosotros me concebisteis
a vuestro modo, y no extraño
lo grande: que esos conceptos
por fuerza han de ser milagros.

La imagen de vuestra idea
es la que habéis alabado;

When the sun tries to penetrate
bodies impervious to light,
he who thinks that they benefit
should know the sun just injures them;

because dense objects and coarse things,
resisting, in the narrowness
and meanness of their crooked pores
the entrance of the rays of light,

and tolerating nothing more
than superficial contact, find
that in their case the brightness serves
only to create shadows. Thus,

it seems to me, under the light
of your most fulsome eulogies,
my obscure scribblings are bereft
of all but their deformities.

Your lofty compliments are but
the honorary sepulchres
of frozen corpses for my cold
spiritless notions: your praises

are elegant pantheons where
the jasper and the marble are
magnificent, superfluous
custodians of lifeless dust.

Everything that you receive
is not measured according to
its actual size, but, rather, that
of the receiving vessel. You

conceive of me in terms that are
your own, and I don't wonder at
the great thing: that these concepts must,
of course, be miracles. Because

the image of your own idea
is, after all, what you have praised;

y siendo vuestra, es bien digna
de vuestros mismos aplausos.

Celebrad ese, de vuestra
propia aprehensión, simulacro,
para que en vosotros mismos
se vuelva a quedar el lauro.

Si no es que el sexo ha podido
o ha querido hacer, por raro,
que el lugar de lo perfecto
obtenga lo extraordinario;

mas a esto solo, por premio
era bastante el agrado,
sin desperdiciar conmigo
elogios tan empeñados.

Quien en mi alabanza viere
ocupar juicios tan altos,
¿qué dirá, sino que el gusto
tiene en el ingenio mando? . . .

and, being yours, it well deserves
your own approval and applause.

Continue then to celebrate
that simulacrum of your own
perceptions, that the laurel may
return to stay among yourselves.

Were it not that my sex, for once,
had made the great attempt, that thus
we unexpected ones had tried
to reach perfection's height at last;

if it were not for this, the joy
alone would be enough reward;
no need for squandering on me
such forced, unnatural compliments.

Whoever sees such judges stoop
to praise me so, what can he say
but that "good taste" has taken hold
of mere intelligence or wit? . . .   —CONSTANCE URDANG

GUSTAVO ADOLFO BÉCQUER
(1836–70)

As the seventeenth century drew to a close, the gold of the Golden Age had lost its luster. Its last great playwright, Calderón de la Barca, died in 1681; its last great poet, Sor Juana Inés de la Cruz, in 1695. During the eighteenth and early nineteenth centuries, Spain completely lost her political prestige and international supremacy, becoming a second-rate power. Even the dynasty changed; her sovereigns, now of French extraction, imposed their own ideology so that the eighteenth century, reflecting the French Enlightenment, was characterized by pronounced interest in reorganization and systematization. The intellectuals busied themselves founding academies, compiling dictionaries, and writing dissertations and treatises of civic value. Only with the Romantic movement, which belatedly reached the Hispanic peninsula in 1833 and was frankly imitative of Lamartine, Hugo, and de Vigny, did literature regain its former prestige. It was only after the Romantic fanfare subsided, especially after the death of "the Spanish Byron," José de Espronceda (1808–42), that the poetry of Bécquer and Rosalía de Castro was given a hearing.

Born in Seville and brought up by his godmother, a wealthy and sensitive lady (his father, an unsuccessful painter, had died when he was five, and his mother when he was nine), Bécquer was given a good education. Despite the admonition of his art teacher (his uncle), "You will never be a good painter but a bad poet," Bécquer, when barely eighteen, boarded a train for Madrid in quest of literary fame. In the painfully hard years that followed, suffering hunger and illness, he succeeded only in undermining his constitution and bringing on the tuberculosis which finally killed him while still in his thirties. After a hopeless love affair in 1858 with Julia Espín, the inspirer of the *Rimas*, he married his physician's daughter, by whom he had three children. He was separated from her, on the advice of his adored brother, the

196

painter Valeriano. In 1870, three months after Valeriano's death, he died, just as his art was attaining its highest fruition.

Bécquer is known for his tales and legends in prose, whose atmosphere of mystery and suspense are reminiscent of Poe and Hoffmann, and, as a poet, for his delicate *Rimas*. In these seventy-six short poems he weaves with tender impressionism the story of his frustrated love: from its thrilling, illusory inception to its dreamed-of culmination and melancholy finale. Critics have dismissed these lyrics as *suspiritos germánicos* (little sighs in the German style) because so many of the poems resemble Heine, a Heine drained of his ferocious acidity—and Bécquer did know Heine's *Lyrisches Intermezzo* through Gérard de Nerval's French translation. Yet the simplicity and musicality of this Spanish Verlaine did a great deal to subdue the brassy avalanche of the Romantics and restored to Spanish literature the supple sonority of the Golden Age. Bécquer bridges the lyricism of the Golden Age to a lyrical future brought to fruition, a score of years after his death, by Rubén Darío, who continued and expanded his poetical horizons and made possible the poetic renaissance of the twentieth century.

BEST EDITION: Joaquín and Serafín Alvárez Quintero (eds.): *Obras completas*, Madrid, Aguilar, 1950.

ABOUT G. A. BÉCQUER: E. L. King: G. A. Bécquer: *From Painter to Poet*, Mexico, Porrúa, 1953. Also: G. H. Daugherty: "G. A. Bécquer," *Poet Lore* 45 (1939), pp. 127-45; C. F. Fraker: "G. A. Bécquer and the Modernists," *Hispanic Review* 3 (1935), pp. 36–44; H. A. Harter: *G. A. Bécquer's Significance for XXth Century Spanish Poetry*, Ohio State University dissertation, 1958; E. A. Peers: A *History of the Romantic Movement in Spain*, Cambridge University Press, 1940; F. Schneider: "G. A. Bécquer as 'Poeta' and His Knowledge of Heine's *Lieder*," *Modern Philology* 19 (1922), pp. 245–56; L. C. Woodman: "G. A. Bécquer: Spanish Romanticist," *Poet Lore* 26 (1915), pp. 512–22; Jorge Guillén: *Language and Poetry*, Harvard University Press, 1961, pp. 125–56.

SOME COLLECTIONS AND CRITICISM PUBLISHED SINCE 1958: B. Brant Bynum: *The Romantic Imagination in the Works of Gustavo Adolfo Bécquer*, Chapel Hill, N.C., University of North Carolina, 1993.

Saeta que voladora . . .

Saeta que voladora
Cruza, arrojada al azar,
Y que no se sabe dónde
Temblando se clavará;

Hoja que del árbol seca
Arrebata el vendaval,
Y que no hay quien diga el surco
Donde al polvo volverá;

Gigante ola que el viento
Riza y empuja en el mar,
Y rueda y pasa y se ignora
Qué playa buscando va;

Luz que en cercos temblorosos
Brilla, próxima a expirar,
Y que no se sabe de ellos
Cuál el último será;

Eso soy yo, que al acaso
Cruzo el mundo, sin pensar
De dónde vengo, ni adónde
Mis pasos me llevarán.

Como la brisa que la sangre orea . . .

Como la brisa que la sangre orea
sobre el oscuro campo de batalla,
cargada de perfumes y armonías
en el silencio de la noche vaga;

símbolo del dolor y la ternura,
del bardo inglés en el horrible drama,
la dulce Ofelia, la razón perdida,
cogiendo flores y cantando pasa.

An Arrow Flying Past . . .

An arrow flying past,
a shaft shot in the dark
without a thought of where
its trembling point will strike;

A dry leaf from the tree
tossed by the autumn gales,
and no one knows what furrow
will catch it when it falls;

A giant wave that the wind
whips and drives through the sea,
that rolls on without knowing
which is the shore it seeks;

Lamp that, as it expires,
casts trembling rings of light
and knows not which will prove
its final shining out.

All these am I who wander
across the world, nor see
whence I have come or whither
my steps will carry me.

—J. M. COHEN

As the Breeze That Cools the Blood . . .

As the breeze that cools the blood
on the gloomy field of battle,
with perfume and harmony fraught,
strays in the silence of night;

symbol of sorrow and softness
in the awful play of the English bard,
sweet Ophelia, reason lost,
goes by picking flowers and singing.

—EDWARD F. GAHAN

Del salón en el ángulo oscuro . . .

Del salón en el ángulo oscuro,
De su dueña tal vez olvidada,
Silenciosa y cubierta de polvo
    Veíase el arpa.

¡Cuánta nota dormía en sus cuerdas,
Como el pájaro duerme en las ramas,
Esperando la mano de nieve
    Que sabe arrancarlas!

¡Ay!—pensé—, cuántas veces el genio
Así duerme en el fondo del alma,
Y una voz como Lázaro, espera
Que diga: "¡Levántate y anda!"

Besa el aura que gime blandamente . . .

Besa el aura que gime blandamente
Las leves ondas que jugando riza;
El sol besa a la nube en Occidente
Y de púrpura y oro la matiza;
La llama en derredor del tronco ardiente
Por besar a otra llama se desliza,
Y hasta el sauce, inclinándose a su peso,
Al río que le besa, vuelve un beso.

Los invisibles átomos del aire . . .

Los invisibles átomos del aire
En derredor palpitan y se inflaman;
El cielo se deshace en rayos de oro;
La tierra se estremece alborozada;
Oigo flotando en olas de armonía
Rumor de besos y batir de alas;
Mis párpados se cierran . . . ¿Qué sucede?
—¡Es el amor que pasa!

Dark in a Corner of the Room . . .

Dark in a corner of the room,
By its owner perhaps forgot,
Covered over wth dust and silent
        Lay the harp.

In its strings what notes lay dormant,
As in a bird in the boughs asleep,
Awaiting the touch of a snowy hand
        To call them forth.

Ah, I thought, how often genius
Sleeps thus deep within the soul,
Like Lazarus awaiting a voice
To bid it, rise and go!
                                    —KATE FLORES

The Gentle Breeze With a Whispered Cry . . .

The gentle breeze with a whispered cry
Kisses the water it ripples in fun;
The radiant clouds in the western sky
Are purple and gold from the kiss of the sun:
A flame slips round a tree trunk nigh
To kiss with ardor another one;
And the willow, trailing low its leaves,
Returns to the river the kiss it receives.
                                    —ALICE JANE MCVAN

The Invisible Atoms of the Air . . .

The invisible atoms of the air,
Flaming, tremble everywhere;
The sky dissolves in golden rays;
The earth with ecstasy is shaken.
Floating on waves of harmony
I can hear kisses, fluttering wings.
My eyelids close. . . . Pray what is nigh?
Tell me? . . . Silence! . . . Love goes by!
                                    —KATE FLORES

Yo soy ardiente, yo soy morena . . .

—Yo soy ardiente, yo soy morena,
Yo soy el símbolo de la pasión;
De ansia de goces mi alma está llena.
¿A mí me buscas?—No es a ti; no.

—Mi frente es pálida; mis trenzas de oro;
Puedo brindarte dichas sin fin;
Yo de ternura guardo un tesoro.
¿A mí me llamas?—No; no es a ti.

—Yo soy un sueño, un imposible,
Vano fantasma de niebla y luz;
Soy incorpórea, soy intangible;
No puedo amarte.—¡Oh, ven; ven tú!

Voy contra mi interés al confesarlo . . .

Voy contra mi interés al confesarlo;
        pero yo, amada mía,
pienso, cual tú, que una oda sólo es buena
de un billete del Banco al dorso escrita.
No faltará algún necio que al oírlo
        se haga cruces y diga:
"Mujer al fin del siglo diecinueve,
material y prosaica . . ." ¡Bobería!
¡Voces que hacen correr cuatro poetas
que en invierno se embozan con la lira!
¡Ladridos de los perros a la luna!
Tú sabes y yo sé que en esta vida,
con genio, es muy contado quien la *escribe*,
y con oro, cualquiera *hace* poesía.

Asomaba a sus ojos una lágrima . . .

Asomaba a sus ojos una lágrima
y a mi labio una frase de perdón;
habló el orgullo y se enjugó su llanto
y la frase en mis labios expiró.

I Am Ardent, I Am Brunette . . .

"I am ardent, I am brunette,
I am the symbol of passion true;
Of longing for pleasure my soul is full.
'Tis I you are seeking?" — "No, not you."

"My brow is pale, my tresses gold;
A wealth of tenderness I hold;
Joys without end I can offer you.
'Tis I you are calling?" — "No, not you."

"I am a dream, an impossibility,
A futile phantom of cloud and light;
I have no body, being intangible;
I cannot love you." — "Ah, tonight!"

— KATE FLORES

It Goes Against My Interest to Confess It . . .

It goes against my interest to confess it;
        but I, my love,
think as you do that an ode is good only
when written on the back of a bank note.
No doubt some fool hearing that remark
        will cross himself and say:
"Women, of course, of the nineteenth century,
materialistic and prosaic. . . ." Nonsense!
Like tales that tell us that four poets
kept themselves warm in winter with a lyre!
Bayings of dogs at the moon!
You know and I know that in this life,
with genius, it is very seldom that one *writes*,
and with gold, anyone can *make* poetry.

— DOREEN BELL

Into Her Eyes a Tear Crept . . .

Into her eyes a tear crept,
On my lips forgiveness hung;
Pride then spoke and dried her weeping,
And my words died on my tongue.

Yo voy por un camino, ella por otro;
pero al pensar en nuestro mutuo amor,
yo digo aún: "¿Por qué callé aquel día?"
Y ella dirá: "¿Por qué no lloré yo?"

Los suspiros son aire y van al aire . . .

Los suspiros son aire y van al aire.
Las lágrimas son agua y van al mar.
Dime, mujer: cuando el amor se olvida,
          ¿sabes tú adónde va?

Cuando me lo contaron sentí el frío . . .

Cuando me lo contaron sentí el frío
de una hoja de acero en las entrañas;
me apoyé contra el muro, y un instante
la conciencia perdí de dónde estaba.

Cayó sobre mi espíritu la noche;
en ira y en piedad se anegó el alma . . .
¡Y entonces comprendí por qué se llora,
y entonces comprendí por qué se mata!

Pasó la nube de dolor . . . Con pena
logré balbucear breves palabras . . .
¿Quién me dio la noticia? . . . Un fiel amigo . . .
¡Me hacía un gran favor! . . . Le di las gracias.

Olas gigantes que os rompéis bramando . . .

Olas gigantes que os rompéis bramando
En las playas desiertas y remotas,
Envuelto entre la sábana de espumas,
          ¡Llevadme con vosotras!

I go one way, she another;
Remembering, though, our love together,
I still ask, why did I not speak?
And she asks, why did I not weep?
　　　　　　　　　　　—KATE FLORES

Sighs Are Air, and Go to the Air . . .

Sighs are air, and go to the air,
Tears are water, and go to the sea.
Tell me, fair one, if you know:
　　　When love is forgotten, where can it go?　—KATE FLORES

When They Told Me I Felt the Cold . . .

When they told me I felt the cold
of a steel blade in my entrails;
I leaned against the wall, and for an instant
I lost consciousness of where I was.

Night fell on my spirit;
my soul was flooded with wrath and pity . . .
And then I understood why one weeps,
then I understood why one kills!

The cloud of pain passed . . . With difficulty
I managed to stammer a few words . . .
Who broke the news? . . . A faithful friend . . .
He was doing me a great favor! . . . I thanked him.
　　　　　　　　　　　—DOREEN BELL

Great Waves Breaking With a Roar . . .

Great waves breaking with a roar
on shores desolate and remote,
wrap me in a sheet of foam,
　　　take me with you!

Ráfagas de huracán, que arrebatáis
Del alto bosque las marchitas hojas,
Arrastrado en el ciego torbellino,
    ¡Llevadme con vosotras!

Nubes de tempestad, que rompe el rayo
Y en fuego ornáis las desprendidas orlas,
Arrebatado entre la niebla obscura,
    ¡Llevadme con vosotras!

Llevadme, por piedad, adonde el vértigo
Con la razón me arranque la memoria . . .
¡Por piedad! . . . ¡Tengo miedo de quedarme
    Con mi dolor a solas!

Volverán las oscuras golondrinas . . .

Volverán las oscuras golondrinas
En tu balcón sus nidos a colgar,
Y otra vez con el ala a sus cristales
    Jugando llamarán;

Pero aquellas que el vuelo refrenaban
Tu hermosura y mi dicha al contemplar,
Aquellas que aprendieron nuestros nombres,
    Ésas . . . ¡no volverán!

Volverán las tupidas madreselvas
De tu jardín las tapias a escalar,
Y otra vez a la tarde, aún más hermosas,
    Sus flores se abrirán;

Pero aquellas, cuajadas de rocío,
Cuyas gotas mirábamos temblar
Y caer, como lágrimas del día . . .
    Ésas . . . ¡no volverán!

Volverán del amor en tus oídos
Las palabras ardientes a sonar;

Gusts of the hurricane, snatching
the tall wood's shrunken leaves,
drag me in the whirlwind,
    carry me with you!

Storm clouds broken with lightning,
whose edges are ragged with fire,
fold me in a sunless mist,
    carry me away!

Take me, for pity, someplace where,
senseless, I won't remember . . .
Have mercy! . . . I'm afraid to be
    alone with my grief!

                    —JOHN HAINES

The Darkling Swallows Will Come Again . . .

The darkling swallows will come again
Upon your balcony to hang their nests,
And once more their wings brush your windows
    As they playfully call;

But those that lingered in their flight
Your beauty and my gladness to behold,
The ones that learned our names:
    Those will come back no more!

The entwining honeysuckle will come again
Upon the walls of your garden to climb,
And once more at evening, lovelier still,
    Their buds will open;

But those that hung studded with dew,
Whose drops we watched tremble
And fall, like tears of the day:
    Those will come back no more!

Upon your ears there will fall again
The sound of burning words of love;

Tu corazón de su profundo sueño
   Tal vez despertará;

Pero mudo y absorto y de rodillas,
Como se adora a Dios ante su altar,
Como yo te he querido . . . desengáñate,
   ¡Así no te querrán!

Al ver mis horas de fiebre . . .

Al ver mis horas de fiebre
e insomnio lentas pasar,
a la orilla de mi lecho,
   ¿quién se sentará?

Cuando la trémula mano
tienda, próximo a expirar,
buscando una mano amiga,
   ¿quién la estrechará?

Cuando la muerte vidríe
de mis ojos el cristal,
mis párpados aún abiertos,
   ¿quién los cerrará?

Cuando la campana suene
(si suena en mi funeral),
una oración al oírla,
   ¿quién murmurará?

Cuando mis pálidos restos
oprima la tierra ya,
sobre la olvidada fosa,
   ¿quién vendrá a llorar?

¿Quién, en fin, al otro día,
cuando el sol vuelva a brillar,
de que pasé por el mundo,
   ¿quién se acordará?

Your heart then, from its slumber deep,
    Perhaps will wake;

But mute, enraptured, kneeling,
As God before His altar is adored,
As I loved you . . . be not deceived:
    You will be loved no more!   —KATE FLORES

To See the Hours of Fever . . .

To see the hours of fever
And sleeplessness pass by,
Seated at my bedside
    Who will watch me die?

When my hand gropes trembling
With its dying grasp
Seeking for a friendly hand
    Whose hand will it clasp?

When my eyes turn glassy
As my seeing dies,
Open still and staring
    Who will close my eyes?

When the bell tolls for me
(If there is a bell)
Who a prayer will murmur
    As he hears its knell?

When my rigid body
In the earth lies dead,
Who at my forgotten grave
    Tears will come to shed?

When again the sunlight
Floods some later day,
That I once was in the world
    Who will think to say?   —JOHN CROW

¿De dónde vengo? . . .

¿De dónde vengo? . . .
El más horrible y áspero de los senderos busca:
las huellas de unos pies ensangrentados sobre la roca dura;
los despojos de un alma hecha jirones en las zarzas agudas
te dirán el camino que conduce a mi cuna.

¿Adónde voy?
El mas sombrío y triste de los páramos cruza;
valle de eternas nieves y de eternas melancólicas brumas.
En donde esté una piedra solitaria sin inscripción alguna,
donde habite el olvido, allí estará mi tumba.

No dormía: vagaba en ese limbo . . .

No dormía; vagaba en ese limbo
en que cambian de forma los objetos,
misteriosos espacios que separan
          la vigilia del sueño.

Las ideas, que en ronda silenciosa
daban vueltas en torno a mi cerebro,
poco a poco en su danza se movían
          con un compás más lento.

De la luz que entra al alma por los ojos
los párpados velaban el reflejo;
mas otra luz el mundo de visiones
          alumbrada por dentro.

En este punto resonó en mi oído
un rumor semejante al que en el templo
vaga confuso al terminar los fieles
          con una *amén* sus rezos.

Y oí como una voz delgada y triste
que por mi nombre me llamó a lo lejos,

Where Do I Come From? . . .

Where do I come from? . . .
Seek the roughest and most hideous of paths:
the prints of bleeding feet on cruel rocks,
the remains of a soul made tatters on sharp thorns,
will tell you the road that leads to my cradle.

Where am I going? . . .
Cross the saddest and most somber of the steppes;
the valley of eternal snows and of eternal melancholy mists.
Where there is a solitary stone without the least inscription,
where oblivion abides, there will be my tomb.
—EDWARD F. GAHAN

I Lay Awake, Wandering in That Limbo . . .

I lay awake, wandering in that limbo
where objects change their form,
mysterious rooms that separate
        watching and sleep.

Thoughts that in silent procession
circled about in my mind,
little by little moved in their dance
        with a slower measure.

My eyelids veiled the reflection
of the light that enters the soul thereby;
with other light the world of visions
        was lit from within.

Just then there echoed in my ear
a murmur, such as hangs in a church,
confused, when the faithful are ending
        their prayers with *Amen.*

And I seemed to hear a voice, thin and sad,
calling me by my name from afar,

y sentí olor de cirios apagados,
    de humedad y de incienso.

    Entró la noche, y del olvido en brazos
caí, cual piedra, en su profundo seno;
dormí, y al despertar exclamé: "¡Alguno
    que yo quería ha muerto!"

Cerraron sus ojos . . .

    Cerraron sus ojos,
que aún tenía abiertos;
taparon su cara
con un blanco lienzo,
y unos sollozando,
y otros en silencio,
de la triste alcoba
todos se salieron.

    La luz, que en un vaso
ardía en el suelo,
al muro arrojaba
la sombra del lecho,
y entre aquella sombra
veíase a intervalos
dibujarse rígida
la forma del cuerpo.

    Despertaba el día
y a su albor primero,
con sus mil ruidos
despertaba el pueblo.
Ante aquel contraste
de vida y misterios,
de luz y tinieblas,
medité un momento:
¡Dios mío, qué solos
se quedan los muertos!

    De la casa, en hombros,
lleváronla al templo,

and I sensed the odor of snuffed candles,
  of dampness and incense.

  Night came and, in oblivion's arms,
I fell like a stone to her deep breast:
I slept and, on awakening, cried out: "Someone
  whom I loved has died!"

—JOHN HAINES

They Closed Her Eyes . . .

  They closed her eyes
That she still kept open;
They covered her head
With a white linen cloth;
Then some with sobs,
Others in silence,
One and all left
The sorrowful room.

  The light in a glass
Burned on the floor;
It cast on the wall
The shadow of the bed;
And within that shadow,
Intermittently seen,
Was stiffly outlined
The shape of the body.

  Day was awakening,
And at its first dawning,
With a thousand noises
The village was waking.
Faced with that contrast
Of life and mysteriousness,
Of light and darkness,
I thought for a moment:
"How lonely, oh God,
Do we leave the dead!"

  From the house, on their shoulders,
They carried her to church,

y en una capilla
dejaron el féretro.
Allí rodearon
sus pálidos restos
de amarillas velas
y de paños negros.

    Al dar de las ánimas
el toque postrero,
acabó una vieja
sus últimos rezos;
cruzó la ancha nave,
las puertas gimieron
y el santo recinto
quedóse desierto.

    De un reloj se oía
compasado el péndulo,
y de algunos cirios
el chisporroteo.
Tan medroso y triste,
tan oscuro y yerto
todo se encontraba . . .
que pensé un momento:
¡Dios mío, qué solos
se quedan los muertos!

    De la alta campana
la lengua de hierro
le dio volteando
su adiós lastimero.
El luto en las ropas,
amigos y deudos
cruzaron en fila
formando el cortejo.

    Del último asilo,
oscuro y estrecho,
abrió la piqueta
el nicho a un extremo.
Allí la acostaron,
tapáronle luego,

And in a chapel
They set down the bier.
There they surrounded
Her pale remains
With yellow candles
And black draperies.

As the bells at sunset
Pealed their last chime,
An old woman ended
Her final prayers;
She crossed the narrow nave,
The doors groaned,
And the holy alcove
Was left deserted.

The measured pendulum
Of a clock was heard,
And the sputtering
Of a few candles.
So terrible and sad,
So gloomy and stiff
Was everything there . . .
That I thought for a moment:
"How lonely, oh God,
Do we leave the dead!"

From the lofty belfry
The iron clapper
Whirled and rang out
Its sad farewell.
Mourning on their dress,
Friends and kindred
Passed in procession
To pay her homage.

For her last refuge,
Narrow and dark,
The pickax opened
The niche at one end.
They laid her there,
Quickly walled it up,

y con un saludo
despidióse el duelo.

La piqueta al hombro,
el sepulturero,
cantando entre dientes,
se perdió a lo lejos.
La noche se entraba,
reinaba el silencio;
perdido en las sombras,
medité un momento:
¡Dios mío, qué solos
se quedan los muertos!

En las largas noches
del helado invierno,
cuando las maderas
crujir hace el viento
y azota los vidrios
el fuerte aguacero,
de la pobre niña
a solas me acuerdo.

Allí cae la lluvia
con un son eterno;
allí la combate
el soplo del cierzo;
del húmedo muro
tendida en el hueco,
¡acaso de frío
se hielan sus huesos! . . .

¿Vuelve el polvo al polvo?
¿Vuela el alma al cielo?
¿Todo es vil materia,
podredumbre y cieno?
¡No sé; pero hay algo
que explicar no puedo,
que al par nos infunde
repugnancia y duelo,
al dejar tan tristes,
tan solos los muertos!

And with a bow
The rites were ended.

Pickax on shoulder,
The gravedigger,
Singing between his teeth,
Was lost in the distance.
Night was approaching,
Silence reigned;
Lost in the shadows
I thought for a moment:
*"How lonely, oh God,
Do we leave the dead!"*

During the long nights
Of icy winter,
When timbers creak
Under the wind
And fierce showers
Lash the windowpanes,
Alone, I remember
The poor young girl.

There falls the rain
With eternal sound;
There struggles with it
The north wind's blast.
Laid in that hole
In the damp wall,
Perhaps her bones
Freeze with cold! . . .

Does dust return to dust?
Does the soul fly to heaven?
Is all vile matter,
Rottenness and filth?
I know not: but there's something
That I cannot explain,
Something that fills us
With repugnance and sorrow
At leaving the dead
So lonely and so sad.

—MURIEL KITTEL

ROSALÍA DE CASTRO
(1837–85)

Literary historians, prone to oversimplification, have dubbed Rosalía "the feminine Bécquer." Similarities in form and content are discernible between the two Romantic poets, but their differences are equally numerous and striking.

Rosalía, an illegitimate child born in Santiago de Compostela, spent her childhood and youth in her mother's manor in the Galician countryside. Before her eleventh birthday she had composed her earliest poems in Galician, a Portuguese dialect. At nineteen she left for Madrid on family business and two years later married a relatively successful young writer, Manuel Murguía, who later became famous as folklorist and historian of Galicia. They had several children, and he recognized and encouraged her talents. Despite her seemingly happy family life, over and beyond the Galician landscape and the folkloric motifs in her poems, notes of anguish, of turbulent, unrealized passion, and of premonition of death seem forever present and dominant.

In addition to a few short stories and novelettes, Rosalía wrote three volumes of verse: *Cantares gallegos* (1863), *Follas novas* (1880), and *En las orillas del Sar* (1884). Considering that the first two were written in Galician and dealt with nature and provincial mores, which were of only mild interest to the sophisticated denizens of the Spanish capital, they may be considered successful, especially *Follas novas*, which bore a long introduction by a leading public figure of nineteenth-century Spain—the orator and liberal legislator Emilio Castelar. *En las orillas del Sar*, published a few months before her death, of cancer, naturally had a wider appeal, as it was written in Spanish and penetrated more poignantly into her personal tragedy. However, more than half a century elapsed before the literary wold recognized the evocative power and lyrical intensity of Spain's foremost woman poet.

BEST EDITION: V. García Marti (ed.): *Obras completas*, Madrid, 1952 (3rd ed.).

ABOUT ROSALÍA DE CASTRO: Nothing worthwhile in English. Perceptive study in Portuguese by Alberto Machado da Rosa: *Rosalía de Castro, poeta incomprendido*, which was published in July 1954 in *Revista Hispánica Moderna* xx, pp. 5–47. In Spanish, two doctoral theses: Alicia Murias Santaella: *Rosalía de Castro, su vida y su obra*, Buenos Aires, 1942; and Sister Mary Pierre Tirrel: *La mística de la saudade*, Madrid, 1951.

SOME COLLECTIONS AND CRITICISM PUBLISHED SINCE 1958: Matilde Albert Robatto: *Rosalía de Castro y la condición femenina*, Madrid, Partenon, 1981. Benito Varela Jacomo, ed.: *Obra Poética: bilingüe. Rosalía de Castro: antología, estudio preliminar, traducción de los poemas gallegos y bibliografía* (poems in Galician and Castilian on facing pages), Barcelona, Bruguera, 1972. Anna-Marie Aldaz, Barbara N. Gantt, and Anne C. Bromley, editors and translators: *Poems. Rosalía de Castro*, Albany, N.Y., State University of New York Press, 1991. Kathleen K. Kulp: *Manner and Mood in Rosalía de Castro: A Study of Themes and Style*, Madrid, Jose Porrúa Torranzas, 1968. Kathleen Kulp-Hill: *Rosalía de Castro*, Boston, Twayne, 1977.

Ya que de la esperanza . . .

Ya que de la esperanza para la vida mía
triste y descolorido ha llegado el ocaso,
a mi morada oscura, desmantelada y fría
    tornemos paso a paso,
porque con su alegría no aumente mi amargura
    la blanca luz del día.

Contenta, el negro nido busca el ave agorera;
bien reposa la fiera en el antro escondido;
en su sepulcro, el muerto; el triste, en el olvido,
    y mi alma en su desierto.

Candente está la atmósfera . . .

Candente está la atmósfera;
explora el zorro la desierta vía;
    insalubre se torna
del limpio arroyo el agua cristalina,
    y el pino aguarda inmóvil
los besos inconstantes de la brisa.

Imponente silencio
    agobia la campiña;
sólo el zumbido del insecto se oye
en las extensas y húmedas umbrías;
    monótono y constante
como el sordo estertor de la agonía.

Bien pudiera llamarse, en el estío,
    la hora del mediodía,
noche en que al hombre de luchar cansado,
    más que nunca le irritan
de la materia la imponente fuerza
y del alma las ansias infinitas.

Volved, ¡oh noches del invierno frío,
nuestras viejas amantes de otros días!
Tornad con vuestros hielos y crudezas

Now That the Sunset of Hope . . .

Now that the sunset of hope for my life
has sad and colorless come,
toward my dim dwelling, dismantled and chill,
  let us turn step by step;
for the white light of day
  with its gladness does not embitter me more;

Contented the ill-fated bird seeks its black nest;
well the wild beast to its hidden cave retreats;
the dead to the grave; the wretched to oblivion,
  and to its wilderness my soul.
       — KATE FLORES

The Atmosphere Is Incandescent . . .

The atmosphere is incandescent;
The fox explores an empty road;
  Sick grow the waters
That sparkled in the clear arroyo,
  Unfluttered stands the pine
Waiting for fickle winds to blow.

  A majesty of silence
  Overpowers the meadow;
Only the hum of an insect troubles
The spreading, dripping forest shadow,
  Relentless and monotonous
As muffled rattle in a dying throat.

In such a summer the hour of midday
  Could as well go
By the name of night, to struggle-weary
  Man who has never known
Greater vexation from the vast cares
Of the soul, or from matter's majestic force.

Would it were winter again! The nights! The cold!
O those old loves of ours so long ago!
Come back to make this fevered blood run fresh,

a refrescar la sangre enardecida
por el estío insoportable y triste. . . .
¡Triste! . . . ¡Lleno de pámpanos y espigas!

Frío y calor, otoño o primavera,
¿dónde . . . dónde se encuentra la alegría?
Hermosas son las estaciones todas
para el mortal que en sí guarda la dicha;
mas para el alma desolada y huérfana,
no hay estación risueña ni propicia.

Del rumor cadencioso de la onda . . .

Del rumor cadencioso de la onda
    y el viento que muge,
del incierto reflejo que alumbra
    la selva y la nube;
del piar de alguna ave de paso,
del agreste ignorado perfume
    que el céfiro roba
    al valle o a la cumbre,
mundos hay donde encuentran asilo
    las almas que al peso
    del mundo sucumben.

Ya no mana la fuente . . .

Ya no mana la fuente, se agotó el manantial;
ya el viajero allí nunca va su sed a apagar.
Ya no brota la hierba, ni florece el narciso,
ni en los aires esparcen su fragancia los lirios.
Sólo el cauce arenoso de la seca corriente
le recuerda al sediento el horror de la muerte.
¡Mas no importa! A lo lejos otro arroyo murmura
donde humildes violetas el espacio perfuman.
Y de un sauce el ramaje, al mirarse en las ondas,
tiende en torno del agua su fresquísima sombra.

Bring back your sharp severities and snows
To these intolerable summer sorrows . . .
Sorrows! . . . While vine and corn stand thick and gold!

The cold, the heat; the autumn or the spring;
Where, where has delight set up its home?
Beautiful are all seasons to the man
Who shelters happiness within his soul;
But the deserted, orphaned spirit feels
No season smile upon its luckless door.   —EDWIN MORGAN

From the Cadenced Roar of the Waves . . .

From the cadenced roar of the waves
        and the wail of the wind,
from the shimmering light
        flecked over woodland and cloud,
from the cries of passing birds
and the wild unknown perfumes
        stolen by zephyrs
        from mountaintops and valleys,
there are realms where souls
        crushed by the weight of the world
        find refuge.   —KATE FLORES

The Spring Does Not Flow Now . . .

The spring does not flow now, the stream is quite dry;
No traveler goes to quench his thirst there.
The grass does not grow now, no daffodil blooms,
No fragrance of lilies floats on the air.
Only the sandy bed of the dried-up river
Fills the parched traveler with the horror of death.
No matter; in the distance another stream murmurs
Where timid violets perfume the air.
And willow boughs, seeing themselves in the ripples,
Spread about the water the coolest of shade.

El sediento viajero que el camino atraviesa
humedece los labios en la linfa serena
del arroyo, que el árbol con sus ramas sombrea,
y dichoso se olvida de la fuente ya seca.

Te amo . . . ¿Por qué me odias? . . .

Te amo . . . ¿Por qué me odias?
—Te odio . . . ¿Por qué me amas?
Secreto es éste el más triste
y misterioso del alma.

Mas ello es verdad . . . ¡Verdad
dura y atormentadora!
—Me odias, porque te amo;
te amo, porque me odias.

Yo no sé lo que busco eternamente . . .

Yo no sé lo que busco eternamente
en la tierra, en el aire y en el cielo;
yo no sé lo que busco; pero es algo
que perdí no sé cuándo y que no encuentro,
aun cuando sueñe que invisible habita
en todo cuanto toco y cuanto veo.

¡Felicidad, no he de volver a hallarte
en la tierra, en el aire, ni en el cielo,
    aun cuando sé que existes
    y no eres vano sueño!

Dicen que no hablan las plantas . . .

Dicen que no hablan las plantas, ni las fuentes, ni los pájaros,
ni el onda con sus rumores, ni con su brillo los astros.
Lo dicen: pero no es cierto, pues siempre cuando yo paso
de mí murmuran y exclaman

The thirsty traveler, crossing the highway,
Moistens his lips with the limpid water
Of the stream shaded by the tree's branches,
And gladly forgets the spring now dry.

—MURIEL KITTEL

I Love You . . . Why Do You Hate Me? . . .

I love you . . . Why do you hate me?
—I hate you . . . Why do you love me?
Saddest, most mysterious
Secret of the spirit is this.

And yet it is a truth, hard
As truth in a torturer's hand!
—You hate me, because I love you;
I love you, because you hate me.

—EDWIN MORGAN

I Know Not What I Seek Eternally . . .

I know not what I seek eternally
on earth, in air, and sky;
I know not what I seek; but it is something
that I have lost, I know not when,
and cannot find, although in dreams invisibly
it dwells in all I touch and see.

Ah, bliss! Never can I recapture you
either on earth, in air, or sky,
    although I know you have reality
    and are no futile dream!

—MURIEL KITTEL

They Say That the Plants Do Not Speak . . .

They say that the plants do not speak, nor the brooks, nor the birds,
Nor the waves with their roar, nor with their brilliance the stars.
So they say; but one cannot be sure, for always, when I go by,
They whisper about me and say

—Ahí va la loca soñando
con la eterna primavera de la vida y de los campos,
y ya bien pronto, bien pronto, tendrá los cabellos canos,
y ve temblando, aterida, que cubre la escarcha el prado.

Mientras el hielo las cubre . . .

Mientras el hielo las cubre
con sus hilos brillantes de plata
todas las plantas están ateridas,
ateridas como mi alma,

Esos hielos para ellas
son promesa de flores tempranas
son para mí silenciosos obreros
que están tejiéndome la mortaja.

Yo en mi lecho de abrojos . . .

Yo en mi lecho de abrojos,
tú en tu lecho de rosas y de plumas,
verdad dijo el que dijo que un abismo
media entre mi miseria y tu fortuna.
Mas yo no cambiaría
por tu lecho mi lecho,
pues rosas hay que manchan y emponzoñan
y abrojos que, a través de su aspereza,
nos conducen al cielo.

Las campanas

Yo las amo, yo las oigo
cual oigo el rumor del viento,
el murmurar de la fuente
o el balido del cordero.

—Ah, there goes the madwoman, dreaming
Of the everlasting springtide of life and the fields,
And yet soon, very soon, her hair will be gray,
And trembling, frozen, she sees that the frost is upon the grass.

—KATE FLORES

When the Frosts Cover Them . . .

When the frosts cover them
With their sparkling silver threads,
All the plants are stiff with cold,
Stiff with cold like my soul.

To them these frosts
Are the promise of early flowers;
To me they are silent workers
Weaving my winding sheet.

—MURIEL KITTEL

I in My Bed of Thistles . . .

I in my bed of thistles,
You in your bed of roses and feathers,
He spoke the truth who spoke of an abyss
Between your good fortune and my wretchedness.
Yet I would never change
My bed for your bed,
There are roses that envenom and corrupt,
And thistles on the road to heaven
Though harsh to the flesh.

—EDWIN MORGAN

The Bells

I love them, I listen to them
As I listen to the wind's whisper,
Or to the fountain's murmur
Or the bleating of the lamb.

Como los pájaros, ellas,
tan pronto asoma en los cielos
el primer rayo del alba,
le saludan con sus ecos.

Y en sus notas, que van prolongándose
por los llanos y los cerros,
hay algo de candoroso,
de apacible y de halagüeño.

Si por siempre enmudecieran,
¡qué tristeza en al aire y en el cielo!
¡Qué silencio en las iglesias!
¡Qué extrañeza entre los muertos!

¡Justicia de los hombres!, yo te busco . . .

¡Justicia de los hombres!, yo te busco
        pero sólo te encuentro
en la "palabra," que tu nombre aplaude
mientras te niega tenazmente el "hecho."

        —Y tú, ¿dónde resides?—me pregunto
con aflicción—, justicia de los cielos!
cuando el pecado es obra de un instante,
y durará la expiación terrible.
        ¡Mientras dure el Infierno!

Sintiéndose acabar
con el estío . . .

Sintiéndose acabar con el estío
        la deshauciada enferma,
        ¡moriré en el otoño!
—pensó, entre melancólica y contenta—,
y sentiré rodar sobre mi tumba
        las hojas también muertas.

The bells are like the birds,
Their cries and echoes welcome
The earliest ray of daybreak
That opens up the skies.

And their notes, pealing out
Across the plains and the peaks,
Keep in them something candid,
Something serene and sweet.

Were their tongues forever dumb,
What gloom in the air and in the sky!
What silence in all the churches!
What strangeness among the dead!

—EDWIN MORGAN

Justice of Men! I Go in Search of You . . .

Justice of men! I go in search of you
      And all that I find
Is the word your fame gives luster to;
In the deed itself you are stubbornly denied.

   And you, have you no abiding place,
With pain I ask, O justice of the skies?
When one sin that was sinned within an instant
Shall linger in its ghastly expiation
      For as long as hell has its fires!

—EDWIN MORGAN

Feeling Her End Would Come With Summer's End . . .

Feeling her end would come with summer's end,
      the incurable invalid
            thought with mingled joy and sadness:
"I shall die in the autumn,
and over my grave I shall feel the rustling
      of the leaves that will also be dead."

Mas . . . ni aun la muerte complacerla quiso,
    cruel también con ella:
perdonóle la vida en el invierno,
y, cuando todo renacía en la tierra,
la mató lentamente entre los himnos
alegres de la hermosa primavera.

No va solo el que llora . . .

    No va solo el que llora,
no os sequéis, ¡por piedad!, lágrimas mías;
    basta un pesar al alma;
jamás, jamás le bastará una dicha.

Juguete del destino, arista humilde,
    rodé triste y perdida;
pero conmigo lo llevaba todo:
llevaba mi dolor por compañía.

Hora tras hora, día tras día . . .

    Hora tras hora, día tras día,
entre el cielo y la tierra que quedan,
        eternos vigías,
como torrente que se despeña
        pasa la vida.

    Devolvedle a la flor su perfume
        después de marchita;
de las ondas que besan la playa
y que unas tras otras besándolas expiran
recoged los rumores, las quejas,
y en planchas de bronce grabad su armonía.

    Tiempos que fueron, llantos y risas,
negros tormentos, dulces mentiras,
¡ay!, ¿en dónde su rastro dejaron,
        en dónde, alma mía?

But . . . cruel with her, too, even death
     would not oblige her,
sparing her life through the winter
and, when all the earth was being born anew,
killing her slowly amidst the happy hymns
of glorious spring.
                       —KATE FLORES

He Who Weeps Goes Not Alone . . .

    He who weeps goes not alone,
Keep flowing, I beg of you, my tears!
    A single burden suffices the soul;
One joy is never, never enough.

Destiny's plaything, humble speck,
    Sad and lost I stray;
Nevertheless I carry all with me:
I carry my sorrow for company.
                    —KATE FLORES

Hour After Hour, Day After Day . . .

    Hour after hour, day after day,
Between the earth and sky that keep
    Eternal watch,
Like a rushing headlong torrent
    Life passes on.

    Restore fragrance to the flower
    After it withers;
From the waves that caress the beach
And one after the other die in that caress,
Gather the murmurs and complaints,
And engrave on plates of bronze their harmony.

    Times now past, tears and laughter,
Dark afflictions, soothing falsehoods,
Ah, where do they leave their mark,
    Tell me where, my soul!
                —MURIEL KITTEL

MANUEL GONZÁLEZ PRADA
(1848–1918)

Although he was a contemporary of Bécquer and Rosalía de Castro, González Prada's long life extended to the end of World War I; therefore, his literary work reflects many vicissitudes and historical changes. Because of his dynamic participation in Peruvian civic life, his admirers have emphasized his ideological militancy and iconoclastic struggles to the point of obscuring his poetical creation.

González Prada's biography shows how the son of a wealthy, aristocratic, extremely Catholic family, baptized by the Archbishop of Lima, became liberal and anti-clerical and paved the way for the anti-imperialist APRA (Alianza Popular Revolucionaria Americana) party. He was a strange boy, who studied law to please his mother but who spent his time translating the German Romantic poets and writing plays. During the Chilean invasion of Peru (1879), González Prada enlisted in the Peruvian Army, proving his courage at the Battle of Miraflores. But no sooner had the Chileans left Peruvian soil than military cliques took control of the government. It was then that his writing became vitriolic. In 1888, at the festival at the Teatro Politeama organized by students collecting funds for rescuing the provinces of Tacna and Arica from the Chileans, González Prada delivered a speech which became an historical event and contained the slogan of his generation: "The old men to their grave; the young men to their task!" In other speeches he spoke out against academicism, colonialism, traditionalism, clericalism. Finally, in 1891, rallying around him some of the boldest intellectuals, he founded the Unión Nacional, Peru's first radical party.

After a stay in France and Spain (1891–98), which brought him in touch with Ernest Renan, then lecturing at the Collège de France, with the Spanish intellectuals of the generation of 1898, and with the Freethinkers of Geneva, González Prada returned, better prepared to continue his struggles at home. In Peru, reaction had become ferocious: González Prada was burned in effigy, threatened with mobbing, provoked to fight duels, and prevented from delivering lectures and publishing articles.

In 1901 his wife and son bought a press and published a collection of his poems, *Minúsculas*, which was reprinted in a trade edition eight years later, followed by *Presbiterianas* (1909) and *Exóticas* (1911). By then his reputation as a political leader, orator, and poet had become so glamorously established that he said with typical wryness: "So many visits [of admirers] are convincing me that I shall soon find a place in the *Guide to Lima*, along with the bull ring, the museum of history, Pizarro's skeleton, and so many other useless things." And so Peru's fighting poet found himself appointed Director of the National Library in 1912, a position he held until his death.

González Prada's poetry presents many aspects of his genius: his formalistic interests (experimentation with triolets, rondels, balatas, pantoums, etc.), as well as love lyrics, philosophical poems, views on the Spaniards' oppression of Native Americans, and iconoclastic aphorisms.

BEST EDITIONS: *Obras completas*, Lima, 1946–50, 6 vols.; Carlos García Prada (ed.): *Antología Poética*, Mexico, Editorial Cultura, 1940.

ABOUT GONZÁLEZ PRADA: J. H. Cutler: *Manuel González Prada, Precursor of Modern Peru*, Harvard University dissertation, 1936. *Also*: I. Goldberg: "A Peruvian Iconoclast," *American Mercury*, November 1925, pp. 330–33; I. B. Rothberg: "The Dominant Theme in González Prada's *Minúsculas*," *Hispania* 38 (1955), pp. 465–71.

SOME COLLECTIONS AND BIOGRAPHY PUBLISHED SINCE 1958: Manuel González Prada: *Páginas libres; Horas de lucha* (prose), Caracas, Biblioteca Ayacucho, 1976. Luis Alberto Sánchez: *Nuestras vidas son los ríos: historia y leyenda de los González Prada*, Lima, Universidad Nacional Mayor de San Marcos, 1977.

Vivir y morir

Humo y nada el soplo del sér:
Mueren hombre, pájaro y flor,
Corre a mar de olvido el amor,
Huye a breve tumba el placer.

¿Dónde están las luces de ayer?
Tiene ocaso todo esplendor,
Hiel esconde todo licor,
Todo expía el mal de nacer.

¿Quién rïó sin nunca gemir,
Siendo el goce un dulce penar?
¡Loco y vano ardor el sentir!

¡Vano y loco anhelo el pensar!
¿Qué es vivir? soñar sin dormir.
¿Qué es morir? dormir sin soñar.

Los bienes y las glorias de la vida . . .

Los bienes y las glorias de la vida
o nunca vienen o nos llegan tarde.
Lucen de cerca, pasan de corrida,
los bienes y las glorias de la vida.
¡Triste del hombre que en la edad florida
coger las flores del vivir aguarde!
Los bienes y las glorias de la vida
o nunca vienen o nos llegan tarde.

Para verme con los muertos . . .

Para verme con los muertos,
ya no voy al camposanto.
Busco plazas, no desiertos,
para verme con los muertos.

Living and Dying

Smoke and nothing the breath of being:
Blossom, bird and man must die,
Love in a sea of forgetfulness lie,
To a brief gravestone pleasure fleeing.

Of yesterday what light still radiates?
Twilight every splendor steals;
What liquor but its gall conceals?
The evil of birth all expiates.

Who has laughed who has known no pain?
Joy is with sweet sorrow fraught,
Feeling an ardor mad and vain!

Vain and mad the care of thought!
What is life? To dream without sleep.
What is death? To sleep without dreams.

— KATE FLORES

The Treasures and Glories of Life . . .

The treasures and glories of life
Either never reach us or arrive too late.
They glitter near, they hurry by,
The treasures and glories of life.
Sorry the man who in his budding prime
To gather in the flowers hesitates!
The treasures and glories of life
Either never reach us or arrive too late.

— KATE FLORES

To Be With the Dead . . .

To be with the dead,
Not to graveyards I go.
I seek plazas instead,
To be with the dead.

¡Corazones hay tan yertos!
¡Almas hay que hieden tanto!
Para verme con los muertos,
ya no voy al camposanto.

Tus ojos de lirio dijeron que sí . . .

    Tus ojos de lirio dijeron que sí,
tus labios de rosa dijeron que no.
Al verme a tu lado, muriendo por ti,
tus ojos de lirio dijeron que sí.
Auroras de gozo rayaron en mí;
mas pronto la noche de luto volvió:
tus ojos de lirio dijeron que sí,
tus labios de rosa dijeron que no.

Al hogar arrojan leña . . .

Al hogar arrojan leña,
Y helado, exánime estoy.
¿Quién mi yerto sér anima
Con un soplo de calor?
Quemarán en vano selvas,
Porque el frío guardo yo
Muy adentro, muy adentro,
En mi propio corazón.

Su poder revela el Cosmos . . .

Su poder revela el Cosmos
Del paquidermo al gusano,
Desde el granillo de arena
Hasta la mole del astro;
Y en la marcha de los mundos
Lo mismo importan acaso
Una ciudad destruida
Y un hormiguero anegado.

There are hearts so bled!
Souls stinking so!
To be with the dead,
Not to graveyards I go.

—KATE FLORES

Your Lily Eyes Said Yes . . .

Your lily eyes said yes,
Your rosy lips said no.
When beside you dying I found myself,
Your lily eyes said yes.
Dawns burst within my breast,
Which soon were black night, oh:
Your lily eyes said yes,
Your rosy lips said no.

—KATE FLORES

Into the Hearth They Are Tossing Logs . . .

Into the hearth they are tossing logs,
And chilled, dispirited am I.
Who can inspire my frozen being
With a breath of warmth?
They will burn up the forests in vain,
For the cold in me
Goes deep, very deep,
Down in my own heart.

—KATE FLORES

The Cosmos Shows His Power . . .

The Cosmos shows his power
From pachyderm to grub,
From the smallest grain of sand
To dimensions of a star;
And in the course of worlds
Perhaps he's as concerned
for a city that's destroyed
As an anthill overturned.

—WILLIAM M. DAVIS

El Mitayo

—"Hijo, parto: la mañana
reverbera en el volcán;
dame el báculo de chonta,
las sandalias de jaguar."

—"Padre, tienes las sandalias,
tienes el báculo ya:
mas ¿por qué me ves y lloras?
¿A qué regiones te vas?"

—"La injusta ley de los Blancos
me arrebata del hogar:
voy al trabajo y al hambre,
voy a la mina fatal."

—"Tú que partes hoy en día,
dime ¿cuándo volverás?"
—"Cuando el llama de las punas
ame el desierto arenal."

—"¿Cuándo el llama de las punas
las arenas amará?"
—"Cuando el tigre de los bosques
beba en las aguas del mar."

—"¿Cuándo el tigre de los bosques
en los mares beberá?"
—"Cuando del huevo de un cóndor
nazca la sierpe mortal."

—"¿Cuándo del huevo de un cóndor
Una sierpe nacerá?"
—"Cuando el pecho de los Blancos
Se conmueva de piedad."

—"¿Cuándo el pecho de los Blancos
Piadoso y tierno será?"
—"Hijo, el pecho de los Blancos
No se conmueve jamás."

The Mitayo*

"Son, I am going: the morning
Will reverberate in the volcano:
Give me my *chonta* walking stick,
My sandals of jaguar skin."

"Father, you have your sandals,
You have your staff already;
But why do you see me and weep?
To what region are you going?"

"The unjust law of the white man
Tears me from my home.
I am going to work and to hunger,
I am going to the deadly mines."

"You who are leaving this very day,
When, when will you come back?"
"When the llama of the high plateau
Loves the desert sands."

"When will the llama of the high plateau
Love the desert sands?"
"When the tiger of the forests
Drinks the waters of the sea."

"When will the tiger of the forests
Drink the waters of the sea?"
"When the egg of the condor
Hatches a deadly snake."

"When will the egg of a condor
Give forth a deadly snake?"
"When the breast of the white man
With compassion is moved."

"When will the breast of the white man
Be pitying and tender?"
"Son, the breast of the white man
Will be moved with compassion never."

— KATE FLORES

*Indian serving his *mita*, or enforced labor.

Las flechas del Inca

Tuvo tres flechas en la mano el Inca,
Y, alegre, a la primera preguntó:
"Amiga fiel, envenenada flecha,
        Di ¿qué me pides hoy?"
— "Fuerte guerrero de infalible pulso,
        De bravo corazón,
Te pido sólo destrozar las alas
        De cóndor volador."

Tuvo tres flechas en la mano el Inca,
Y, alegre, a la segunda preguntó:
— "Amiga fiel, envenenada flecha,
        Di ¿qué me pides hoy?"
— "Fuerte guerrero de infalible pulso,
        De bravo corazón,
Te pido sólo desgarrar el seno
        De tigre acechador."

Tuvo tres flechas en la mano el Inca,
Y, alegre, a la tercera preguntó:
— "Amiga fiel, envenenada flecha,
        Di ¿qué me pides hoy?"
— "Fuerte guerrero de infalible pulso,
        De bravo corazón,
Te pido sólo atravesar el pecho
        De vil conquistador."

Pope

Si *whatever is, is right*
Absolverás mi demanda:
¿Era buena la joroba
Que tenías en la espalda?

The Inca's Arrows

The Inca had three arrows in his hand,
And joyfully he asked the first:
"Faithful friend, poisoned arrow,
    Tell me, what would you will of me today?"
"Strong warrior of infallible eye
    And valiant heart,
I ask you but to shatter the wings
    Of the flying condor."

The Inca had three arrows in his hand,
And joyfully he asked the second:
"Faithful friend, poisoned arrow,
    Tell me, what would you will of me today?"
"Strong warrior of infallible eye
    And valiant heart,
I ask you but to shatter the breast
    Of the stalking tiger."

The Inca had three arrows in his hand,
And joyfully he asked the third:
"Faithful friend, poisoned arrow,
    Tell me, what would you will of me today?"
"Strong warrior of infallible eye
    And valiant heart,
I ask you but to pierce the breast
    Of the vile Conquistador."

    —KATE FLORES

Pope

If whatever is, is right
You'll solve what I've in mind:
Was it right to have a hump
In the middle of your back?

    —WILLIAM M. DAVIS

Mal traductor de poeta . . .

Mal traductor de poeta
Hace papel de lacayo
Grotescamente vestido
Con los arreos del amo.

¿Los años de Pilar? . . .

—¿Los años de Pilar?
—Según se haga la cuenta:
Por los cabellos, treinta;
Por los dientes, un par.

Tiene muy buen estómago Bicoca . . .

Tiene muy buen estómago Bicoca:
se mira en el espejo y no deboca.

¿Por qué el avaro Tomás . . . ?

—¿Por qué el avaro Tomás
Se consagra a la virtud?
—Porque el vicio cuesta más.

Si el sepulcro no es la nada . . .

Si el sepulcro no es la nada,
Si en él los sueños persisten,
La más atroz pesadilla
Será soñar que se vive.

Who Translates a Poet Badly . . .

Who translates a poet badly
Plays a lackey's role
Grotesquely garbed
In his master's clothes.

—WILLIAM M. DAVIS

How Old is Pilar? . . .

How old is Pilar?
It depends how you count:
By her hair, she's thirty,
By her teeth, she's two.

—WILLIAM M. DAVIS

A Very Strong Stomach Has Mr. Luke . . .

A very strong stomach has Mr. Luke:
He looks in the mirror and doesn't puke.

—WILLIAM M. DAVIS

Why Did Stingy Thomas . . . ?

Why did stingy Thomas
Devote himself to virtue?
"'Cause vice would cost him more."

—WILLIAM M. DAVIS

If the Tomb Is Not Oblivion . . .

If the tomb is not oblivion
And dreams persist there, too,
The most atrocious nightmare
Would be to dream we are alive.

—WILLIAM M. DAVIS

RUBÉN DARÍO
(1867–1916)

By the end of the nineteenth century, Spanish poetry had deteriorated, although there was no dearth of poetasters—indeed, to this day, textbooks are cluttered with "illustrious names." But these scribblers spent their time either retelling stories or anecdotes in verse, aping Byron and Hugo, or reworking old legends and folk poems that had popular appeal. The time was ripe, therefore, for innovation. This came about in two ways: through the influence of the French Symbolists and Parnassians, whom the Spanish poets were to assimilate, and by the injection of new blood.

From a remote village in Nicaragua came a man who called himself "Rubén Darío." A child prodigy, he began versifying by the time he was learning to spell his official name: Félix Rubén García Sarmiento. At first his writings failed to show the slightest trace of originality, but during a sojourn in Chile—1886–90, years of tremendous cultural effervescence there—he was brought in touch with French literary trends through Santiago's sophisticated periodicals. In 1888 he published a sheaf of poems in prose and verse, symbolistically entitled *Azul* (Azure), which marked the birth of modernism in Spanish poetry (also referred to as "the new spirit," as modernism jumbles together the most disparate and even conflicting literary "isms"). With his next works, *Prosas profanas* (1896) and *Cantos de vida y esperanza* (1905), Darío attained the culmination of his career, changing totally the course of Spanish poetry. In these works he utilized all the new resources of French writing: exoticism, not only in landscape but in mythology and human types (here he followed the examples of Leconte de Lisle and the Goncourt brothers); compositions patterned after music; poetization of language, forever seeking the metaphorical and the musical, thus adding considerable suppleness to the language and enriching its tone. In short, Darío brought about the fusion of the American and the

Spanish, the regional and the universal, the modern and the archaic. As a result he became the spokesman for modern poetry and traveled widely in Europe and the Americas as a kind of cultural minister plenipotentiary. But his triumphs were only as great and numerous as his miseries and anguish, inevitably brought about by the very decadence—excesses with women, alcohol, and drugs—which he personified and bitterly lived through during his bohemian existence.

BEST EDITIONS: A. Ghiraldo (ed.): *Obras poéticas completas*, Madrid, 1932; F. C. Sainz de Robles (ed.): *Obras poéticas completas*, Madrid, 1945; A. Méndez Plancarte (ed.): *Poesías completas*, Mexico, 1952 (7th ed.).

ABOUT RUBÉN DARÍO: J. B. Trend: *Rubén Darío*, Oxford, n.d.; J. B. Trend: *Rubén Darío*, Cambridge, 1952. *Also:* M. Bowra: *Inspiration and Poetry*, New York, Macmillan, 1955, pp. 242–64; D. F. Fogelquist: *Rubén Darío and Juan Ramón Jiménez: Their Literary and Personal Relations*, University of Miami, 1956; E. C. LeFort: "Rubén Darío and the 'Modernista' Movement," *University of Miami Hispanic-American Studies* 2 (1941), pp. 220–37; I. Goldberg: "Rubén Darío: The Man and the Poet," *The Bookman* 49 New York (1919), pp. 563–68; I. Goldberg: *Studies in Spanish American Literature*, New York, 1920, pp. 101–83; E. K. Mapes: "Innovation and French Influence in the Metrics of Rubén Darío," *PMLA* 49 (1934), pp. 310–26; C. Rangel Báez: "The Poetry of Ideas in Darío and Nervo," *Inter-America* 8, New York (1924), pp. 29–38; C. D. Watland: "The Literary Education of Rubén Darío: An Examination of the Extent and Nature of His Literary Culture to the Period of *Azul* (1888)," University of Miami dissertation, 1953.

SOME COLLECTIONS AND CRITICISM PUBLISHED SINCE 1958: Erwin K. Mapes: *La influencia francesa en la obra de Rubén Darío*, Managua, Nicaragua, Editores de la Comisión Nacional para la Celebración del Centenario del Nacimiento de Rubén Darío, 1966. Angel Rama: *Rubén Darío y el modernismo*, Caracas, Alfadil, 1985. Cathy Login Jrade: *Rubén Darío and the Romantic Search for Unity: The Modernist Recourse to Esoteric Tradition*, Austin, Tex., University of Texas Press, 1983. Miguel González-Gerth, ed.: *Rubén Darío Centennial Studies*, Austin, Tex., University of Texas Press, 1970. *Rubén Darío: Selected Poems* (translated by Lysander Kemp), Austin, Tex., University of Texas Press, 1965. Fidel Coloma González, *Introducción al estudio de Azul*, Managua, Nicaragua, M. Morales, 1988.

Primaveral

[Fragmentos]

Mes de rosas. Van mis rimas
en ronda a la vasta selva
a recoger miel y aromas
en las flores entreabiertas.
Amada, ven. El gran bosque
es nuestro templo; allí ondea
y flota un santo perfume
de amor. El pájaro vuela
de un árbol a otro y saluda
tu frente rosada y bella
como un alba; y las encinas
robustas, altas, soberbias,
cuando tú pasas agitan
sus hojas verdes y trémulas,
y enarcan sus ramas como
para que pase una reina.
¡Oh amada mía! Es el dulce
tiempo de la primavera.

Hay allá una clara fuente
que brota de una caverna,
donde se bañan desnudas
las blancas ninfas que juegan.
Ríen al son de la espuma,
hienden la linfa serena;
entre polvo cristalino
esponjan sus cabelleras;
y saben himnos de amores
en hermosa lengua griega,
que en glorioso tiempo antiguo
Pan inventó en las florestas.
Amada: pondré en mis rimas
la palabra más soberbia
de las frases de los versos
de los himnos de esa lengua,
y te diré esa palabra
empapada en miel hiblea . . .
¡Oh amada mía, en el dulce
tiempo de la primavera!

Spring

[Fragments]

Month of roses. And my rhymes
go wending through the boundless forest
to gather honey and sweet perfumes
from the blooms of half-opened flowers.
Beloved, come. The great forest
is our temple; there drifts
and ripples a blessed fragrance
of love. The warbler goes flying
from one tree to another to greet
your forehead, lovely and rosy
as a sunrise; and the oak trees,
robust and lofty and proud,
rustle their verdant and trembling
foliage when you go by
and make arches of their branches
as if a queen were passing.
O my own beloved! It is the sweet
season of the springtime.

There is a limpid fountain
that gushes from a cavern
where the white nymphs who play there
go bathing in the nude.
They laugh to the sound of the splashing
and wade through the tranquil lymph;
amid the crystal powders
they sponge their lengthy tresses;
and they know many love hymns
in the beautiful language of Greece
which Pan invented in the flowering fields
in glorious, ancient times.
Beloved: I will put in my stanzas
the most splendid of the words
of the phrases of the verses
of the hymns of that language
and I will give that word to you
imbibed in freshest honey.
O my own beloved, in the sweet
season of the springtime!

—ANITA VOLLAND

Autumnal

En las pálidas tardes
yerran nubes tranquilas
en el azul; en las ardientes manos
se posan las cabezas pensativas.
¡Ah los suspiros! ¡Ah los dulces sueños!
¡Ah las tristezas íntimas!
¡Ah el polvo de oro que en el aire flota,
tras cuyas ondas trémulas se miran
los ojos tiernos y húmedos,
las bocas inundadas de sonrisas,
las crespas cabelleras
y los dedos de rosa que acarician!

En las pálidas tardes
me cuenta una hada amiga
las historias secretas
llenas de poesía:
lo que cantan los pájaros,
lo que llevan las brisas,
lo que vaga en las nieblas,
lo que sueñan las niñas . . .

Una vez sentí el ansia
de una sed infinita.
Dije al hada amorosa:
—Quiero en el alma mía
tener la inspiración honda, profunda,
inmensa: luz, calor, aroma, vida.
Ella me dijo: —¡Ven!, con el acento
con que hablaría un arpa. En él hablaba
un divino idioma de esperanza.
¡Oh sed del ideal!

Sobre la cima
de un monte, a medianoche,
me mostró las estrellas encendidas.
Era un jardín de oro
con pétalos de llama que titilan.
Exclamé: —Más . . .

Autumnal

On pale afternoons
tranquil clouds go roaming
in the blue; and pensive heads
are sunk in burning hands.
O the sighs! O the sweet dreams!
O the intimate sadness!
O the golden dust that ripples through the air,
behind whose tremulous waves appear
moist and tender eyes,
mouths flooded with smiles,
curly heads
and caressing, rosy fingers!

On pale afternoons
a friendly fairy tells me
secret stories
full of poetry:
what the birds sing about,
what the breezes carry,
what wanders in the mists,
what little girls dream . . .

Once I felt the yearning
of an infinite thirst.
I told the gentle fairy:
"I want to feel within my soul
profound, deep, and boundless
inspiration: light, warmth, aroma, life."
She told me, "Come!," with the accent
with which a harp would speak. In it she spoke
a divine language of hope.
O thirst for the ideal!

Upon the summit
of a mountain, at midnight,
she showed me the blazing stars.
It was a garden of gold
with twinkling petals of flame.
I exclaimed, "More . . . "

La aurora
vino después. La aurora sonreía,
con la luz en la frente,
como la joven tímida
que abre la reja y la sorprenden luego
ciertas curiosas mágicas pupilas.
Y dije:—Más . . .—; sonriendo
la celeste hada amiga
prorrumpió:—¡Y bien! ¡Las flores!

Y las flores
estaban frescas, lindas,
empapadas de olor: la rosa virgen,
la blanca margarita,
la azucena gentil, y las volúbiles
que cuelgan de la rama estremecida.
Y dije:—Más . . .

El viento
arrastraba rumores, ecos, risas,
murmullos misteriosos, aleteos,
músicas nunca oídas.
El hada entonces me llevó hasta el velo
que nos cubre las ansias infinitas,
la inspiración profunda
y el alma de las liras,
y lo rasgó. Y allí todo era aurora.
En el fondo se veía
un bello rostro de mujer.

¡Oh, nunca,
Piérides, diréis las sacras dichas
que en el alma sintiera!
Con su vaga sonrisa,
—¿Más? . . .—dijo el hada. Y yo tenía entonces
clavadas las pupilas
en el Azul; y en mis ardientes manos
se posó mi cabeza pensativa . . .

And after
came the dawn. The dawn was smiling
with the light upon her brow,
so like the timid maiden
who opens the grated window and is then surprised
by certain curious, magical eyes.
And I said, "More . . ."; and smiling
the fond celestial fairy
burst out, "Well, then, the flowers!"

And the flowers
were fresh and lovely,
drenched with fragrance: the virgin rose,
the white daisy,
the gracious lily and the morning-glories
that hang from the shaken branch.
And I said, "More . . ."

The wind
was dragging rumors, echoes, laughter,
mysterious murmurs, the flutter of wings,
music never heard.
The fairy then took me to the veil
that hides from us infinite yearnings,
profound inspiration,
and the soul of the lyres,
and she tore it. And there all was dawn.
And in the depths appeared
a lovely woman's face.

O never,
Pierides, will you tell the blessed joys
I felt within my soul!
With her vague smile,
"More? . . ." said the fairy. And then I had
fixed my pupils
on the Blue; and in my burning hands
I sank my pensive head . . .

— ANITA VOLLAND

Sonatina

La princesa está triste . . . Qué tendrá la princesa?
Los suspiros se escapan de su boca de fresa,
que ha perdido la risa, que ha perdido el color.
La princesa está pálida en su silla de oro,
está mudo el teclado de su clave sonoro,
y en un vaso olvidada se desmaya una flor.

El jardín puebla el triunfo de los pavos reales;
parlanchina, la dueña dice cosas banales,
y vestido de rojo piruetea el bufón.
La princesa no ríe, la princesa no siente;
la princesa persigue por el cielo de Oriente
la libélula vaga de una vaga ilusión.

¿Piensa acaso en el príncipe de Golconda o de China,
o en el que ha detenido su carroza argentina
para ver de sus ojos la dulzura de luz?
¿O en el rey de las islas de las rosas fragantes,
o en el que es soberano de los claros diamantes,
o en el dueño orgulloso de las perlas de Ormuz?

¡Ay! La pobre princesa de la boca de rosa
quiere ser golondrina, quiere ser mariposa,
tener alas ligeras, bajo el cielo volar,
ir al sol por la escala luminosa de un rayo,
saludar a los lirios con los versos de Mayo,
o perderse en el viento sobre el trueno del mar.

Ya no quiere el palacio, ni la rueca de plata,
ni el halcón encantado, ni el bufón escarlata,
ni los cisnes unánimes en el lago de azur.
Y están tristes las flores por la flor de la corte:
los jazmines de Oriente, los nelumbos del Norte,
de Occidente las dalias y las rosas del Sur.

¡Pobrecita princesa de los ojos azules!
Está presa en sus oros, está presa en sus tules,
en la jaula de mármol del palacio real;
el palacio soberbio que vigilan los guardas,
que custodian cien negros con cien alabardas,
un lebrel que no duerme y un dragón colosal.

Sonatina

The princess is sad, and in anguish reposes,
She sighs for surcease, and her lips of blown roses
Have lost their gay laughter, have lost their fresh bloom;
The princess is pale on her throne that is golden,
The keyboard is mute in the strains that were olden,
And a blossom neglected has lost its perfume.

The garden is filled with the peacocks' proud clatter,
The duenna is banal, jejune in her chatter,
And vested in red pirouettes the buffoon;
The princess not laughing, the princess not feeling,
Pursues in the sky where a star is concealing
An illusion as vague as the dark of the moon.

Is she thinking perhaps of the prince of Golconda?
Or of him who has halted his carriage in wonder
To seek in her eyes for the beauty of light?
Of the king of the islands of fragrant rose bowers,
Or of him who is sovereign of diamonds and flowers,
Or of the proud lord of the pearls of Delight?

Alas, the poor princess with lips red as cherry,
Would now be a butterfly, swallow, or fairy,
Have wings that would carry her far in the sky.
She would soar to the sun on a shining stepladder,
Or the lilies of May with her verses make gladder,
Or be lost on the wind as it beats the waves high.

She no longer wants the gold distaff or palace,
The magical falcon, the jester's red challis,
The swans' classic grace on the azure lagoon.
The flowers are all sad for the yearning king's daughter,
The lotus has withered with roots in the water,
To all the four quarters dead roses are strewn.

Poor princess, her eyes have a look that distresses,
She's enmeshed in her jewels, her lavish lace dresses,
The palace of marble encages her soul.
The superb royal palace guard never relaxes,
A hundred giant Negroes with giant battle-axes
With watchdogs and dragon would take a huge toll.

¡Oh, quién fuera hipsipila que dejó la crisálida!
(La princesa está triste. La princesa está pálida.)
¡Oh visión adorada de oro, rosa y marfil!
¡Quién volara a la tierra donde un príncipe existe
(La princesa está pálida. La princesa está triste)
más brillante que el alba, más hermoso que Abril!

Calla, calla, princesa—dice el hada madrina—;
en caballo con alas hacia acá se encamina,
en el cinto la espada y en la mano el azor,
el feliz caballero que te adora sin verte,
y que llega de lejos, vencedor de la Muerte,
a encenderte los labios con su beso de amor.

Margarita

¿Recuerdas que querías ser una Margarita
Gautier? Fijo en mi mente tu extraño rostro está;
cuando cenamos juntos, en la primera cita,
en una noche alegre que nunca volverá.

Tus labios escarlata de púrpura maldita
sorbían el champaña del fino baccarat;
tus dedos deshojan la blanca margarita:
"Sí . . . , no . . . sí . . . no," ¡y sabías que te adoraba ya!

Después, ¡oh flor de histeria!, llorabas y reías;
tus besos y tus lágrimas tuve en mi boca yo;
tus risas, tus fragancias, tus quejas eran mías.

Y en una tarde triste de los más dulces días,
la Muerte, la celosa, por ver si me querías,
como una margarita de amor ¡te deshojó!

Sinfonía en gris mayor

El mar como un vasto cristal azogado
refleja la lámina de un cielo de zinc;
lejanas bandadas de pájaros manchan
el fondo bruñido de pálido gris.

I wish that the cocoon would break its enclosure!
The princess grows sad in her pallid composure.
Oh, tower of ivory, oh, vision in white.
She would fly to a land where a dream prince would hail her
(The princess is sadder, the princess grows paler)
A prince more resplendent than dawn after night.

Be silent, my child, says the fairy godmother,
On a swift winged steed never loved by another,
With a sword at his belt and a falcon above,
Rides the knight who adores you, his whole body yearning,
He overcomes distance and Death and is burning
To impassion your lips with the kiss of his love!
— JOHN CROW

Marguerite

Do you remember that you wanted to be a Marguerite
Gautier? Your strange face is fixed in my mind;
when we had dinner together, on that first rendezvous,
on a joyous night that will never come again.

Your lips made scarlet with accursed purple
were sipping champagne from the perfect crystal glass;
your fingers plucked the petals from the white daisy:
"Yes . . . , no . . . , yes . . . , no," and you knew I already adored you!

And after, oh flower of hysteria, you laughed and you cried;
I had your kisses and your tears upon my mouth;
your laughter, your fragrance, your moaning all were mine.

And on one sad afternoon of the very sweetest days,
Death, the jealous one, to see if you truly loved me,
like a daisy of love, plucked you away!
— ANITA VOLLAND

Symphony in Gray Major

The sea, great mercury mirror,
reflects the zinc sheet of sky;
stain of faraway birds
on pale burnished gray.

El sol como un vidrio redondo y opaco
con paso de enfermo camina al cenit;
el viento marino descansa en la sombra,
teniendo de almohada su negro clarín.

Las ondas que mueven su vientre de plomo
debajo del muelle parecen gemir.
Sentado en un cable, fumando su pipa,
está un marinero pensando en las playas
de un vago, lejano, brumoso país.

Es viejo ese lobo. Tostaron su cara
los rayos de fuego del sol del Brasil;
los recios tifones del mar de la China
le han visto bebiendo su frasco de gin.

La espuma impregnada de yodo y salitre
hace tiempo conoce su roja nariz,
sus crespos cabellos, sus bíceps de atleta,
su gorra de lona, su blusa de dril.

En medio del humo que forma el tabaco
ve el viejo el lejano, brumoso país,
a donde una tarde caliente y dorada
tendidas las velas partió el bergantín . . .

La siesta del trópico. El lobo se aduerme.
Ya todo lo envuelve la gama del gris.
Parece que un suave y enorme esfumino
del curvo horizonte borrara el confín.

La siesta del trópico. La vieja cigarra
ensaya en su ronca guitarra senil,
y el grillo preludia su solo monótono
en la única cuerda que está en su violín.

La fuente

Joven, te ofrezco el don de esta copa de plata
para que un día puedas calmar la sed ardiente,
la sed que con su fuego más que la muerte mata.
Mas debes abrevarte tan sólo en una fuente.

Opaque round window, the sun
at a sick pace totters to the zenith;
a sea wind stretches
in shade, pillowed on its black trumpet.

Under the pier the waves
groan, twitching leaden bellies.
A sailor sits on a coil of rope,
smoking, remembering
distant landfalls, a misty country.

This seadog is old. Fiery rays
of Brazilian sun have scorched his face;
vicious Chinese typhoons have seen him
tilting his gin bottle.

Foam infused with saltpeter and iodine
has long been familiar with his red nose,
his crisp curls and athlete's biceps,
his canvas cap and drill shirt.

In the tobacco smoke he sees
that far-off misty land for which,
one golden, hot afternoon,
his brig set out in full sail.

Tropical siesta. The old man sleeps.
The scale of gray major envelops him.
It's as if an enormous soft charcoal had been rubbed
over where the horizon used to curve.

Tropical siesta. An old cigale
tries out her obsolete, hoarse guitar;
a grasshopper begins
a monotone on his one-stringed fiddle.   —DENISE LEVERTOV

The Fount

Youth, I offer you this silver cup
So that, one day, your ardent thirst may end,
The thirst whose fire rages worse than death:
But you must quench it only at one fount.

Otra agua que la suya tendrá que serte ingrata;
busca su oculto origen en la gruta viviente
donde la interna música de su cristal desata,
junto al árbol que llora y la roca que siente.

Guíate el misterioso eco de su murmullo;
asciende por los riscos ásperos del orgullo;
baja por la constancia y desciende al abismo

cuya entrada sombría guardan siete panteras:
son los Siete Pecados las siete bestias fieras.
Llena la copa y bebe: la fuente está en ti mismo.

Yo persigo una forma . . .

Yo persigo una forma que no encuentra mi estilo,
botón de pensamiento que busca ser la rosa;
se anuncia con un beso que en mis labios se posa
al abrazo imposible de la Venus de Milo.

Adornan verdes palmas el blanco peristilo;
los astros me han predicho la visión de la Diosa,
y en mi alma reposa la luz como reposa
el ave de la luna sobre un lago tranquilo.

Y no hallo sino la palabra que huye,
la iniciación melódica que de la flauta fluye
y la barca del sueño que en el espacio boga;

y bajo la ventana de mi Bella-Durmiente,
el sollozo continuo del chorro de la fuente
y el cuello del gran cisne que me interroga.

Marcha triunfal

¡Ya viene el cortejo!
¡Ya viene el cortejo! Ya se oyen los claros clarines.
La espada se anuncia con vivo reflejo;
ya viene, oro y hierro, el cortejo de los paladines.

All other waters you shall drink in vain;
Seek its hidden source within that living cave
From whence the inner music of its crystal springs
Beside the feeling rock and weeping tree.

Be guided by the echo of its stream:
It rises by the bitter cliffs of pride,
Goes down through constancy, and descends through the abyss

Whose somber entrance seven panthers guard.
They are the Seven Sins, the seven savage beasts:
Fill the cup and drink—the fount is in yourself.

                        —WILLIAM M. DAVIS

I Pursue a Form . . .

I pursue a form that does not fit my style,
frail bud of thought that seeks to be the rose;
I know the impossible embrace meanwhile
that the Venus of Milo with a kiss bestows.

Green palms embellish the white peristyle;
the stars predict the vision of the Goddess;
and in my soul the light rests as, a while,
the bird of the moon on a still lake reposes.

And I find nothing but the words that flee,
the first melodic notes of the lute throbbing,
and the barque of dreams that navigates in space;

and under the window of my Sleeping-Beauty,
the crystal stream of the fountain ever sobbing,
and the neck of the swan, a question that I face.

                        —DOREEN BELL

Triumphal March

    Now the parade is coming!
Now the parade is coming! You can hear the clear bugles already.
The sword proclaims itself with a bright reflection;
now comes the parade of valiant knights in iron and gold!

Ya pasa debajo los arcos ornados de blancas Minervas y Martes,
los arcos triunfales en donde las Famas erigen sus largas trompetas,
la gloria solemne de los estandartes
llevados por manos robustas de heroicos atletas.
Se escucha el ruido que forman las armas de los caballeros,
los frenos que mascan los fuertes caballos de guerra,
los cascos que hieren la tierra,
y los timbaleros
que el paso acompasan con ritmos marciales.
¡Tal pasan los fieros guerreros
debajo los arcos triunfales!

Los claros clarines de pronto levantan sus sones,
su canto sonoro,
su cálido coro,
que envuelve en un trueno de oro
la augusta soberbia de los pabellones.
Él dice la lucha, la herida venganza,
las ásperas crines,
los rudos penachos, la pica, la lanza,
la sangre que riega de heroicos carmines
la tierra;
los negros mastines
que azuza la muerte, que rige la guerra.

Los áureos sonidos
anuncian el advenimiento
triunfal de la Gloria;
dejando el picacho que guarda sus nidos,
tendiendo sus alas enormes al viento,
los cóndores llegan. ¡Llegó la victoria!

Ya pasa el cortejo,
Señala el abuelo los héroes al niño.
Ved cómo la barba del viejo
los bucles de oro circunda de armiño.
Las bellas mujeres aprestan coronas de flores,
y bajo los pórticos vense sus rostros de rosa;
y la más hermosa
sonríe al más fiero de los vencedores.
¡Honor al que trae cautiva la extraña bandera!
¡Honor al herido y honor a los fieles
soldados que muerte encontraron por mano extranjera!
¡Clarines! ¡Laureles!

Now under the arches adorned with white Minervas and Mars,
the triumphal arches where the Fames raise their long trumpets,
the solemn glory of banners passes by,
carried in the strong hands of heroic athletes.
You can hear the clatter of troops of horsemen,
the bits that the sturdy war horses champ,
the hoofs striking the ground,
and the drummers
marking time with martial rhythms.
So the fierce warriors pass
under the triumphal arches!

Suddenly the clear bugles raise their sounds,
their resounding song,
their spirited chorus
which wraps the majestic pride
of the flags in a golden thunder.
It tells the struggle, the vengeance struck,
the coarse manes,
the rough plumes, the pike, the spear,
the blood that washes the earth
in heroic scarlet;
the black war dogs,
death-incited, war-ruled.

The golden sounds
proclaim the victorious
coming of Glory;
leaving the peak that shelters their nests,
spreading their vast wings in the wind,
the condors arrive. Victory has come!

Now the parade passes by.
The grandfather points out the heroes to the child;
see how the old man's beard
surrounds the gold curls with ermine.
Beautiful girls prepare crowns of flowers
and under the porches you can see their rosy faces;
and the prettiest one
smiles at the ugliest of the victors.
Honor to him who captures the foreign flag!
Honor to the wounded man and honor to the loyal
soldiers who met death by a foreign hand!
Bugles, laurels!

Las nobles espadas de tiempos gloriosos
desde sus panoplias saludan las nuevas coronas y lauros
—las viejas espadas de los granaderos más fuertes que osos,
hermanos de aquellos lanceros que fueron centauros—.
Las trompas guerreras resuenan;
de voces los aires se llenan . . .
—A aquellas antiguas espadas,
a aquellos ilustres aceros,
que encarnan las glorias pasadas . . .
¡Y al sol que hoy alumbra las nuevas victorias ganadas,
y al héroe que guía su grupo de jóvenes fieros;
al que ama la insignia del suelo paterno;
al que ha desafiado, ceñido el acero y el arma en la mano,
los soles del rojo verano,
las nieves y vientos del gélido invierno,
la noche, y el hambre
y el odio y la muerte, por ser por la patria inmortal,
saludan con voces de bronce las trompas de guerra que tocan
la marcha triunfal! . . .

Los cisnes

   ¿Qué signo haces, oh Cisne, con tu encorvado cuello
al paso de los tristes y errantes soñadores?
¿Por qué tan silencioso de ser blanco y ser bello,
tiránico a las aguas o impasible a las flores?

   Yo te saludo ahora como en versos latinos
te saludara antaño Publio Ovidio Nasón.
Los mismos ruiseñores cantan los mismos trinos,
y en diferentes lenguas es la misma canción.

   A vosotros mi lengua no debe ser extraña.
A Garcilaso visteis, acaso, alguna vez . . .
Soy un hijo de América, soy un nieto de España . . .
Quevedo pudo hablaros en verso en Aranjuez.

   Cisnes, los abanicos de vuestras alas frescas
den a las frentes pálidas sus caricias más puras
y alejen vuestras blancas figuras pintorescas
de nuestras mentes tristes las ideas oscuras.

The noble swordsmen of glorious times
salute the new crowns and fames from their panoplies
(the old grenadier swordsmen stronger than bears,
brothers of those lancers who were centaurs).
The war trumpets blare;
voices fill the air.
To those old swordsmen,
to those illustrious blades
that embody past glories;
and to the sun that shines today on new victories;
and to the hero who leads his group of fierce young men;
to him who loves the badge of his mother soil;
to him who, girt in steel and weapon in hand, has dared
suns of red summer,
snow and wind of frigid winter,
night, frost
and hate and death, for the sake of living for his immortal land—
greetings are sent by the bronze-voiced war trumpets that play
the triumphal march.
                                          —CHARLES GUENTHER

The Swans

What sign do you make, O Swan, with your curved neck
to the sad and wandering dreamers as they pass?
And why are you so silent, you white being,
tyrannical to these waters smooth as glass?

I salute you now as once in Latin verses
you were saluted by Publio Ovidio Nasón.
The same nightingales warble the same trills,
in different tongues it still is the same song.

To you I cannot speak an alien language.
You saw Garcilaso, perhaps, one day . . .
I am a son of America, grandson of Spain . . .
Quevedo could speak to you in Aranjuez . . .

O Swans, the fans of your fresh snowy wings
give to our pale brows their most pure caress,
and with your picturesque white forms you still
charm us from care and banish our distress.

Brumas septentrionales nos llenan de tristezas;
se mueren nuestras rosas; se agotan nuestras palmas;
casi no hay ilusiones para nuestras cabezas,
y somos los mendigos de nuestras pobres almas.

Nos predican la guerra con águilas feroces,
gerifaltes de antaño revienen a los puños,
mas no brillan las glorias de las antiguas hoces,
ni hay Rodrigos ni Jaimes, ni hay Alfonsos ni Nuños.

Faltos de los alientos que dan las grandes cosas,
¿qué haremos los poetas sino buscar tus lagos?
A falta de laureles son muy dulces las rosas,
y a falta de victorias busquemos los halagos.

La América española, como la España entera,
fija está en el Oriente de su fatal destino;
yo interrogo a la Esfinge que el porvenir espera
con la interrogación de tu cuello divino:

¿Seremos entregados a los bárbaros fieros?
¿Tantos millones de hombres hablaremos inglés?
¿Ya no hay nobles hidalgos ni bravos caballeros?
¿Callaremos ahora para llorar después?

He lanzado mi grito, cisnes, entre vosotros,
que habéis sido los fieles en la desilusión,
mientras siento una fuga de americanos potros
y el estertor postrero de un caduco león . . .

Y un cisne negro dijo: «La noche anuncia el día.»
Y un blanco: «La aurora es inmortal, la aurora
es inmortal!» ¡Oh tierras de sol y de armonía,
aún guarda la esperanza la caja de Pandora!

Filosofía

Saluda al sol, araña, no seas rencorosa.
Da tus gracias a Dios, o sapo, pues que eres.
El peludo cangrejo tiene espinas de rosa,

The northern mists have filled our hearts with sadness,
our roses die, our wreaths are withered quite;
there are almost no illusions left our leaders,
and we are mendicants in piteous plight.

They preach war to us with ferocious eagles,
falcons of old times come back to their wrists;
but the old glories shine no longer, there
are no Jaimes nor Rodrigos in our lists.

Lacking the encouragement of the great things,
what shall we poets do but seek your lakes?
For lack of laurels they are sweet, the roses,
and lacking victories we look for praise.

Spanish America, as the whole of Spain,
in the Orient of its destiny is set;
I question the Sphinx waiting for the future
with the interrogation of your perfect neck.

Shall we be handed over to the barbarians?
So many million men shall we speak English?
Are there no longer brave knights, gallant nobles?
Shall we keep silent now, later to languish?

I have flung out my shout, Swans, amongst you,
who have been faithful in my disillusion,
while I hear the flight of American wild horses
and the last gasp of a decrepit lion . . .

And a black Swan said:—The night announces the day.
And a white one:—The dawn is immortal!
Immortal!—O land of sun and harmony,
there yet is hope for you in the box of Pandora!

    —DOREEN BELL

Philosophy

Spider, salute the Sun! No rancor show.
Give God your thanks, oh toad, that you exist.
The hirsute crab has such thorns as has the rose.

y los moluscos, reminiscencias de mujeres.
Sabed ser lo que sois, enigmas, siendo formas;
dejad la responsabilidad a las Normas,
que a su vez la enviarán al Todopoderoso . . .
(Toca grillo, a la luz de la luna, y dance el oso.)

Leda

El cisne en la sombra parece de nieve;
su pico es de ámbar, del alba al trasluz;
el suave crepúsculo que pasa tan breve
las cándidas alas sonrosa de luz.

Y luego, en las ondas del lago azulado,
después que la aurora perdió su arrebol,
las alas tendidas y el cuello enarcado,
el cisne es de plata, bañado de sol.

Tal es, cuando esponja las plumas de seda,
olímpico pájaro herido de amor,
y viola en las linfas sonoras a Leda,
buscando su pico los labios en flor.

Suspira la bella desnuda y vencida,
y en tanto que al aire sus quejas se van,
del fondo verdoso de fronda tupida
chispean turbados los ojos de Pan.

¡Ay, triste del que un día . . . !

¡Ay, triste del que un día en su esfinge interior
pone los ojos e interroga! Está perdido.
¡Ay del que pide eurekas al placer o al dolor!
Dos dioses hay, y son: Ignorancia y Olvido.

Lo que el árbol desea decir y dice al viento,
y lo que el animal manifiesta en su instinto,
cristalizamos en palabra y pensamiento.
Nada más que maneras expresan lo distinto.

In the mollusc, reminiscence of woman is.
Since shapes are mysteries, learn to wear your own;
The responsibility is of the Norms alone,
Which they in turn leave to the All-Powerful's care.
(Chirp, cricket, in the moonlight; dance on, bear.)   —MUNA LEE

Leda

The swan among the shadows is like snow;
its beak translucent amber in the dawn;
in the ephemeral half-light a pink glow
illumines its wings softly and is gone.

And later, on the waves of the blue lake,
When dawn has lost its rose tints in the sky,
stretching its wings and arching its proud neck
the swan is silver under the sun's eye.

So is it when, preening its silken plumage,
the Olympic bird is wounded by love's power,
and ravishes in the sonorous waters Leda,
seeking with its hard beak the lips in flower.

The beauty vanquished and denuded, sighing,
burdens the wind with her complaints in vain,
while from the green depths of thick foliage spying
scintillate the embarrassed eyes of Pan.   —DOREEN BELL

Unhappy He . . .

Unhappy he who his inner sphinx one day
Observes and questions deeply! Lost is he.
Alas for who believes that Grief or Joy will stay!
Ignorance and Forgetfulness: two gods have we.

What the tree desires to say and says to the wind,
That for which animals by instinct expression find,
Into thought and speech we must crystallize,
Yet only in manner of saying a difference lies.   —MUNA LEE

Melancolía

Hermano, tú que tienes la luz, dame la mía.
Soy como un ciego. Voy sin rumbo y ando a tientas.
Voy bajo tempestades y tormentas,
ciego de ensueño y loco de armonía.

Ése es mi mal. Soñar. La poesía
es la camisa férrea de mil puntas cruentas
que llevo sobre el alma. Las espinas sangrientas
dejan caer las gotas de mi melancolía.

Y así voy, ciego y loco, por este mundo amargo;
a veces me parece que el camino es muy largo,
y a veces que es muy corto . . .

Y en este titubeo de aliento y agonía,
cargo lleno de penas lo que apenas soporto.
¿No oyes caer las gotas de mi melancolía?

Caracol

[a Antonio Machado]

En la playa he encontrado un caracol de oro
macizo y recamado de las perlas más finas;
Europa le ha tocado con sus manos divinas
cuando cruzó las ondas sobre el celeste toro.

He llevado a mis labios el caracol sonoro
y he suscitado el eco de las dianas marinas;
le acerqué a mis oídos, y las azules minas
me han contado en voz baja de su secreto tesoro.

Así la sal me llega de los vientos amargos
que en sus hinchadas velas sintió la nave Argos
cuando amaron los astros el sueño de Jasón;

y oigo un rumor de olas y un incógnito acento,
y un profundo oleaje, y un misterioso viento . . .
(El caracol la forma tiene de un corazón.)

Melancholy

Brother, you who have the light, tell me where mine is.
I am as a blind man. I move without bearings and grope in the darkness.
I walk beneath hurricanes and tempests,
blinded by illusions and maddened by harmony.

That is my affliction. Dreaming. Poetry
is the harsh shirt of a thousand cruel needles
I wear upon my soul. The bloodstained barbs
let fall the droplets of my melancholy.

And thus I go, mad and sightless through this bitter world;
at times it seems to me the road is very long,
and at times it seems very short . . .

And in this hesitation of courage and agony,
weighted down with sorrows which I can scarcely bear,
can you not hear them falling, the droplets of my melancholy?
—ANITA VOLLAND

Seashell

[to Antonio Machado]

At the seashore I came upon a golden shell,
massive and embroidered with the finest pearls;
Europa had touched it with her sacred hands
when she crossed the billows on the celestial bull.

I raised to my lips this sonorous shell
and stirred the echo of the sea's reveille;
I brought it to my ear and the azure depths
told me in whispers of their secret treasure.

And thus the salt did reach me from the bitter winds
that in her swelling sails the vessel Argo felt
when the stars loved Jason's dream;

and I hear a murmur of sea waves and an unknown reverberation
and a turbulent surge and a mysterious wind . . .
(The shell has the form of a heart.)
—ANITA VOLLAND

Nocturno

Los que auscultasteis el corazón de la noche;
los que por el insomnio tenaz habéis oído
el cerrar de una puerta, el resonar de un coche
lejano, un eco vago, un ligero ruido . . .

en los instantes del silencio misterioso,
cuando surgen de su prisión los olvidados,
en la hora de los muertos, en la hora del reposo,
¡sabréis leer estos versos de amargor impregnados! . . .

Como en un vaso vierto en ellos mis dolores
de lejanos recuerdos y desgracias funestas,
y las tristes nostalgias de mi alma, ebria de flores,
y el duelo de mi corazón, triste de fiestas.

Y el pesar de no ser lo que yo hubiera sido,
la pérdida del reino que estaba para mí,
el pensar que un instante pude no haber nacido,
y el sueño que es mi vida desde que yo nací . . .

Todo esto viene en medio del silencio profundo
en que la noche envuelve la terrena ilusión,
y siento como un eco del corazón del mundo
que penetra y conmueve mi propio corazón.

Allá lejos

Buey que vi en mi niñez echando vaho un día
bajo el nicaragüense sol de encendidos oros,
en la hacienda fecunda, plena de la armonía
del trópico; paloma de los bosques sonoros
del viento, de las hachas, de pájaros y toros
salvajes, yo os saludo, pues sois la vida mía.

Nocturne

Those who give ear to the heart of the night,
Those who in long-abiding wakefulness have heard
The closing of a door, the sound of a distant
Coach, a tenuous echo, a vague noise . . .

In moments of mysterious silence,
When from their prisons the forgotten ones emerge,
In the hour of the dead, the hour of repose,
They will know how to read these verses wrapped in bitterness . . .

Into them I pour as into a cup my sorrows
For faraway remembrances and dreadful misfortunes,
And the sad nostalgias of my soul, drunk with flowers,
And the brooding of my heart, sad with celebrations.

And the burden of not becoming that which I might have been,
The losing of the kingdom that was to have been mine,
The thought that there was an instant when I might not have been born,
And the dream my life has been having once been born . . .

All this comes drifting in the midst of the silence profound
In which the night envelops the earthly illusion,
And I feel as if an echo of the heartbeat of the world
Had fathomed and commingled with my own.
                                                    —KATE FLORES

Far Away and Long Ago

Ox of my childhood, steaming
under the flaring gold of Nicaraguan sun
on the fruitful farm, full of tropical harmony;
Pigeon of the wind-sonorous, bird-musical
wild-bull-roaring, ax-echoing forest:
I salute you both, for you are my life.

Pesado buey, tú evocas la dulce madrugada
que llamaba a la ordeña de la vaca lechera,
cuando era mi existencia toda blanca y rosada,
y tú, paloma arrulladora y montañera,
significas en mi primavera pasada
todo lo que hay en la divina Primavera.

Lo fatal

Dichoso el árbol que es apenas sensitivo,
y más la piedra dura, porque ésa ya no siente,
pues no hay dolor más grande que el dolor de ser vivo,
ni mayor pesadumbre que la vida consciente.

Ser, y no saber nada, y ser sin rumbo cierto,
y el temor de haber sido y un futuro terror . . .
y el espanto seguro de estar mañana muerto,
y sufrir por la vida y por la sombra y por

lo que no conocemos y apenas sospechamos,
y la carne que tienta con sus frescos racimos,
y la tumba que aguarda con sus fúnebres ramos,
y no saber adónde vamos,
¡ni de dónde venimos . . . !

Versos de otoño

Cuando mi pensamiento va hacia ti, se perfuma;
tu mirar es tan dulce, que se torna profundo.
Bajo tus pies desnudos aun hay blancor de espuma,
y en tus labios compendias la alegría del mundo.

El amor pasajero tiene el encanto breve,
y ofrece un igual término para el gozo y la pena.
Hace una hora que un nombre grabé sobre la nieve;
hace un minuto dije mi amor sobre la arena.

Heavy ox, you evoke the gentle
dawn that called the cows in to be milked,
when my life was all white and rose,
and you, cooing mountain dove,
stand for all there was of divine Spring
in my remote springtime.

—DENISE LEVERTOV

Doom

Happy the tree, that scarcely feels,
And happier the hard stone not to feel at all,
For there is no pain greater than the pain of being alive,
Nor burden as heavy as conscious existence.

To be, and to know nothing, and to have no certain path,
And the fear of having been and a dread future . . .
And the hideous sureness of being dead tomorrow,
And suffering for life and for the dark and for

That which we do not know of and barely suspect,
And the flesh tempting with its cool grapes,
And the tomb that waits with its funeral wreaths,
And to know not whither we go,
Neither whence we come! . . .

—KATE FLORES

Autumn Verses

My thoughts are perfumed when toward you they turn;
So sweet your look, that they become profound.
Still beneath your naked feet the whiteness of the foam,
And comprised within your lips the gladness of the world.

Transient love a brief enchantment holds,
And offers equally in joy or grief to end.
An hour ago I carved a name in the snow;
A moment ago I told my love in the sand.

Las hojas amarillas caen en la alameda,
en donde vagan tantas parejas amorosas.
Y en la copa de Otoño un vago vino queda
en que han de deshojarse, Primavera, tus rosas.

¡Eheu!

Aquí, junto al mar latino,
digo la verdad:
Siento en roca, aceite y vino,
yo mi antigüedad.

¡Oh qué anciano soy, Dios santo,
oh, qué anciano soy! . . .
¿De dónde viene mi canto?
Y yo ¿adónde voy?

El conocerme a mí mismo,
ya me va costando
muchos momentos de abismo
y el cómo y el cuándo . . .

Y esta claridad latina,
¿de qué me sirvió
a la entrada de la mina
del yo y el no yo . . . ?

Nefelíbata contento,
creo interpretar
las confidencias del viento,
la tierra y el mar . . .

Unas vagas confidencias
del ser y el no ser,
y fragmentos de conciencias
de ahora y ayer.

Como en medio de un desierto
me puse a clamar;
y miré el sol como muerto
y me eché a llorar.

The yellow leaves are falling in the park,
Where wander so many amorous couples,
And in Autumn's cup there remains a vagrant wine
Into which your roses, Spring, have to drop their petals.

—KATE FLORES

Eheu!

Here, beside the Latin sea,
I speak the truth:
I feel in rock and oil and wine
my own antiquity.

Oh how old I am, my God,
oh, how very old I am! . . .
From whence comes my singing?
And I, where am I bound?

The understanding of myself
has already cost me
many a moment of meditation
and the how and the when . . .

And this Latin splendor,
of what use was it to me
at the entrance of the dark mine
of the I and the not I? . . .

Contented wanderer of the clouds
I feel I can interpret
the secrets of the wind,
of the earth and of the sea . . .

Some few vague secrets
of being and not being
and fragments of consciences
of now and yesterday.

As in the midst of a desert
I started to cry out;
and looked up at the sun like a dead man
and then burst into tears.

—ANITA VOLLAND

ANTONIO MACHADO
(1875–1939)

In his self-portrait, *Retrato,* included here, Machado declares some fundamental things about himself. Adding to them certain factual touches, his life appears in all its uneventful simplicity. Born in Seville, the son of a jurist who did pioneer work in Spanish folklore, he moved to Madrid at the age of eight and became so rooted to Castile that his work mirrors unfailingly and faithfully the Castilian quintessence. After his studies at the progressive Institución Libre de Enseñanza, he worked in Paris as translator for the publishers Garnier. In 1907 he returned to Spain and taught French in the high school at Soria, where, in 1909, he married sixteen-year-old Leonor. For three years he was blissfully happy, but it all ended abruptly with her death, which left him with a recurrent grief expressed in his writing. From then on, the years passed unalterably and monotonously for the quiet, provincial schoolteacher. However, at a moment of crisis, during the Civil War, he boldly came out for the defense of Loyalist Spain and left only after the downfall of the republic. On arriving at Collioure (France) with his mother, he died; she died three days later.

Machado began his literary career during the heyday of modernism. Steeped in the classics—Ronsard was his favorite—at first he seemed to be antagonized by the new trends, but modernism finally did enter into the essential texture of his writings.

On surveying his production, from the early verse of 1899, included in *Soledades* (1903), to his Civil War poems written shortly before his death, one sees much experimentation and self-renewal. He tried the long narrative—for instance, the 800-line poem *The House of Alvargonzález*—as well as three-line aphorisms; and as for prosody, from the most classic meters to free verse and poetic prose. He also tried, less successfully, to write for the theater. His best work invariably conjures up the landscape of Castile, with its inhabitants and their

276

tragic struggles. In his pristine, often denuded verse, Machado highlighted man's tragic predicament to such an extent that recent criticism has endeavored to show his affinity with the Existentialists, and more especially with Heidegger, whom he read assiduously.

BEST EDITIONS: *Obras*, Mexico: Editorial Seneca, 1940; *Poesías completas*, Buenos Aires, Losada, 1958 (4th ed.); Manuel y Antonio Machado: *Obras completas*, Madrid, Plentitud, 1947.

ABOUT ANTONIO MACHADO: A. J. McVan: *Antonio Machado*, New York, Hispanic Society of America, 1959. *Also:* J. E. Cirute: "Humor in the *Cancionero apócrifo*," *Modern Language Forum* 42 (1958), pp. 133–40; J. Dos Passos: *Rocinante to the Road Again*, New York, 1922; J. R. Jiménez: "A. Machado," *Antioch Review* 18 (1958), pp. 272–74; E. A. Peers: A. *Machado*, Oxford, Clarendon Press, 1940, also in *St. John of the Cross & Other Lectures*, London, 1946; J. B. Trend: *Alfonso the Sage*, London, 1926, pp. 135–46; J. B. Trend: A. *Machado*, Oxford, Dolphin Book Company, 1953.

SOME COLLECTIONS AND CRITICISM PUBLISHED SINCE 1958: Ricardo Senabre: *Antonio Machado y Juan Ramón Jiménez, poetas del siglo XX*, Madrid, Anaya, 1991. Bernard Sese: *Claves de Antonio Machado*, Madrid, Espasa-Calpe, 1990.

La plaza y los naranjos encendidos . . .

La plaza y los naranjos encendidos
con sus frutas redondas y risueñas.

Tumulto de pequeños colegiales
que, al salir en desorden de la escuela,
llenan el aire de la plaza en sombra
con la algazara de sus voces nuevas.

¡Alegría infantil en los rincones
de las ciudades muertas! . . .
¡Y algo nuestro de ayer, que todavía
vemos vagar por estas calles viejas!

Amada, el aura dice . . .

Amada, el aura dice
tu pura veste blanca . . .
No te verán mis ojos;
¡mi corazón te aguarda!

El viento me ha traído
tu nombre en la mañana;
el eco de tus pasos
repite la montaña . . .
No te verán mis ojos;
¡mi corazón te aguarda!

En las sombrías torres
repican las campanas . . .
No te verán mis ojos;
¡mi corazón te aguarda!

Los golpes del martillo
dicen la negra caja;
y el sitio de la fosa,
los golpes de la azada . . .
No te verán mis ojos;
¡mi corazón te aguarda!

The Plaza and the Flaming Orange Trees . . .

The plaza and the flaming orange trees
with their round and smiling fruit.

Clamor of small schoolchildren
scampering wildly out of school,
filling the air of the somber plaza
with the tumult of their new voices.

Childish cheer on the corners
of the dead towns! . . .
And something out of our yesterday, still
lingering in these old streets!

—KATE FLORES

The Breeze Tells Me, Loved One . . .

The breeze tells me, loved one,
of your pure white dress . . .
My eyes may not see you,
but my heart awaits.

The wind has brought me
your name in the morning;
the echo of your step
resounds on the hill . . .
My eyes may not see you,
but my heart awaits.

In the somber towers
the bells are tolling . . .
My eyes may not see you,
but my heart awaits.

The falling hammer
tells me of the black box;
and the place for the grave,
the sound of the spade . . .
My eyes may not see you,
but my heart awaits.

—JAMES DUFFY

Cante hondo

Yo meditaba absorto, devanando
los hilos del hastío y la tristeza,
cuando llegó a mi oído,
por la ventana de mi estancia, abierta

a una caliente noche de verano,
el plañir de una copla soñolienta,
quebrada por los trémolos sombríos
de las músicas magas de mi tierra.

. . . Y era el Amor, como una roja llama . . .
—Nerviosa mano en la vibrante cuerda
ponía un largo suspirar de oro,
que se trocaba en surtidor de estrellas—.

. . . Y era la Muerte, al hombro la cuchilla,
el paso largo, torva y esquelética.
—Tal cuando yo era niño la soñaba—.

Y en la guitarra, resonante y trémula,
la brusca mano, al golpear, fingía
el reposar de un ataúd en tierra.

Y era un plañido solitario el soplo
que el polvo barre y la ceniza avienta.

La calle en sombra . . .

La calle en sombra. Ocultan los altos caserones
el sol que muere; hay ecos de luz en los balcones.

¿No ves, en el encanto del mirador florido,
el óvalo rosado de un rostro conocido?

La imagen, tras el vidrio de equívoco reflejo,
surge o se apaga como daguerrotipo viejo.

Deep Song

The dusk sifted into my breathless room,
Wide open to a torrid summer night,
And wrapped its hands about my desolation
As I unwound its tattered shreds of light.

Then on the air a sudden blaze of sound:
The sobbing of a wistful, broken strain
That quivered with the somber tremolos
Of tragic songs from my own southern Spain.

. . . And it was Love, a red and fiery flame . . .
Whose nervous hand upon the throbbing strings
A long and golden pause sustained
That flashed into quick stars with trembling wings—

. . . And it was Death, the scythe upon his shoulder,
Grim-faced and skeletal, with steps long-drawn and slow.
—Thus did I dream of him when but a child—

On the guitar, sonorous, tremulous below,
A brusque hand as it strummed would imitate
The lowering of a casket in the ground.

The breath of wind was but a solitary wail
That winnows ash and stirs the dust around.
—JOHN CROW

Her Street Is Dark . . .

Her street is dark. The tall housetops now shade
A dying sun; upon the balconies soft light is played.

Look! Can't you see inside that flowering window sill
The rose tint oval of a face remembered still?

Head pressed against the glass a blurred white stripe
Surges and vanishes like an old daguerreotype.

Suena en la calle sólo el ruido de tu paso;
se extinguen lentamente los ecos del ocaso.

¡Oh angustia! Pesa y duele el corazón . . . ¿Es ella?
No puede ser . . . Camina . . . En el azul, la estrella.

El casco roído y verdoso . . .

El casco roído y verdoso
del viejo falucho
reposa en la arena . . .
La vela tronchada parece
que aun sueña en el sol y en el mar.

El mar hierve y canta . . .
El mar es un sueño sonoro
bajo el sol de abril.
El mar hierve y ríe
con olas azules y espumas de leche y de plata,
el mar hierve y ríe
bajo el cielo azul.
El mar lactescente,
el mar rutilante,
que ríe en sus liras de plata sus risas azules . . .
¡Hierve y ríe el mar! . . .

El aire parece que duerme encantado
en la fúlgida niebla de sol blanquecino.
La gaviota palpita en el aire dormido, y al lento
volar soñoliento, se aleja y se pierde en la bruma del sol.

La noria

La tarde caía
triste y polvorienta.

El agua cantaba
su copla plebeya
en los cangilones
de la noria lenta.

My steps the only sound on a deserted street . . .
A swollen sun that blots the west with slanting rays that meet.

O, love! My heart with agony now beats. Can it be she?
Move on . . . A star now lights the blue . . . It cannot be.

—JOHN CROW

The Moldering Hulk . . .

The moldering hulk
of the old sloop
rests upon the sand . . .
The tattered sail seems still
to be dreaming upon the sun and the sea.

The sea bubbles and sings . . .
The sea is a sonorous dream
under the April sun.
The sea bubbles and laughs
with azure waves and foam of milk and silver,
the sea bubbles and laughs
under the azure sky.
The milky sea,
the glittering sea,
laughing its azure laughter upon its silver lyres . . .
It bubbles and laughs, the sea! . . .

The wind seems to be sleeping entranced
in the lambent haze of the bleaching sun.
A gull hovers in the dormant air, and in slow,
drowsy flight drifts away and is lost amid the mist of the sun.

—KATE FLORES

The Water Wheel

The afternoon falls,
dusty and sad.

The water sings
its vulgar tunes
in the earthen buckets
of the slow draw-well.

Soñaba la mula
¡pobre mula vieja!
al compás de sombra
que en el agua suena.

La tarde caía
triste y polvorienta.

Yo no sé qué noble,
divino poeta
unió a la amargura
de la eterna rueda

la dulce armonía
del agua que sueña
y vendó sus ojos
¡pobre mula vieja! . . .

Mas sé que fue un noble,
divino poeta,
corazón maduro
de sombra y de ciencia.

Guitarra del mesón que hoy suenas jota . . .

Guitarra del mesón que hoy suenas jota,
mañana petenera,
según quien llega y tañe
las empolvadas cuerdas,

    guitarra del mesón de los caminos,
no fuiste nunca, ni serás, poeta.

Tú eres alma que dice su armonía
solitaria a las almas pasajeras . . .

Y siempre que te escucha el caminante
sueña escuchar un aire de su tierra.

The mule—the poor
old mule—dreams
to the rhythm of the shadows
in the water's refrain.

The afternoon falls,
dusty and sad.

I do not know what noble
divine poet
tied to the bitterness
of the wheel eternal

the sweet harmony
of water that dreams,
and bandaged your eyes,
poor old mule!

But I do know that it was a noble
divine poet,
a heart matured
in shadow and science.

—JAMES DUFFY

Tavern Guitar Playing a *Jota* Today . . .

Tavern guitar playing *a jota* today,
a *petenera* tomorrow,
according to whoever comes and strums
your dusty strings,

guitar of the roadside inn,
you never were nor will you be a poet.

You're a soul uttering its lonely
harmony to passing souls . . .

And whenever a traveler hears you
he dreams of hearing a tune of his native town.

—CHARLES GUENTHER

Desnuda está la tierra . . .

Desnuda está la tierra,
y el alma aúlla al horizonte pálido
como loba famélica. ¿Qué buscas,
poeta, en el ocaso?

Amargo caminar, porque el camino
pesa en el corazón. ¡El viento helado,
y la noche que llega, y la amargura
de la distancia! . . . En el camino blanco

algunos yertos árboles negrean;
en los montes lejanos
hay oro y sangre . . . El sol murió . . . ¿Qué buscas,
poeta, en el ocaso?

Retrato

Mi infancia son recuerdos de un patio de Sevilla,
y un huerto claro donde madura el limonero;
mi juventud, veinte años en tierra de Castilla;
mi historia, algunos casos que recordar no quiero.

Ni un seductor Mañara, ni un Bradomín he sido
—ya conocéis mi torpe aliño indumentario—,
mas recibí la flecha que me asignó Cupido,
y amé cuanto ellas pueden tener de hospitalario.

Hay en mis venas gotas de sangre jacobina,
pero mi verso brota de manantial sereno;
y, más que un hombre al uso que sabe su doctrina,
soy, en el buen sentido de la palabra, bueno.

Adoro la hermosura, y en la moderna estética
corté las viejas rosas del huerto de Ronsard;
mas no amo los afeites de la actual cosmética,
ni soy un ave de esas del nuevo gay-trinar.

Denuded Is the Earth . . .

Denuded is the earth,
and the soul howls to the pale horizon
like a famished wolf. What seek you,
poet, in the sunset?

Bitter to walk, because the road
weighs on the heart. The frozen wind,
and the night comes, and the bitterness
of the distance! . . . On the white road

stiff trees blacken;
in the distant mountains
there is gold and blood . . . The sun has died . . . What seek you,
poet, in the sunset?
                                    —EDWARD F. GAHAN

Portrait

My childhood are remembrances of a court in Seville,
and an orchard where the bright lemons ripen and fall;
my youth are twenty years in the lands of Castile;
my history, some events I do not want to recall.

Neither a Casanova nor a Don Juan could I be
—you well know how plainly, even dully, I dress—
but I had the arrow that Cupid assigned me,
and have loved women for their grace and tenderness.

There are drops of red Jacobin blood in my veins,
but my verse springs like water from a source in a wood;
and, more than a man may be who knows his doctrines,
I am, you know, in the good sense of the word, good.

I adore beauty, and in the modern aesthetics
cut old roses from the orchard that to Ronsard belongs;
but I do not like the make-up of today's cosmetics,
and I am not one of these birds with the new songs.

Desdeño las romanzas de los tenores huecos
y el coro de los grillos que cantan a la luna.
A distinguir me paro las voces de los ecos,
y escucho solamente, entre las voces, una.

¿Soy clásico o romántico? No sé. Dejar quisiera
mi verso, como deja el capitán su espada:
famosa por la mano viril que la blandiera,
no por el docto oficio del forjador preciada.

Converso con el hombre que siempre va conmigo
—quien habla solo espera hablar a Dios un día—;
mi soliloquio es plática con este buen amigo
que me enseñó el secreto de la filantropía.

Y al cabo, nada os debo; debéisme cuanto he escrito.
A mi trabajo acudo, con mi dinero pago
el traje que me cubre y la mansión que habito;
el pan que me alimenta y el lecho en donde yago.

Y cuando llegue el día del último viaje,
y esté al partir la nave que nunca ha de tornar,
me encontraréis a bordo ligero de equipaje,
casi desnudo, como los hijos de la mar.

I detest the arias of all these empty tenors
and their choir of crickets that serenade the moon.
I stop to distinguish the notes of the echoes,
and hear, between the many voices, only one.

Am I classic or romantic? I know not. I prefer to
leave behind me my verse, as the captain leaves his sword:
the hand that carried rather than the smith who wrought it
winning whatever fame posterity accord.

I talk with a man who goes with me to the end
—who speaks alone expects to speak with God one day—;
my soliloquy is a talk with this good friend
who teaches me the secrets of philanthropy.

And at least I owe you nothing; you owe me what I wrote.
I go to my work and I pay with my money
for the suit that covers me and the house I inhabit,
the bread that sustains me and the bed where I lie.

And when the day comes for the last voyage outward,
and the boat that will not come back is just about to sail,
you will find me on deck, with little luggage, to windward,
and almost naked, like the sons of the sea and the gale.

—DOREEN BELL

La tierra de Alvargonzález

I

Siendo mozo Alvargonzález,
dueño de mediana hacienda,
que en otras tierras se dice
bienestar, y aquí, opulencia,
en la feria de Berlanga
prendóse de una doncella,
y la tomó por mujer
al año de conocerla.
Muy ricas las bodas fueron,
y quien las vio las recuerda;
sonadas las tornabodas
que hizo Álvar en su aldea;
hubo gaitas, tamboriles,
flautas, bandurria y vihuela,
fuegos a la valenciana
y danzas a la aragonesa.

II

Feliz vivió Alvargonzález
en el amor de su tierra.
Naciéronle tres varones,
que en el campo son riqueza,
y, ya crecidos, los puso,
uno a cultivar la huerta,
otro a cuidar los merinos,
y dio al menor a la Iglesia.

III

Mucha sangre de Caín
tiene la gente labriega,
y en el hogar campesino
armó la envidia pelea.

Casáronse los mayores;
tuvo Alvargonzález nueras
que le trajeron cizaña
antes que nietos le dieran.

The House of Alvargonzález

I

Alvargonzález, being single
and owner of a fair-sized farm—that is,
being what in other countries
would be called well-off, and here
opulent, took a fancy
to a young girl at Berlanga Fair,
and made her his wife that very year.
The wedding was a fine one,
long remembered by all who saw it,
and the feast Alvargonzález gave in his village
on the day after was spoken of far and wide.
There were drums and flageolets,
flute, guitar and mandolin,
Valencian fireworks
and Aragonese dances.

II

Alvargonzález dwelt in contentment,
in the love of his land.
Three boys were born to him,
and in the country sons are riches.
As they grew up he set them to work,
one in the fields and orchards, one
to care for his flock of merino sheep; the youngest
he gave to the Church.

III

Much blood of Cain
flows in peasant veins:
Envy armed for a fight.

The older sons took brides;
now there were daughters-in-law
bringing discord to Alvargonzález
before they had brought him a grandchild.

La codicia de los campos
ve tras la muerte la herencia;
no goza de lo que tiene
por ansia de lo que espera.

El menor, que a los latines
prefería las doncellas
hermosas y no gustaba
de vestir por la cabeza,
colgó la sotana un día
y partió a lejanas tierras.
La madre lloró; y el padre
diole bendición y herencia.

IV
Alvargonzález ya tiene
la adusta frente arrugada;
por la barba le platea
la sombra azul de la cara.

Una mañana de otoño
salió solo de su casa;
no llevaba sus lebreles,
agudos canes de caza;
iba triste y pensativo
por la alameda dorada;
anduvo largo camino
y llegó a una fuente clara.

Echóse en la tierra; puso
sobre una piedra la manta,
y a la vera de la fuente
durmió al arrullo del agua.

Rustic covetousness
looks beyond death to inheritance;
what lies in the hand is not enjoyed
for desire of what is to come.

The youngest son, who preferred
pretty girls to studying Latin,
and did not like the idea
of wearing a shovel hat,
hung up his cassock one day
and left for foreign parts.
His mother wept; his father gave him
his blessing and his inheritance.

IV
By now Alvargonzález had
a stern face and a furrowed brow;
his beard silvered
the somber blue of his jaw.

One autumn morning
he went out alone from his house,
not taking his keen
hunting greyhounds along,
and sadly, thoughtfully, passed
through the golden poplar grove.
A long way he walked,
till he came to a clear spring.

He threw himself down; laid
his cloak under a stone;
and by the edge of the fountain
fell asleep to the water's murmuring.

El sueño

I

Y Alvargonzález veía,
como Jacob, una escala
que iba de la tierra al cielo,
y oyó una voz que le hablaba.
Mas las hadas hilanderas
entre las vedijas blancas
y vellones de oro han puesto
un mechón de negra lana.

II

Tres niños están jugando
a la puerta de su casa;
entre los mayores brinca
un cuervo de negras alas.
La mujer vigila, cose
y, a ratos, sonríe y canta.
—Hijos, ¿qué hacéis? —les pregunta.
Ellos se miran y callan.
—Subid al monte, hijos míos,
y antes que la noche caiga,
con un brazado de estepas
hacedme una buena llama.

III

Sobre el lar de Alvargonzález
está la leña apilada;
el mayor quiere encenderla,
pero no brota la llama.
—Padre, la hoguera no prende,
está la estepa mojada.

Su hermano viene a ayudarle
y arroja astillas y ramas
sobre los troncos de roble;
pero el rescoldo se apaga.
Acude el menor, y enciende,

The Dream

I

And Alvargonzález saw,
like Jacob, a ladder
reaching from earth to sky
and heard a voice that spoke.
But magical spinning beings
had put, between the white strands
and golden fleeces, a mesh
of black wool.

II

Three boys are playing
at his house door;
between the eldest hops
a black-winged crow.
The woman looks on, sews, sometimes
smiles and sings.
"What are you doing, my sons?" she asks.
They look at her and say nothing.
"Climb the hill, my sons,
and before it grows dark
make me a good fire with an armful
of rock-rose brush."

III

In the hearth of Alvargonzález
wood is piled;
the oldest boy wants to set it alight
but the flame won't catch.
"Father, the fire won't burn,
the kindling is wet."

His brother comes to help him,
scattering chips and twigs
on the oak logs;
but the embers die.
Then the youngest comes to the rescue

bajo la negra campana
de la cocina, una hoguera
que alumbra toda la casa.

IV

Alvargonzález levanta
en brazos al más pequeño
y en sus rodillas lo sienta:
—Tus manos hacen el fuego;
aunque el último naciste
tú eres en mi amor primero.

Los dos mayores se alejan
por los rincones del sueño.
Entre los dos fugitivos
reluce un hacha de hierro.

Aquella tarde

I

Sobre los campos desnudos,
la luna llena, manchada
de un arrebol purpurino,
enorme globo, asomaba.
Los hijos de Alvargonzález
silenciosos caminaban,
ya han visto al padre dormido
junto de la fuente clara.

II

Tiene el padre entre las cejas
un ceño que le aborrasca
el rostro, un tachón sombrío
como la huella de un hacha.
Soñando está con sus hijos,
que sus hijos lo apuñalan;
y cuando despierta mira
que es cierto lo que soñaba.

and lights, under the black
kitchen chimney, a blaze
that illumines the whole house.

IV
Alvargonzález lifts up
the smallest boy and sets him
on his knee. "Yours are the hands
that light the fire:
though you were born the last
you are first in my love."

The older sons recede
into the dream's distance.
Between their fugitive forms
shines the blade of an ax.

That Evening

I
Over the bare fields
the full moon rose,
a great globe, brindled
with reddish clouds.
The sons of Alvargonzález
came walking silently;
they had seen their father
asleep by the clear fountain.

II
Between his brows the father
wears a frown that clouds
his whole face, a dark shadow
like the mark of an ax.
In dream he is with his sons,
he dreams that his sons have stabbed him;
when he awakes he sees
that all is true that he dreamed.

III

A la vera de la fuente
quedó Alvargonzález muerto.
Tiene cuatro puñaladas
entre el costado y el pecho,
por donde la sangre brota,
más un hachazo en el cuello.
Cuenta la hazaña del campo
el agua clara corriendo,
mientras los dos asesinos
huyen hacia los hayedos.
Hasta la Laguna Negra,
bajo las fuentes del Duero,
llevan el muerto, dejando
detrás un rastro sangriento;
y en la laguna sin fondo,
que guarda bien los secretos,
con una piedra amarrada
a los pies, tumba le dieron.

IV

Se encontró junto a la fuente
la manta de Alvargonzález,
y, camino del hayedo,
se vio un reguero de sangre.
Nadie de la aldea ha osado
a la laguna acercarse,
y el sondarla inútil fuera,
que es la laguna insondable.
Un buhonero, que cruzaba
aquellas tierras errante,
fue en Dauria acusado, preso
y muerto en garrote infame.

V

Pasados algunos meses,
la madre murió de pena.
Los que muerta la encontraron
dicen que las manos yertas
sobre su rostro tenía,
oculto el rostro con ellas.

III

At the edge of the fountain
Alvargonzález lies dead.
Blood streams from four knife wounds
between his side and his breast
and an ax blow on the throat.
The clear water ripples by,
recounting the rustic exploit,
while the two murderers
make off toward the beechwoods.
To Black Lake, below
the springs of the River Duero,
they drag the corpse,
leaving a bloody trail;
and in the bottomless lake,
which guards its secrets well,
give him his burial,
a rock tied to his feet.

IV

Alvargonzález's cloak was found
close to the fountain;
and on the beechwoods path
drops of blood were noticed.
No one in the village
dared to approach Black Lake,
and dragging it was useless
for it was fathomless.
A peddler, wandering across those parts,
was accused in Dauria, taken,
and put to death by the infamous garrote.

V

Some months later the mother
died of grief.
Those who found her dead
say she held her hands stiffly
before her face,
hiding her face with them.

VI

Los hijos de Alvargonzález
ya tienen majada y huerta,
campos de trigo y centeno
y prados de fina hierba;
en el olmo viejo, hendido
por el rayo, la colmena,
dos yuntas para el arado,
un mastín y mil ovejas.

Otros días

I

Ya están las zarzas floridas
y los ciruelos blanquean;
ya las abejas doradas
liban para sus colmenas,
y en los nidos que coronan
las torres de las iglesias,
asoman los garabatos
ganchudos de las cigüeñas.
Ya los olmos del camino
y chopos de las riberas
de los arroyos, que buscan
al padre Duero, verdean.
El cielo está azul, los montes
sin nieve son de violeta.
La tierra de Alvargonzález
se colmará de riqueza;
muerto está quien la ha labrado,
mas no le cubre la tierra.

II

La hermosa tierra de España,
adusta, fina y guerrera
Castilla, de largos ríos,
tiene un puñado de sierras
entre Soria y Burgos como
reductos de fortaleza,
como yelmos crestonados,
y Urbión es una cimera.

VI
The sons of Alvargonzález
now possessed a sheepfold, an orchard,
fields of wheat and rye,
pastures of fine grass;
in the old elm tree cracked by lightning,
a wild bees' nest;
two teams for plowing,
a mastiff and a thousand sheep.

Other Days

I
The blackberries are in flower
and the cherry trees are
white with blossom; already
golden bees are gathering
honey for their hives,
and in the nests crowning
the church towers appear
the hooklike beaks of storks.
Already the roadside elms
and the poplars by the rivers and streams, that seek
Father Duero, grow green.
The sky is blue, the snowless
mountains are violet.
The fields of Alvargonzález
will be heaped up with riches;
he who tilled them is dead,
but earth does not cover him.

II
The beautiful heart of Spain,
austere, refined, martial
Castile, with its wide rivers,
has a handful of mountains that lie
between Burgos and Soria like the
redoubts of a fortress;
they resemble crested helmets.
Urbión is one of these crests.

III

Los hijos de Alvargonzález,
por una empinada senda,
para tomar el camino
de Salduero a Covaleda,
cabalgan en pardas mulas,
bajo el pinar de Vinuesa.
Van en busca de ganado
con que volver a su aldea,
y por tierra de pinares
larga jornada comienzan.
Van Duero arriba, dejando
atrás los arcos de piedra
del puente y el caserío
de la ociosa y opulenta
villa de indianos. El río,
al fondo del valle, suena,
y de las cabalgaduras
los cascos baten las piedras.
A la otra orilla del Duero
canta una voz lastimera:
"La tierra de Alvargonzález
se colmará de riqueza,
y el que la tierra ha labrado
no duerme bajo la tierra".

IV

Llegados son a un paraje
en donde el pinar se espesa,
y el mayor, que abre la marcha,
su parda mula espolea,
diciendo: —Démonos prisa;
porque son más de dos leguas
de pinar y hay que apurarlas
antes que la noche venga.

Dos hijos del campo, hechos
a quebradas y asperezas,
porque recuerdan un día
la tarde en el monte tiemblan.
Allá en lo espeso del bosque

III

The sons of Alvargonzález, on gray mules,
are riding along a pinewoods path
below the forest of Vinuesa
toward the road that leads from
Salduero to Covaleda.
They have set out to buy cattle
and return with them to the village;
a long day's journey through the forest
lies before them.
They pass above the Duero, leaving
behind them the stone-arched
bridge, and the hunting lodge
of a sumptuous, useless villa belonging
to a family returned rich from America.
The river murmurs, deep in its valley;
the mule's hoofs rattle against stones.
From across the river
a voice is plaintively singing:
"The fields of Alvargonzález
will be filled to the brim with riches,
and he who tilled the fields
docs not slccp in the earth."

IV

They have come to a place
where the pines grow thicker,
and the eldest son, who goes first,
spurs his mule, saying,
"Let us make haste;
there's more than two leagues
of pinewoods; we have to get through
before dark."

Two sons of the open fields,
here they feel crushed and nervous;
remembering a certain day,
the fall of night on the hill,
they tremble.
There in the thick of the forest

otra vez la copla suena:
"La tierra de Alvargonzález
se colmará de riqueza,
y el que la tierra ha labrado
no duerme bajo la tierra".

V

Desde Salduero el camino
va al hilo de la ribera;
a ambas márgenes del río
el pinar crece y se eleva,
y las rocas se aborrascan,
al par que el valle se estrecha.
Los fuertes pinos del bosque
con sus copas gigantescas,
y sus desnudas raíces
amarradas a las piedras;
los de troncos plateados
cuyas frondas azulean,
pinos jóvenes; los viejos,
cubiertos de blanca lepra,
musgos y líquenes canos
que el grueso tronco rodean,
colman el valle y se pierden
rebasando ambas laderas.
Juan, el mayor, dice: —Hermano,
si Blas Antonio apacienta
cerca de Urbión su vacada,
largo camino nos queda.
—Cuanto hacia Urbión alarguemos
se puede acortar de vuelta,
tomando por el atajo,
hacia la Laguna Negra,
y bajando por el puerto
de Santa Inés a Vinuesa.
—Mala tierra y peor camino.
Te juro que no quisiera
verlos otra vez. Cerremos
los tratos en Covaleda;
hagamos noche, y, al alba,

again the singing sounds:
"The fields of Alvargonzález
will be heaped to the brim with riches,
and he who tilled the earth
does not sleep in the earth."

V

From Salduero on, the road
follows the thread of the river;
on both banks of the stream
thick pinewoods tower,
and the rocks look menacing
to the pair who file up the valley.
Mighty forest pines
with giant summits and
naked roots lashed to the rocks;
young pines with silvery
stems and bluish fronds;
and old ones, covered
with leprous white,
mosses and hoary lichens girdling
their thick trunks;
they fill the valley and lose themselves
in the steep slopes on both sides.
Juan, the eldest, speaks: "Brother,
if Blas Antonio has his herds grazing
near Urbión, we still have
a long way to go."
"After we reach Urbión
we can shorten the way back,
taking the short cut by Black Lake
and coming down
by the Santa Inés pass at Vinuesa."
"Bad country and a worse road.
I can tell you, I don't want to
see it again. We'll
make our deal in
Covaleda, spend the night there,

volvámonos a la aldea
por este valle, que a veces
quien piensa atajar rodea.
Cerca del río cabalgan
los hermanos y contemplan
cómo el bosque centenario,
al par que avanzan, aumenta,
y la roqueda del monte
el horizonte les cierra.
El agua, que va saltando,
parece que canta o cuenta:
"La tierra de Alvargonzález
se colmará de riqueza,
y el que la tierra ha labrado
no duerme bajo la tierra".

Castigo

I

Aunque la codicia tiene
redil que encierre la oveja,
trojes que guarden el trigo,
bolsas para la moneda,
y garras, no tiene manos
que sepan labrar la tierra.
Así, a un año de abundancia
siguió un año de pobreza.

II

En los sembrados crecieron
las amapolas sangrientas;
pudrió el tizón las espigas
de trigales y de avenas;
hielos tardíos mataron
en flor la fruta en la huerta,
y una mala hechicería
hizo enfermar las ovejas.

and at daybreak we can go back
this way. Sometimes
short cuts turn out to be long."
Close to the river
ride the brothers and watch
how the ancient forest
seems to grow bigger as they advance,
and the steep rocks shut them in.
The leaping water
seems to speak or to sing:
"The fields of Alvargonzález
will be heaped up with riches,
and he who tilled the fields
does not sleep in the earth."

Punishment

I

Although covetousness
owns the sheepfold and the sheep in it,
barns for the grain,
purses for the money,
and though it has
clutching fingers, it does not have
hands that know well how to
care for the land.
And so, on a year of plenty
followed a year of dearth.

II

Blood-red poppies
flourished in the fields,
blight rotted the ears of
wheat and oats;
late frosts
killed off the budding bloom on the
fruit trees,
and some evil spell
sickened the sheep.

A los dos Alvargonzález
maldijo Dios en sus tierras,
y al año pobre siguieron
largos años de miseria.

III
Es una noche de invierno.
Cae la nieve en remolinos.
Los Alvargonzález velan
un fuego casi extinguido.
El pensamiento amarrado
tienen a un recuerdo mismo,
y en las ascuas mortecinas
del hogar los ojos fijos.
No tienen leña ni sueño.
Larga es la noche y el frío
arrecia. Un candil humea
en el muro ennegrecido.
El aire agita la llama,
que pone un fulgor rojizo
sobre las dos pensativas
testas de los asesinos.
El mayor de Alvargonzález,
lanzando un ronco suspiro,
rompe el silencio, exclamando:
—Hermano, ¡qué mal hicimos!
El viento la puerta bate,
hace temblar el postigo,
y suena en la chimenea
con hueco y largo bramido.
Después el silencio vuelve,
y a intervalos el pabilo
del candil chisporrotea
en el aire aterecido.
El segundón dijo:—¡Hermano,
demos lo viejo al olvido!

El viajero

I
Es una noche de invierno.
Azota el viento las ramas
de los álamos. La nieve
ha puesto la tierra blanca.

The Alvargonzález brothers
were cursed by God in their land;
after the year of dearth there followed
long years of poverty.

III

   A winter night.
Snow falls in eddies.
The brothers are sitting up
by a half-extinguished fire.
Their ingrained thoughts
dwell on the same memory;
both of them fix their gaze
on the dying embers in the hearth.
Both firewood and sleep are lacking.
The night is long, and the cold
grows more intense. A candle
smokes by the blackened wall.
The draft stirs its flame
which sheds a sallow glow
on the murderers' brooding faces.
The eldest Alvargonzález,
heaving a deep sigh, breaks
the silence, exclaiming:
"Brother, it was an evil thing we did!"
The wind, howling, batters the door,
shaking the wicket gate, and
wails in the chimney
a long and hollow sound.
Then the silence resumes,
and from time to time the candle
gives off sparks in the
frosty air.
The other speaks: "Brother,
let us forget the old man!"

The Traveler

I

   A winter night. The wind
whips the poplar branches.
Snow has whitened the earth.

Bajo la nevada, un hombre
por el camino cabalga;
va cubierto hasta los ojos,
embozado en negra capa.
Entrando en la aldea, busca
de Alvargonzález la casa,
y ante su puerta llegado,
sin echar pie a tierra, llama.

II
Los dos hermanos oyeron
una aldabada a la puerta,
y de una cabalgadura
los cascos sobre las piedras.
Ambos los ojos alzaron
llenos de espanto y sorpresa.
—¿Quién es? Responda —gritaron.
—Miguel —respondieron fuera.
Era la voz del viajero
que partió a lejanas tierras.

III
Abierto el portón, entróse
a caballo el caballero
y echó pie a tierra. Venía
todo de nieve cubierto.
En brazos de sus hermanos
lloró algún rato en silencio.
Después dio el caballo al uno,
al otro, capa y sombrero,
y en la estancia campesina
buscó el arrimo del fuego.

IV
El menor de los hermanos,
que niño y aventurero
fue más allá de los mares
y hoy torna indiano opulento,
vestía con negro traje

A man is riding
along the snowy road, muffled
up to the eyes in a black cloak.
Entering the village, he looks for the
Alvargonzález house, and
arriving before its gate, without
dismounting, he knocks.

II
The two brothers hear
the rapping at the gate,
the sound of hoofs on the stones.
Both of them leap to their feet, startled and fearful.
"Who is it? Answer!" they cry.
"Miguel," calls a voice outside —
the voice of the wanderer,
he who had gone
away to far countries.

III
The gate was opened, the rider
entered on horseback
and jumped to the ground.
He was white with snow.
In the arms of his brothers
he wept for a while in silence.
Then, giving his horse in charge to one,
his hat and cloak to the other,
he entered the farmhouse, seeking
the warmth of the fire.

IV
The youngest brother,
who had crossed the seas as an adventurous boy
and was now returned a rich "Indian,"*
was dressed in a black suit

---

*i.e., one who has returned from a long sojourn in America.

de peludo terciopelo,
ajustado a la cintura
con ancho cinto de cuero.
Gruesa cadena formaba
un bucle de oro en su pecho.

Era un hombre alto y robusto
con ojos grandes y negros
llenos de melancolía;
la tez de color moreno,
y sobre la frente comba
enmarañados cabellos;
el hijo que saca porte
señor de padre labriego,
a quien fortuna le debe
amor, poder y dinero.
De los tres Alvargonzález
era Miguel el más bello;
porque al mayor afeaba
el muy poblado entrecejo
bajo la frente mezquina,
y al segundo, los inquietos
ojos que mirar no saben
de frente, torvos y fieros.

V
Los tres hermanos contemplan
el triste hogar en silencio;
y con la noche cerrada
arrecia el frío y el viento.
—Hermanos, ¿no tenéis leña?
—dice Miguel.
        —No tenemos
—responde el mayor.
        Un hombre,
milagrosamente, ha abierto
la gruesa puerta cerrada
con doble barra de hierro.

of deep velvet, held at the waist
by a broad leather belt. A thick chain
formed a loop of gold on his breast.

A tall robust man
with large dark eyes full of melancholy;
dark complexioned,
with chestnut curls falling about his forehead.
This son resembled, in lordly bearing,
his peasant father:
to which good fortune he owed
both love, and power, and money.
Of the three brothers
Miguel was the handsomest,
for the eldest was spoiled by
the frowning lines between his eyes
under a low forehead,
and the second, by restless eyes
that would not look straight before them,
fierce and sullen eyes.

                              V
The three brothers silently contemplate
the cheerless hearth;
as night shuts in about them
the wind and cold sharpen.
"Have you no wood, my brothers?"
asks Miguel.
                    "None,"
answers the eldest.
                    Miraculously,
a man has opened
the heavy door
closed with its iron double bolt.

El hombre que ha entrado tiene
el rostro del padre muerto.
Un halo de luz dorada
orla sus blancos cabellos.
Lleva un haz de leña al hombro
y empuña un hacha de hierro.

El indiano

I
De aquellos campos malditos,
Miguel a sus dos hermanos
compró una parte, que mucho
caudal de América trajo,
y aun en tierra mala, el oro
luce mejor que enterrado,
y más en mano de pobres
que oculto en orza de barro.

Diose a trabajar la tierra
con fe y tesón el indiano,
y a laborar los mayores
sus pegujales tornaron.

Ya con macizas espigas,
preñadas de rubios granos,
a los campos de Miguel
tornó el fecundo verano;
y ya de aldea en aldea
se cuenta como un milagro
que los asesinos tienen
la maldición en sus campos.

Ya el pueblo canta una copla
que narra el crimen pasado:
"A la orilla de la fuente
lo asesinaron.
¡Qué mala muerte le dieron
los hijos malos!
En la laguna sin fondo
al padre muerto arrojaron.
No duerme bajo la tierra
el que la tierra ha labrado."

And this man who has entered
has the face of their dead father.
A halo of golden light surrounds
his white head.
He carries a bundle of wood on his shoulder
and grips an iron ax.

The Indian

I
Miguel bought from his brothers
part of the accursed fields, for he had brought
a fortune back from America,
and money is better put to use
even on bad land, than buried,
and better in the hands of the poor
than hidden in a crock.

The Indian gave himself up to working the land
with faith and tenacity;
the older brothers continued
to toil in their small fields.

And soon, with firm ears of ripening
wheat, summer returned
to Miguel's fields; and from village to village
it was whispered—as of a miracle—
that the murderers' fields were cursed indeed.

People began to sing
a ballad that told of the crime:
"By the edge of the fountain
they killed him.
An evil death
his sons gave him.
They threw their father
into the bottomless lake.
He who tilled the earth
does not sleep in the earth."

II

Miguel, con sus dos lebreles
y armado de su escopeta,
hacia el azul de los montes,
en una tarde serena,
caminaba entre los verdes
chopos de la carretera,
y oyó una voz que cantaba:
"No tiene tumba en la tierra.
Entre los pinos del valle
del Revinuesa,
al padre muerto llevaron
hasta la Laguna Negra".

La casa

I

La casa de Alvargonzález
era una casona vieja,
con cuatro estrechas ventanas,
separada de la aldea
cien pasos, y entre dos olmos
que, gigantes centinelas,
sombra le dan en verano,
y en el otoño hojas secas.

Es casa de labradores,
gente aunque rica plebeya,
donde el hogar humeante
con sus escaños de piedra
se ven sin entrar, si tiene
abierta al campo la puerta.
Al arrimo del rescoldo
del hogar borbollonean
dos pucherillos de barro
que a dos familias sustentan.

A diestra mano, la cuadra
y el corral; a la siniestra,
huerto y abejar, y, al fondo,

II
Miguel, with his two greyhounds,
and armed with a shotgun,
went up one serene evening
between the highway poplars
toward the blue of the hills,
and he heard a voice singing:
"He has no grave in the earth.
Among the pines
of the valley of Revinuesa
they took their dead father,
down to Black Lake."

The House

1
The Alvargonzález house
was large and old, with four
narrow windows; it stood
a hundred paces from the village
between two elms, gigantic
sentinels that gave it shade
in summer, and in the fall
scattered their dry leaves over it.

In peasants' houses—the houses
of people still plebeian, though wealthy—
where the stone inglenooks,
the smoking hearth,
can be seen without entering, the door
stands open to the fields.
Safe in the ashes
bubble the earthenware pots—enough
to feed two families.

To the right, the yard
and the corral; to the left,
orchard and beehives; and at the back

una gastada escalera,
que va a las habitaciones,
partidas en dos viviendas.

Los Alvargonzález moran
con sus mujeres en ellas.
A ambas parejas, que hubieron,
sin que lograrse pudieran,
dos hijos, sobrado espacio
les da la casa paterna.

En una estancia que tiene
luz al huerto, hay una mesa
con gruesa tabla de roble,
dos sillones de vaqueta;
colgado en el muro, un negro
ábaco de enormes cuentas,
y unas espuelas mohosas
sobre un arcón de madera.

Era una estancia olvidada
donde hoy Miguel se aposenta.
Y era allí donde los padres
veían en primavera
el huerto en flor, y en el cielo
de mayo, azul, la cigüeña
—cuando las rosas se abren
y los zarzales blanquean—
que enseñaba a sus hijuelos
a usar de las alas lentas.

Y en las noches del verano,
cuando la calor desvela,
desde la ventana al dulce
ruiseñor cantar oyeran.

Fue allí donde Alvargonzález,
del orgullo de su huerta

a worn staircase, leading
to the living quarters, divided
into two dwellings.

There live the Alvargonzález brothers
and their wives. There was space
and to spare, in the paternal house,
for both couples, to each of which
had been born two sons—in whom
they took no joy.

In a room that gives
onto the orchard, there is a massive
oak table and two
leather armchairs;
hung on the wall
an abacus with huge
counters, and some rusty spurs
over a wooden chest.

In this forgotten parlor
Miguel settled himself.
From this room in springtime
his parents had watched
the orchard in bloom, and the blue
sky of May, and the stork—
when roses open and brambles
are white—teaching
its young to use their
clumsy wings.

And on summer nights
when the heat kept them awake,
from this window they had heard
the tender song of the nightingales.

Here it was that Alvargonzález,
proud of his orchard

y del amor de los suyos,
sacó sueños de grandeza.

   Cuando en brazos de la madre
vio la figura risueña
del primer hijo, bruñida
de rubio sol la cabeza,
del niño que levantaba
las codiciosas, pequeñas
manos a las rojas guindas
y a las moradas ciruelas,
oh, aquella tarde de otoño
dorada, plácida y buena,
él pensó que ser podría
feliz el hombre en la tierra.

   Hoy canta el pueblo una copla
que va de aldea en aldea:
"¡Oh casa de Alvargonzález,
qué malos días te esperan;
casa de los asesinos,
que nadie llame a tu puerta!"

                 II
   Es una tarde de otoño.
En la alameda dorada
no quedan ya ruiseñores;
enmudeció la cigarra.
Las últimas golondrinas,
que no emprendieron la marcha,
morirán, y las cigüeñas
de sus nidos de retamas,
en torres y campanarios,
huyeron.
              Sobre la casa
de Alvargonzález, los olmos
sus hojas que el viento arranca
van dejando. Todavía
las tres redondas acacias,
en el atrio de la iglesia,
conservan verdes sus ramas,
y las castañas de Indias
a intervalos se desgajan

and full of love for his sons,
had dreamed dreams of grandeur.

When he watched the golden-brown
sunburned face of his firstborn
laughing in his mother's arms,
lifting his little greedy hands for
red wild cherries and black plums;
or on some golden, beneficent, placid
afternoon in autumn: he thought
life could be filled with joy
for man on earth.

Today the people are singing a song
that spreads from village to village:
"Oh, house of Alvargonzález,
what evil days await you;
Oh, house of the murderers,
may no one knock at your door!"

II
It is an autumn evening.
In the tawny poplar grove
no nightingales remain;
the cicadas are silenced.
The last swallows, who
have not set out on their journey,
will die, and the storks are deserting
their nests of furze
on towers and belfries.
           The elms by the house
of Alvargonzález let fall their leaves,
torn by the wind. The three
rounded acacia trees in the churchyard
still keep their green
branches; and from the horse chestnut
at intervals twigs snap off,

cubiertas de sus erizos;
tiene el rosal rosas grana
otra vez, y en las praderas
brilla la alegre otoñada.

En laderas y en alcores,
en ribazos y cañadas,
el verde nuevo y la hierba,
aún del estío quemada,
alternan; los serrijones
pelados, las lomas calvas,
se coronan de plomizas
nubes apelotonadas;
y bajo el pinar gigante,
entre las marchitas zarzas
y amarillentos helechos,
corren las crecidas aguas
a engrosar el padre río
por canchales y barrancas.

Abunda en la tierra un gris
de plomo y azul de plata,
con manchas de roja herrumbre,
todo envuelto en luz violada.

¡Oh tierras de Alvargonzález,
en el corazón de España,
tierras pobres, tierras tristes,
tan tristes que tienen alma!

Páramo que cruza el lobo
aullando a la luna clara
de bosque a bosque, baldíos
llenos de peñas rodadas,
donde roída de buitres
brilla una osamenta blanca;
pobres campos solitarios
sin caminos ni posadas,
¡oh pobres campos malditos,
pobres campos de mi patria!

covered with burrs;
the rose tree once more
bears crimson roses, and in the fields
the cheerful grass is gleaming.

On ridges and hills,
on banks and dells, an alternation
of fresh green, and grass scorched by the
summer sun. The austere
mountain ranges and treeless hills
crown themselves with dark
gray puff balls of cloud;
and below the great pinewoods, between
withered berries and ferns that are turning yellow,
the rising waters run to increase
the father river, down rocky slopes and deep clefts.

The land abounds in leaden
grays and silvery blues, stained
with rusty reds, all
enveloped in a mauve light.

Oh, fields of Alvargonzález,
fields in the heart of Spain,
so sad that you have attained
a soul through your sadness.

Cold highlands the wolf crosses
howling from thicket to thicket
at the shining moon, wastes
full of round boulders
where, gnawed by vultures, a white
skeleton shines; poor country
without roads or inns,
ah, poor ill-fated fields,
poor fields of my homeland!

La tierra

I

Una mañana de otoño,
cuando la tierra se labra,
Juan y el indiano aparejan
las dos yuntas de la casa.
Martín se quedó en el huerto
arrancando hierbas malas.

II

Una mañana de otoño,
cuando los campos se aran,
sobre un otero, que tiene
el cielo de la mañana
por fondo, la parda yunta
de Juan lentamente avanza.

Cardos, lampazos y abrojos,
avena loca y cizaña
llenan la tierra maldita,
tenaz a pico y a escarda.

Del corvo arado de roble
la hundida reja trabaja
con vano esfuerzo; parece
que al par que hiende la entraña
del campo y hace camino,
se cierra otra vez la zanja.

"Cuando el asesino labre
será su labor pesada;
antes que un surco en la tierra,
tendrá una arruga en su cara."

III

Martín, que estaba en la huerta
cavando, sobre su azada
quedó apoyado un momento;
frío sudor le bañaba
el rostro.

The Land

I

One autumn morning
when the land was ready for plowing,
Juan and the Indian harnessed
the two teams.
Martín remained in the orchard
hoeing out weeds.

II

An autumn morning; they are plowing.
Against a knoll that has the
morning sky for background,
Juan's gray team
slowly draws forward.

Thistles, burdocks, thorns,
darnel and wild oats
crowd the afflicted field,
obstinately opposed to pick and hoe.

The plow of oak and its curving plowshare
work with vain force; it seems
as if the furrows close up again
behind the team as it cleaves
the bowels of the earth.

"When a murderer works,
his work shall be hard;
before a furrow in earth,
a furrow will show on his face."

III

Martín, who was digging
in the orchard, leaned
on his spade for a moment;
cold sweat
bathed his face.

    Por el oriente,
la luna llena, manchada
de un arrebol purpurino,
lucía tras de la tapia
del huerto.
    Martín tenía
la sangre de horror helada.
La azada que hundió en la tierra
teñida de sangre estaba.

       IV
   En la tierra en que ha nacido
supo afincar el indiano;
por mujer a una doncella
rica y hermosa ha tomado.

   La hacienda de Alvargonzález
ya es suya, que sus hermanos
todo le vendieron: casa,
huerto, colmenar y campo.

     Los asesinos

       I
   Juan y Martín, los mayores
de Alvargonzález, un día
pesada marcha emprendieron
con el alba, Duero arriba.

   La estrella de la mañana
en el alto azul ardía.
Se iba tiñendo de rosa
la espesa y blanca neblina
de los valles y barrancos,
y algunas nubes plomizas
a Urbión, donde el Duero nace,
como un turbante ponían.

   Se acercaban a la fuente.
El agua clara corría,
sonando cual si contara

In the east,
the full moon, brindled
with clouds of purplish red,
shone over the orchard wall.
Martín chilled
in horror: the spade
with which he was digging was
stained with blood.

IV
The Indian understood how to
acquire property in the land of his birth;
for wife he has taken
a rich and beautiful girl.

The Alvargonzález farm
now is his own, for his brothers
have sold him everything: house,
orchard, beehives and land.

The Murderers

I
Juan and Martín, the older
brothers, one day
set out at dawn for a
hard journey, up the
River Ducro.

The morning star
burned in the high blue.
The thick white mist in
ravines and valleys was tinted
rose, and Urbión,
where the Duero is born,
wore a turban of dark clouds.

They drew near to the spring.
The clear water gushed out,
sounding as if it were telling

una vieja historia, dicha
mil veces y que tuviera
mil veces que repetirla.

Agua que corre en el campo
dice en su monotonía:
Yo sé el crimen: ¿no es un crimen
cerca del agua, la vida?

Al pasar los dos hermanos
relataba el agua limpia:
"A la vera de la fuente
Alvargonzález dormía".

II
—Anoche, cuando volvía
a casa —Juan a su hermano
dijo—, a la luz de la luna
era la huerta un milagro.

Lejos, entre los rosales,
divisé un hombre inclinado
hacia la tierra; brillaba
una hoz de plata en su mano.

Después irguióse y, volviendo
el rostro, dio algunos pasos
por el huerto, sin mirarme,
y a poco lo vi encorvado
otra vez sobre la tierra.
Tenía el cabello blanco.
La luna llena brillaba,
y era la huerta un milagro.

III
Pasado habían el puerto
de Santa Inés, ya mediada
la tarde, una tarde triste
de noviembre, fría y parda.
Hacia la Laguna Negra
silenciosos caminaban.

an old tale, told
a thousand times already,
and which it would tell
thousands of times again.

The water that flows through the fields
repeats monotonously:
"I know the crime; is not life,
near my waters, a crime?"

And as it flowed past the brothers
the clear water was saying:
"By the edge of the fountain
Alvargonzález slept."

II

"Last night, when he came back
to the house," Juan said
to his brother, "in the moonlight,
in the orchard, that was
a miracle.

"In the distance, between the rosebushes,
I made out a man
leaning toward the ground.
A silver sickle
was shining in his hand.

Then he stood straight, and,
turning his head, he
took a few steps toward the orchard, without
looking at me, and after a moment
I saw him bend to the ground again.
His hair was white.
The full moon was shining
and in the orchard a miracle happened."

III

They have gone through the pass
Of Santa Inés; the afternoon is advanced,
a sad November afternoon,
cold and gray.
They walk on silently toward Black Lake.

IV
Cuando la tarde caía,
entre las vetustas hayas
y los pinos centenarios,
un rojo sol se filtraba.

Era un paraje de bosque
y peñas aborrascadas;
aquí bocas que bostezan
o monstruos de fieras garras;
allí una informe joroba,
allá una grotesca panza,
torvos hocicos de fieras
y dentaduras melladas,
rocas y rocas, y troncos
y troncos, ramas y ramas.
En el hondón del barranco
la noche, el miedo y el agua.

V
Un lobo surgió, sus ojos
lucían como dos ascuas.
Era la noche, una noche
húmeda, oscura y cerrada.

Los dos hermanos quisieron
volver. La selva ululaba.
Cien ojos fieros ardían
en la selva, a sus espaldas.

VI
Llegaron los asesinos
hasta la Laguna Negra,
agua transparente y muda
que enorme muro de piedra,
donde los buitres anidan
y el eco duerme, rodea;
agua clara donde beben
las águilas de la sierra,
donde el jabalí del monte
y el ciervo y el corzo abrevan;
agua pura y silenciosa
que copia cosas eternas;

IV
When evening fell
the red sun filtered
between ancient beeches
and hoary pines.

It was a thickly wooded place
of grim rocks;
here gaping mouths appeared
or monsters with thick claws,
there a deformed hump, a
grotesque belly;
cruel snouts, toothless jaws,
rock after rock, trunk
after trunk, branch after
branch. And in the depths
of the gorge night,
fear, the water.

V
A wolf came forth, his eyes
glowed, two live coals.
It was night, a damp, dark
and close-encompassing night.

The two brothers would have liked
to turn back. The wild woods howled.
A hundred savage eyes burned
from among the trees on either hand.

VI
The murderers were come
to Black Lake,
the transparent waters,
mute as a great
stone wall, where vultures nest
and echo sleeps, lay before them;
clear water where mountain eagles
drink, and the wild boar,
the stag and the fallow deer;
water silent and pure
that mirrors eternal things;

agua impasible que guarda
en su seno las estrellas.
¡Padre! gritaron; al fondo
de la laguna serena
cayeron, y el eco ¡padre!
repitió de peña en peña.

Caminante, son tus huellas . . .

Caminante, son tus huellas
el camino, y nada más;
caminante, no hay camino,
se hace camino al andar.
Al andar se hace camino,
y al volver la vista atrás
se ve la senda que nunca
se ha de volver a pisar.
Caminante, no hay camino,
sino estelas en la mar.

Bueno es saber que los vasos . . .

Bueno es saber que lo vasos
nos sirven para beber;
lo malo es que no sabemos
para qué sirve la sed.

Una noche de verano . . .

Una noche de verano,
en la playa de Sanlúcar,
oí una voz que cantaba:
Antes que salga la luna.

Antes que salga la luna,
a la vera de la mar;
dos palabritas a solas
contigo tengo de hablar.

intractable water that guards
the stars in its breast.
"Father!" they cried; and plunged
into the depths of the calm lake.
And echo repeated, "Father!
Father!" from rock to rock.

—DENISE LEVERTOV

Walker, It Is Your Footsteps . . .

   Walker, it is your footsteps
that are the road, no more;
walker, there is no road,
the road is made by walking.
Walking makes the road,
and on looking back
the path is seen that never
will be again the track.
Walker, there is no road,
merely wakes of boats in the sea.

—KATE FLORES

The Good Thing Is, We Know . . .

   The good thing is, we know
That glasses are for drinking;
The bad thing is, we don't
Know what our thirst is for.

—WILLIAM M. DAVIS

A Summer's Night . . .

   A summer's night
on the beach of Sanlúcar,
I heard a voice that sang,
while the moon was far.

   While the moon was far,
on the edge of the sea,
a few words alone
you must speak with me.

¡Playa de Sanlúcar,
noche de verano,
copla solitaria
junto al mar amargo!

¡A la orillita del agua,
por donde nadie nos vea,
antes que la luna salga!

¿Quién puso, entre las rocas de ceniza . . . ?

¿Quién puso, entre las rocas de ceniza,
para la miel del sueño,
esas retamas de oro
y esas azules flores del romero?
la sierra de violeta
y, en el poniente, el azafrán del cielo,
¿quién ha pintado? ¡El abejar, la ermita,
el tajo sobre el río, el sempiterno
rodar del agua entre las hondas peñas,
y el rubio verde de los campos nuevos,
y todo, hasta la tierra blanca y rosa
al pie de los almendros!

La primavera ha venido . . .

La primavera ha venido.
Nadie sabe cómo ha sido.

El ojo que ves no es . . .

El ojo que ves no es
ojo porque tú lo veas,
es ojo porque te ve.

Rosa de fuego

Tejidos sois de primavera, amantes,
de tierra y agua y viento y sol tejidos.
La sierra en vuestros pechos jadeantes,
en los ojos los campos florecidos,

Sanlúcar beach,
summer night,
a lonely song
by the bitter sea.

On the little strand
with none to see
while the moon is far.

—JAMES DUFFY

Who Placed, Amidst the Tracts of Ash . . . ?

Who placed, amidst the tracts of ash,
For the honey of the dream,
That sedge of gold
And those rosemary blossoms of blue?
By whom was the violet mountain range
Painted and, in the dusk,
The saffron sky? The beehive, the hermitage,
The cleft above the river, the everlasting
Rushing of the waters amidst the deep rocks,
The pale green of the new meadows,
And all, down to the earth white and rose
At the foot of the almond trees!

—KATE FLORES

Spring Has Come

Spring has come.
No one knows how it was done.

—KATE FLORES

The Eye You See Isn't . . .

The eye you see isn't
An eye because you see it;
It's an eye because it sees you.

—WILLIAM M. DAVIS

Rose of Fire

Woven you are of the spring, lovers,
Of earth and water and wind and sun.
With the mountains heaving in your breasts
And in your eyes the fields in flower,

pasead vuestra mutua primavera,
y aun bebed sin temor la dulce leche
que os brinda hoy la lúbrica pantera,
antes que, torva, en el camino aceche.

Caminad, cuando el eje del planeta
se vence hacia el solsticio de verano,
verde el almendro y mustia la violeta,

cerca la sed y el hontanar cercano,
hacia la tarde del amor, completa,
con la rosa de fuego, en vuestra mano.

La plaza tiene una torre . . .

La plaza tiene una torre,
la torre tiene un balcón,
el balcón tiene una dama,
la dama una blanca flor.
Ha pasado un caballero
—¡quién sabe por qué pasó!—,
y se ha llevado la plaza,
con su torre y su balcón,
con su balcón y su dama,
su dama y su blanca flor.

Siesta
En memoria de Abel Martín

Mientras traza su curva el pez de fuego,
junto al ciprés, bajo el supremo añil,
y vuela en blanda piedra el niño ciego,
y en el olmo la copla de marfil
de la verde cigarra late y suena,
honremos al Señor
—la negra estampa de su mano buena—
que ha dictado el silencio en el clamor.

Al Dios de la distancia y de la ausencia,
del áncora en el mar, la plena mar . . .
Él nos libra del mundo —omnipresencia—,
nos abre senda para caminar.

Promenade your mutual spring,
And even drink of the sweet milk unafraid
The lustful panther proffers you today,
Before, ferocious, he stalks the way.

Proceed, when the axis of the planet
Toward the summer solstice slants—
Withered the violet and the almond tree green,

Close to thirst and the fount close by
Whole toward the afternoon of love,
With the rose of fire in your hand.

—KATE FLORES

The Plaza Has a Tower . . .

The plaza has a tower,
The tower has a balcony,
The balcony has a lady,
The lady a white flower.
A gentleman went by
—Who knows why!—
And he took away the plaza,
With its tower and its balcony,
With its balcony and its lady,
Its lady and her white flower.

—ANGEL FLORES

Siesta

In memoriam: Abel Martín

While the fish of fire curves its arc
Beside the cypress, under the ultimate aniline,
And the blind boy flees to soft stone,
And in the elm the marble verse
Of the green cicada throbs and resounds,
Let us honor the Lord—
The black impress of His benign hand—,
Who in the clamor ordered silence.

God of distance and of absence,
Anchor in the seas, the high seas . . .
He frees us from the world—omnipresence—,
And gives us a path in which to walk.

Con la copa de sombra bien colmada,
con este nunca lleno corazón,
honremos al Señor que hizo la Nada
y ha esculpido en la fe nuestra razón.

El crimen fue en Granada

I
El crimen

Se le vio, caminando entre fusiles,
por una calle larga,
salir al campo frío,
aún con estrellas, de la madrugada.
Mataron a Federico
cuando la luz asomaba.
El pelotón de verdugos
no osó mirarle la cara.
Todos cerraron los ojos;
rezaron: ¡ni Dios te salva!
Muerto cayó Federico
—sangre en la frente y plomo en las entrañas—.
. . . Que fue en Granada el crimen
sabed —¡pobre Granada!— en su Granada . . .

II
El poeta y la muerte

Se le vio caminar solo con Ella,
sin miedo a su guadaña.
—Ya el sol en torre y torre; los martillos
en yunque —yunque y yunque de las fraguas.
Hablaba Federico,
requebrando a la muerte. Ella escuchaba.
"Porque ayer en mi verso, compañera,
sonaba el golpe de tus secas palmas,
y diste el hielo a mi cantar, y el filo
a mi tragedia de tu hoz de plata,
te cantaré la carne que no tienes,
los ojos que te faltan,

With our cup of shadow overflowing,
With our hearts that are never full,
Let us honor the Lord Who made Non-being,
And out of our reason sculpted faith.

—KATE FLORES

The Crime Was in Granada

I
The Crime

You could see him, walking between the rifles,
down the long street,
out to the cold field,
still lit with stars, at daybreak.
They killed Federico*
with the light of day.
The firing squad
dared not look him in the face.
All of them shut their eyes;
they prayed: even God won't save you!
Dead Federico fell
—blood upon his forehead and lead into his guts—.
. . . That the crime was in Granada,
think of it—poor Granada!—in his Granada . . .

II
The Poet and Death

You could see him walking alone with Her,
unafraid of her scythe.
—The sun from tower to tower now; the hammers
on the anvils—anvil after anvil of the forges.
Federico was speaking,
flirting with death. She was listening.
"Because yesterday in my verse, friend,
the clap of your dry palms sounded,
and you gave ice to my song, and to my tragedy the edge
of your silvery sickle,
I shall sing of the flesh that you lack,
and the eyes you do not have,

---

*García Lorca.

tus cabellos que el viento sacudía,
los rojos labios donde te besaban . . .
Hoy como ayer, gitana, muerte mía,
qué bien contigo a solas,
por estos aires de Granada, ¡mi Granada!"

III

Se le vio caminar . . .
                    Labrad, amigos,
de piedra y sueño, en el Alhambra,
un túmulo al poeta,
sobre una fuente donde llore el agua,
y eternamente diga:
el crimen fue en Granada, ¡en su Granada!

Canción

Ya va subiendo la luna
sobre el naranjal.
Luce Venus como una
pajarita de cristal.

Ámbar y berilo,
tras de la sierra lejana,
el cielo, y de porcelana
morada en el mar tranquilo.

Ya es de noche en el jardín
— ¡el agua en sus atanores! —
y sólo huele a jazmín,
ruiseñor de los olores.

¡Cómo parece dormida
la guerra, de mar a mar,
mientras Valencia florida
se bebe el Guadalaviar!

Valencia de finas torres
y suaves noches, Valencia,
¿estaré contigo,
cuando mirarte no pueda,
donde crece la arena del campo
y se aleja la mar de violeta?

of your hair that the wind would toss,
and your red lips where once you were kissed . . .
Today as yesterday, gypsy mine, Death,
how good to be alone with you,
in these breezes of Granada, my Granada!"

                    III
You could see him walking . . .
                         Carve, friends,
in the Alhambra, of stone and of dream,
a memorial to the poet,
over a fountain where the water weeps,
repeating forever:
the crime was in Granada, in his Granada!
                              —KATE FLORES

Song

Now the moon is rising
Above the orange grove.
Venus gleams
Like a toy bird of glass.

Amber and beryl the sky
Behind the far sierra
And purple porcelain
The tranquil sea.

Now night is on the garden
—Water in its sluices!—
And there is but scent of jasmine,
The nightingale perfume.

How the war from sea to sea
Seems to be asleep,
While flowering Valencia
Drinks the Guadalaviar!

Valencia of fine towers
And soft nights, Valencia,
Will you be with me
When I cannot see you,
Where fields of sand grow
And the violet sea recedes!
                              —KATE FLORES

JUAN RAMÓN JIMÉNEZ
(1881–1958)

When, at the turn of the century, Rubén Darío, recognized leader of Spanish poetry, was sojourning in Madrid, he wrote to a young poet, then living in Seville, to come and join his circle. His name was Juan Ramón Jiménez; when he arrived at the Spanish capital, he had just attained the age of eighteen. Born in the town of Moguer (Huelva), the Andalusian youth had attended the local Jesuit schools and, for a while, the University of Seville. Rather frail and frequently ill, Jiménez attracted immediate attention with the publication of his delicate poems in the Seville papers. Darío advised him to publish them in book form and even suggested a title: *Almas de violeta (Violet Souls)*. There were enough poems for a second slim volume, and another Modernist, Valle Inclán, suggested *Ninfeas* for its title.

Concurrent with the twentieth century, the career of Jiménez gave Spain one of its most arresting literary figures, the indisputable heir of Rubén Darío and modernism. But his activities were not confined to verse writing: one of his most fertile tasks was founding magazines and discovering and encouraging new poets. Little else happened to the sickly, hypersensitive man, except that in 1916, in New York, he married Zenobia Camprubí Aymar, the Spanish translator of Rabindranath Tagore. To her he owed the peace and serenity of the second half of his life, for she was a most helpful companion and collaborator, and Jiménez's bitterest blow was her death in November 1956, only three days after the Nobel Prize had been awarded to him.

In his copious *opera omnia*, comprising thousands of poems (or so it seems, at least), Jiménez elaborated—one is tempted to say, perfected—that airiness and those chiaroscuros associated with Bécquer, and often found in Darío. Except for these two modern masters, and perhaps for two others of the Golden Age (Garcilaso and Góngora), no Spanish poet surpassed Jiménez in technical skill and in the alchemy of converting words into music—into something weightless, vaporous, resembling light. His entire life went into his poetry, and his poetry registered his bliss and anguish, as well as every one of his moods. His poetry was his diary, his travel book, his confessional. Even the most commonplace and crude reality became transformed, through the magic of his "pure" verse, into air and light and music.

BEST EDITIONS: *Tercera Antología Poética*, Madrid, Biblioteca Nueva, 1957; *Libros de Poesía*, Madrid, Aguilar, 1957 (Biblioteca Premios Nobel).

ABOUT JUAN RAMÓN JIMÉNEZ: J. B. Trend: *Juan Ramón Jiménez*, Oxford, 1950. *Also*: R. Frank: "The Landscape of the Soul," *Poetry* 82 (1953), pp. 224–39; G. Palau de Nemes: "Appreciation," *Books Abroad* 26 (1952), pp. 16–19; J. E. Patterson: "The Poetry of Jiménez," *Commonweal* 68 (1958), pp. 400–2; W. T. Pattison: "Juan Ramón Jiménez, Mystic of Nature," *Hispania* 33 (1950), pp. 18–22; A. Plenn: "An Appreciation of Juan Ramón Jiménez," *New York Times*, December 9, 1956, p. 5; J. Tagliabue: "The Poetry of Juan Ramón Jiménez," *Poetry*, June 1958, pp. 84–88.

SOME COLLECTIONS AND CRITICISM PUBLISHED SINCE 1958: Ricardo Senabre: *Antonio Machado y Juan Ramón Jiménez, poetas del siglo XX*, Madrid, Anaya, 1991. Howard Thomas Young: *Juan Ramón Jiménez*, New York, Columbia University Press, 1967. John C. Wilcox: *Self and Image in Juan Ramón Jiménez, Modern and Post-Modern Readings*, Urbana, Ill., University of Illinois Press, 1987.

La calle espera a la noche . . .

La calle espera a la noche.
Todo es historia y silencio.
Los árboles de la acera
se han dormido bajo el cielo.

—Y el cielo es violeta y triste,
un cielo de abril, un bello
cielo violeta, con suaves
preludios del estrelleo.—

Por las verjas se ve luz
en las casas. Llora un perro
ante una puerta cerrada.
Negro sobre el cielo liso,
revolotea un murciélago . . .

—¡Oh la lámpara amarilla,
la paz de los niños ciegos,
la nostaljia de las viudas,
la presencia de los muertos!

¡Cuentos que en aquellas tardes
de abril, que ya nunca han vuelto,
nos contábamos, mirando
fijamente a los luceros!—

Y va cayendo la sombra,
dulce y grande, en paz, con esos
rumores lejanos que
se escuchan desde los pueblos . . .

Ya están ahí las carretas . . .

Ya están ahí las carretas . . .
—Lo han dicho el pinar y el viento,
lo ha dicho la luna de oro,
lo han dicho el humo y el eco . . .—
Son las carretas que pasan
estas tardes, al sol puesto,
las carretas que se llevan
del monte los troncos muertos.

The Street Is Waiting for the Night . . .

The street is waiting for the night.
All is history and silence.
The trees along the walk
are asleep under the sky.

And the sad sky is violet,
an April sky, a beautiful
violet sky with gentle
preludes of starlight.

Now the lamps are shining
at the barred windows. A dog whines
at a closed door. A black bat
twirls in the smooth sky . . .

Ah! that yellow lamp,
the peace of the blind children,
the nostalgia of the widows,
the presence of the dead!

And the stories that we told
on those April evenings
that have never returned,
while we gazed at the stars!

And the darkness is falling,
sweet and great and peaceful,
among the distant murmurs
of the little villages . . .

—LYSANDER KEMP

The Oxcarts Are Now on Their Way

The oxcarts are now on their way . . .
—The pine grove and the wind
Have told of their coming.
The golden moon has told of it,
The smoke and the echoes have told of it . . . —
They are the oxcarts that pass by
At sunset during these evenings,
The carts that are taking
The dead tree trunks from the woods.

¡Cómo lloran las carretas,
camino de Pueblo Nuevo!

Los bueyes vienen soñando,
a la luz de los luceros,
en el establo caliente
que sabe a madre y a heno.
Y detrás de las carretas,
caminan los carreteros,
con la aijada sobre el hombro
y los ojos en el cielo.

¡Cómo lloran las carretas,
camino de Pueblo Nuevo!

En la paz del campo, van
dejando los troncos muertos
un olor fresco y honrado
a corazón descubierto.
Y cae el ángelus desde
la torre del pueblo viejo,
sobre los campos talados,
que huelen a cementerio.

¡Cómo lloran las carretas
camino de Pueblo Nuevo!

El campo duerme, temblando . . .

El campo duerme, temblando
en su celeste tristeza,
a la música que dan
los grillos y las estrellas.

Jira el lejano horizonte,
huye la colina, tiembla
el valle, se va el sendero . . .
y todo a la claridad
dulce de la luna nueva . . .

How the oxcarts weep
On the road to Pueblo Nuevo!

By the light of the stars
The oxen dream of the warm stable
Smelling of hay and home.
And behind the carts
Stride the cart drivers
With their goads upon their shoulders
And their eyes on the sky.

How the oxcarts weep
On the road to Pueblo Nuevo!

In the peace of the countryside
The fine, fresh scent of the felled trees
Rises to the responsive heart.
And from the tower of the old town
The Angelus floats
Upon the death-scented fields
Where trees have been cut.

How the oxcarts weep
On the road to Pueblo Nuevo!
                                        —ALICE STERNBERG

The Countryside Sleeps, Trembling . . .

The countryside sleeps, trembling
In its blest celestial sadness,
To the music that is made
By the crickets and the stars.

The distant horizon turns,
The little hill flees, the valley
Shivers, the path disappears . . .
And all in the sweet and mild
Clarity of the new moon . . .

¿Quién ha pasado? no sé . . .
allá por la carretera
resuenan los cascabeles
de algún coche que se acerca;

coche fantástico, coche
nocturno, que nunca llega . . .
—No . . . es la música que dan
los grillos y las estrellas.

¿Era el río? ¿era la brisa?
la corriente tendrá pena . . .
son las flores deshojadas,
la voz de la molinera . . .

¿Es el amor? ¡ay, amor!
es el agua soñolienta
que llama a su fondo de
cristal, de sombra y de yerba . . .

—No . . . es el agua estremecida
y azul de luna, que tiembla
a la música que dan
los grillos y las estrellas . . .

Doraba la luna el río . . .

Anda el agua de alborada . . .
—ROMANCE POPULAR

Doraba la luna el río
—¡fresco de la madrugada!—
Por el mar venían olas
teñidas de luz de alba.

El campo débil y triste
se iba alumbrando. Quedaba
el canto roto de un grillo,
la queja oscura de un agua.

Who went by? I do not know . . .
There along the high road
Tinkle little harness bells
Of a stagecoach coming close;

Carriage of fantasy, nocturnal
Carriage that never arrives . . .
—No . . . it is the music made
By the crickets and the stars.

Was it the river? The breeze?
Perhaps running water grieves . . .
Flowers with their shattered crowns,
The voice of the miller's child . . .

Is it love? Oh, my heart, love!
It is the calm, drowsy water
Inviting down to its depth
Of crystal, shadow, and grass.

—No . . . it is the startled water
Blue with moonlight, quivering
To the music that is made
By the crickets and the stars . . .

—ELOISE ROACH

The Moon Was Gilding the River . . .

The water is dressed for dawn . . .
—POPULAR BALLAD

The moon was gilding the river,
—Coolness of the break of day!—
From the sea the waves were coming
Dyed with the light of the dawn . . .

The countryside, weak and sad,
Was being lighted. Remained
The broken song of the cricket,
The hidden plaint of the well.

Huía el viento a su gruta,
el horror a su cabaña;
en el verde de los pinos,
se iban abriendo las alas.

Las estrellas se morían,
se rosaba la montaña;
allá en el pozo del huerto,
la golondrina cantaba.

Primavera amarilla . . .

Abril venía, lleno
todo de flores amarillas:
amarillo el arroyo,
amarillo el vallado, la colina,
el cementerio de los niños,
el huerto aquel donde el amor vivía.

El sol unjía de amarillo el mundo,
con sus luces caídas;
¡ay, por los lirios áureos,
el agua de oro, tibia;
las amarillas mariposas
sobre las rosas amarillas!

Guirnaldas amarillas escalaban
los árboles; el día
era una gracia perfumada de oro,
en un dorado despertar de vida.
Entre los huesos de los muertos,
abría Dios sus manos amarillas.

El viaje definitivo

. . . Y yo me iré. Y se quedarán los pájaros cantando;
y se quedará mi huerto, con su verde árbol,
y con su pozo blanco.

The wind would flee to its cave,
Horror would flee to its den,
In the greenness of the pines
Wings would open, one by one.

The stars now began to die,
The mountainside turned to rose,
And down in the garden well
Rose the swallow's morning song.

—ELOISE ROACH

Yellow Spring

Spring was coming, brimful
Of yellow flowers:
Yellow the brook,
Yellow the hedges, the hill,
The children's cemetery,
The garden, yonder, where love used to dwell.

The sun with its fallen light
Anointed the world with yellow:
Look at the warm, gold water
Among the golden lilies;
The yellow butterflies
Upon the yellow roses!

Yellow garlands scaling
The trees; the day
Was a perfumed golden miracle
At the golden awakening of life.
Among the bones of the dead
God was opening his yellow hands.

—ANGEL FLORES

The Definitive Journey

. . . And I shall depart. And the birds will remain singing;
And my garden will remain, with its green tree,
And its white well.

Todas las tardes, el cielo será azul y plácido;
y tocarán, como esta tarde están tocando,
las campanas del campanario.
   Se morirán aquellos que me amaron;
y el pueblo se hará nuevo cada año;
y en el rincón aquel de mi huerto florido y encalado,
mi espíritu errará, nostáljico . . .
   Y yo me iré; y estaré solo, sin hogar,
sin árbol verde, sin pozo blanco,
sin cielo azul y plácido . . .
Y se quedarán los pájaros cantando.

Anochecer. Frescura de mi jardín regado . . .

Anochecer. Frescura de mi jardín regado.
Entre las grandes hojas verdes, manda el ocaso
un adiós amarillo, aplastado por una
nube enorme de plomo, morada y taciturna.

Aún gotean las flores la lluvia de la tarde;
claras bocas de plata cantan en otro parque;
hay un deseo vago, suntuoso e inmenso,
de amor—ojos cerrados y labios entreabiertos.

Una luz de instante viene a apretar la sombra;
huelen, como entre sueños, las hierbas y las rosas;
la ventana se enciende y da a la fuente un roto
temblor, un melodioso ondeaje de oro . . .

Tenebrae

Todo el ocaso es amarillo limón.
En el cenit cerrado, bajo las nubes mudas,
bandadas negras de pájaros melancólicos
rayan, constantes, el falso cielo de lluvia.

Por el jardín, sombrío de los plúmbeos nimbos,
las rosas tienen una morada veladura,
y el crepúsculo vago, que cambia las verdades,
pone en todo, al rozarlo, no sé qué gasas húmedas.

Every afternoon the sky will be blue and placid;
And there will ring, as they are ringing this afternoon,
The bells in the belfry.
    Those who loved me will die;
And the town each year will be built anew;
And in yonder corner of my blossoming, whitewashed garden
My soul will wander, nostalgically . . .
    And I shall depart; and I shall be alone, without a home,
without a green tree, without a white well,
Without a sky blue and placid . . .
And the birds will remain singing.   —ANGEL FLORES

Nightfall. The Coolness of My Watered Garden . . .

Nightfall. The coolness of my watered garden.
Between the great green leaves, the setting sun
sends a yellow farewell, pressed by an
enormous leaden cloud, purple and taciturn.

The flowers still are dripping the raindrops of late rain;
some clear mouths of silver sing in another part;
there is vague desire, sensuous and immense,
of love-closed eyes and half-opened lips.

A momentary light comes pushing out the dark;
the grasses and the roses are fragrant as in dreams;
the window becomes fiery and fashions for the fountain
a broken quiver, a melodious swelling of gold.   —ELOISE ROACH

Tenebrae

The whole western sky is lemon yellow.
At the enclosed zenith, under the silent clouds,
Black flocks of melancholy birds continually
Streak the sky like false rain.

Throughout the garden, overcast by leaden nimbuses,
The roses wear a violet tint
And the hazy evening, which distorts truth,
Drops unfamiliar damp vapors on all it touches.

Lívido, deslumbrado del amarillo, torvo
del plomo, en mis oídos, como un moscardón zumba
una ronda monótona, que yo no sé de dónde
viene, . . . que deja lágrimas, . . . que dice: «Nunca, . . . Nunca . . . »

Amor

No has muerto, no.
            Renaces,
con las roasas, en cada primavera.
Como la vida, tienes
tus hojas secas;
tienes tu nieve, como
la vida . . .
            Mas tu tierra,
amor, está sembrada
de profundas promesas,
que han de cumplirse aun en el mismo olvido.
            ¡En vano es que no quieras!
La brisa dulce torna, un día, al alma;
una noche de estrellas,
bajas, amor, a los sentidos,
casto como la vez primera.
    ¡Pues eres puro, eres
eterno! A tu presencia,
vuelven por el azul, en blanco bando,
tiernas palomas que creímos muertas . . .
Abres la sola flor con nuevas hojas . . .
Doras la inmortal luz con lenguas nuevas . . .
    ¡Eres eterno, amor,
como la primavera!

Hora inmensa

Sólo turban la paz una campana, un pájaro . . .
Parece que los dos hablan con el ocaso.
    Es de oro el silencio. La tarde es de cristales.
Mece los frescos árboles una pureza errante.
Y, más allá de todo, se sueña un río límpido

Like a livid, leaden-grim, yellow-dazzled horsefly,
There drones in my ear a monotonous round
Which comes from I know not where . . .
Which leaves tears, . . . which says: "Never, . . . Never . . . "
—ALICE STERNBERG

Love

You are not dead, no.
Each spring,
With the roses, you are reborn.
Like life, you have
Your dry leaves;
You have your snow, like
Life . . .
But your soil,
Love, is sown
With deep promises
Which must be fulfilled even in Oblivion itself.
You would refuse in vain!
The balmy breeze returns, some day, to the soul;
On a starlit night, love,
You descend to the senses,
Chastely, as the first time.
Because you are pure, you are
Eternal! To your presence
Tender pigeons we thought dead
Return in white flocks, through the blue . . .
With new leaves you open the only flower . . .
You gild the immortal light with new tongues . . .
Like spring,
You are eternal, love!
—ANGEL FLORES

Immense Hour

Only a bell, a bird, the stillness break . . .
It seems the two are talking with the twilight.
The silence is of gold, the evening crystal.
A vagrant purity rocks the tender trees.
And, beyond it all, one dreams a limpid stream

que, atropellando perlas, huye hacia lo infinito . . .
¡Soledad! ¡Soledad! Todo es claro y callado . . .
Sólo turban la paz una campana, un pájaro . . .
El amor vive lejos . . . sereno, indiferente,
el corazón es libre. Ni está triste, ni alegre.
Lo distraen colores, brisas, cantos, perfumes . . .
Nada como en un lago de sentimiento inmune . . .
Sólo turban la paz una campana, un pájaro . . .
¡Parece que lo eterno se coje con la mano!

Deprisa, tierra, deprisa . . .

Deprisa, tierra, deprisa;
deprisa, deprisa, sol;
descomponed el sistema,
que me espera a mí el amor.

¿Qué importa que el universo
se trastorne, tierra, sol?
Todo es humo, sólo es gloria
que me espera a mí el amor.

¡A la nieve con la espiga!
¡Anda, tierra; vuela, sol!
¡Abreviadme la esperanza,
que me espera a mí el amor!

Aún cuando el mar es grande . . .

Aún cuando el mar es grande,
como es lo mismo todo,
me parece que estoy ya a tu lado . . .
Ya sólo el agua nos separa,
el agua que se mueve sin descanso,
¡el agua, sólo, el agua!

That, trampling pearls, flees toward the infinite . . .
  Solitude! Solitude! All is clear and calm . . .
Only a bell, a bird, the stillness break . . .
  Love lives afar . . . serene, indifferent,
The heart is free. It is neither sad nor glad.
Colors, breezes, songs, perfumes distract it . . .
It swims as on a lake immune to sentiment . . .
  Only a bell, a bird, the stillness break . . .
One seems to catch the eternal in one's hand!
          —EDWARD F. GAHAN

Faster, Earth, Faster . . .

Faster, earth, faster;
faster, faster, sun;
set at odds the system,
love awaits me now.

What odds that the universe
be upset, earth, sun?
All is smoke; sole glory is
love awaiting now.

Let snow destroy the wheat!
Hurry, earth! fly, sun!
Shorten now my hoping time,
for love awaits me now!
          —ELOISE ROACH

The Sea Is Enormous . . .

The sea is enormous,
just as everything is,
yet it seems to me I am still with you . . .
Soon only water will separate us,
water, restlessly shifting,
water, only water!
          —JAMES WRIGHT

A la puente del amor . . .

A la puente del amor,
piedra vieja entre altas rocas
—cita eterna, tarde roja—,
vengo con mi corazón:

Mi novia sola es el agua,
que pasa siempre y no engaña,
que pasa siempre y no cambia,
que pasa siempre y no acaba.

El amanecer tiene . . .

El amanecer tiene
esa tristeza de llegar,
en tren, a una estación que no es de uno.

¡Qué agrios los rumores
de un día que se sabe pasajero
—oh vida mía!

—Arriba, con el alba, llora un niño.—

Epitafio ideal de un marinero

Hay que buscar, para saber
tu tumba, por el firmamento.
—Llueve tu muerte de una estrella.
La losa no te pesa, que es un universo
de ensueño—.
En la ignorancia, estás
en todo—cielo, mar y tierra—muerto.

To the Bridge of Love . . .

To the bridge of love,
old stone between tall cliffs
—eternal meeting place, red evening—,
I come with my heart:

My beloved is only water,
that always passes away, and does not deceive,
that always passes away, and does not change,
that always passes away, and does not end.

　　　　　　　　　　　—JAMES WRIGHT

The Dawn Brings With It . . .

The dawn brings with it
that sadness of arriving, by train,
at a station that is not one's own.

How disagreeable, those rumblings
of a new day that one knows cannot last long
—Oh my life!

Overhead, as the day breaks, a child is crying.

　　　　　　　　　　　—JAMES WRIGHT

Mariner's Ideal Epitaph

　　One must, to find your tomb,
search the firmament.
—Your death rains from a star.
A tombstone does not weigh you down, it being a universe
of dream—.
Oblivious you are
to everything—dead in earth and sea and sky.

　　　　　　　　　　　—KATE FLORES

Desvelo

Se va la noche, negro toro
—plena carne de luto, de espanto y de misterio—;
que ha bramado terrible, inmensamente,
al temor sudoroso de todos los caídos;
y el día viene, niño fresco,
pidiendo confianza, amor y risa,
—niño que, allá muy lejos,
en los arcanos donde
se encuentran los comienzos con los fines,
ha jugado un momento,
por no sé qué pradera
de luz y sombra,
con el toro que huía—.

Ocaso

¡Oh, qué sonido de oro que se va,
de oro que ya se va a la eternidad;
qué triste nuestro oído, de escuchar
ese oro que se va a la eternidad,
este silencio que se va a quedar
sin su oro que se va a la eternidad!

Cenit

Yo no seré yo, muerte,
hasta que tú te unas con mi vida
y me completes así todo;
hasta que mi mitad de luz se cierre
con mi mitad de sombra
—y sea yo equilibrio eterno
en la mente del mundo:
unas veces, mi medio yo, radiante;
otras, mi otro medio yo, en olvido.

Yo no seré yo, muerte,
hasta que tú, en tu turno, vistas
de huesos pálidos mi alma.

Vigil

The night departs, a black bull
—full flesh of mourning, terror, mystery—
who roared with vast horror
at the sweating dread of all the fallen;
and day comes in, a young child
begging trust, love, laughter,
—a child very far away,
in the secret chests
where ends and beginnings meet,
who played a moment
on some kind of field
of light and shadow,
with the fleeing bull.

—WILLIS BARNSTONE

Sunset

Oh, what sound of gold going,
of gold now going to eternity;
how sad our ear, to have to hear
that gold that is going to eternity,
this silence that is going to remain
without its gold that is going to eternity!

KATE FLORES

Zenith

I shall not be myself, death,
until you join my life
and thus make me whole;
until my luminous half closes
upon my darkened half
—and I am balanced eternally
in the mind of the world:
at times one half of me illumined;
at others, my other half, in shade.

I shall not be myself, death,
until you, in your turn, clothe
with pallid bones my soul.

—KATE FLORES

GABRIELA MISTRAL
(1889–1957)

Because the human person looms so large in the Hispanic tradition, it might be feared that Gabriela Mistral's personality, with her great generosity, her altruism, her championing of so many good (and lost) causes, would relegate her poetical achievement to a secondary place. It must be said emphatically, therefore, that her inclusion in this anthology is due solely to the intrinsic merit of her poetry.

Born Lucila Godoy Alcayaga, of humble parents—her father was a poor schoolteacher who dabbled in verse—she spent her childhood in the Elqui Valley of northern Chile, which accounts, as she once said, for her interest in rural education and the agrarian problem. She was self-educated from the age of eleven and began teaching when hardly fifteen.

In 1907 she fell in love with Romelio Ureta, a young railroad employee, who later committed suicide over financial matters. (Contrary to popular legend, this occurred after the romance had ended.) This death opened up the gates of her inspiration; from it stem some of her most intense lyrics.

Although the normal school at La Serena had refused admission to "the girl with pagan ideas," she managed to take short courses in education elsewhere and attained promotions with the help of her growing reputation as a poet. Her *Sonnets of Death* won her the coveted Santiago Poetry Prize in 1914, and her other poems occasionally appeared in periodicals and anthologies. In 1922 her New York admirers published, through Columbia University Press, her first book, *Desolación*, and José de Vasconcelos, then Secretary of Education of Mexico, invited her to help reorganize his country's school system.

After the successful completion of this assignment (1924), she was involved, until her death, in international and diplomatic work: with the League of Nations and United Nations, and in the Chilean consulates in Naples, Madrid, Lisbon, Rio de Janeiro, and Los Angeles. Her creative work went on slowly, her books appearing at infrequent intervals: *Ternura* (1924), *Tala* (1938), *Lagar* (1954). While the poets of her generation were cultivating rhetorical artifice, Gabriela's verse sought only the utmost simplicity and intense sincerity. She wrote with tenderness or rebellion, about love and death, about children, about the lofty mission of the teacher, about suffering and religion. And she who adored children and never had a child of her own wrote some of the most beautiful cradle songs and children's verse in the Spanish language. Sadly enough, the one child she adopted and brought up as her own son—her nephew Yin Yin—died at the age of fifteen. Immediately after this tragedy, in 1945, Gabriela Mistral traveled to Stockholm to receive the Nobel Prize.

BEST EDITION: Margaret Bates (ed.): *Poesías completas,* Madrid, 1958 (Biblioteca Premios Nobel).

ABOUT GABRIELA MISTRAL: S. C. Rosenbaum: *Modern Women Poets of Spanish America,* New York, 1945, pp. 171–203, Also. Margaret J. Bates: "Gabriela Mistral," *The Americas,* Vol. 3 (1946), pp. 168–89; E. Ferguson: *Chile,* New York, 1943, pp. 17–28. Sister J. Berchmans: "Gabriela Mistral and the Franciscan Concept of Life," *Renascence* 5 (1952), pp. 40–46, 95; A. M. Espinosa: "Gabriela Mistral," *The Americas* 8 (1951), pp. 3–40; M. J. Bates: "Gabriela Mistral," *The Americas* 14 (1957), pp. 145–51; E. A. Peers: *Gabriela Mistral,* Liverpool: Institute of Hispanic Studies, 1946; R. A. Wheelock: "Gabriela Mistral," *Catholic World* 186 (1958), pp. 252–58.

SOME COLLECTIONS AND CRITICISM PUBLISHED SINCE 1958: Santandreu, Cora: *Aspects del estilo en la poesía de Gabriela Mistral,* Santiago de Chile, Editorial de la Universidad de Chile, 1958. Luis V. Anastasia: *Gabriela Mistral: poética de la imagen y sentido de la vida,* Montevideo, 1995(?).

Íntima

Tú no oprimas mis manos.
Llegará el duradero
tiempo de reposar con mucho polvo
y sombra en los entretejidos dedos.

Y dirías: "No puedo
amarla, porque ya se desgranaron
como mieses sus dedos."

Tú no beses mi boca.
Vendrá el instante lleno
de luz menguada, en que estaré sin labios
sobre un mojado suelo.

Y dirías: "La amé, pero no puedo
amarla más, ahora que no aspira
el olor de retamas de mi beso."

Y me angustiara oyéndote,
y hablaras loco y ciego,
que mi mano será sobre tu frente
cuando rompan mis dedos,
y bajará sobre tu cara llena
de ansia mi aliento.

No me toques, por tanto. Mentiría
al decir que te entrego
mi amor en estos brazos extendidos,
en mi boca, en mi cuello,
y tú, al creer que lo bebiste todo,
te engañarías como un niño ciego.

Porque mi amor no es sólo esta gavilla
reacia y fatigada de mi cuerpo,
que tiembla entera al roce del cilicio
y que se me rezaga en todo vuelo.

Es lo que está en el beso, y no es el labio;
lo que rompe la voz, y no es el pecho:
¡es un viento de Dios, que pasa hendiéndome
el gajo de las carnes, volandero!

Intimate

Do not press my hands.
The lasting time of rest
Will come with much dust
And shadow amid my fingers intertwined.

And you will say: "I cannot
Love her, now that like the wheat tassel
Her fingers waste away."

Do not kiss my mouth.
The moment filled with failing
Light will come when I will be without lips
Upon a humid earth.

And you will say: "I loved her, but I cannot
Love her more, now that she does not covet
The fir fragrance of my kiss."

And it will anguish me to hear you,
And you will mad and blinded speak,
My hand upon your forehead
As my fingers break,
And down upon your anxious
Face my breath will fall.

Wherefore do not touch me. I should lie
Were I to say I brought my love to you
In these extended arms,
In my lips, my throat;
And you, were you to think you drank it all,
Like a blind child would be deceived.

For my love is not merely this willful
And weary husk of my body,
All atremble with the chafing hair shirt
And still with me in full flight.

It is that which is in the kiss, and is not the lip;
That which breaks the voice, and is not the breast:
It is a wind of God, that in passing rends me,
Severed limb of flesh, wafted.

—KATE FLORES

Balada

Él pasó con otra;
yo le vi pasar.
Siempre dulce el viento
y el camino en paz.
¡Y estos ojos míseros
le vieron pasar!

Él va amando a otra
por la tierra en flor.
Ha abierto el espino;
pasa una canción.
¡Y él va amando a otra
por la tierra en flor!

Él besó a la otra
a orillas del mar;
resbaló en las olas
la luna de azahar.
¡Y no untó mi sangre
la extensión del mar!

Él irá con otra
por la eternidad.
Habrá cielos dulces.
(Dios quiere callar.)
¡Y él irá con otra
por la eternidad!

A los niños

Después de muchos años, cuando yo sea un montoncito de polvo callado, jugad conmigo, con la tierra de mi corazón y de mis huesos. Si me recoge un albañil, me pondrá en un ladrillo, y quedaré clavada para siempre en un muro, y yo odio los nichos quietos. Si me hacen ladrillo de cárcel, enrojeceré de vergüenza oyendo sollozar a un hombre; y si soy ladrillo de una escuela, padeceré también de no poder cantar con vosotros, en los amaneceres.

Ballad

He went by with another;
I have seen him go.
Ever fair was the wind
and the path full of peace.
My eyes, my poor eyes
have seen him go!

He is falling in love with another
upon the flowering earth.
The thorn bush is blooming;
a song goes floating by.
And he is falling in love with another
upon the flowering earth!

He has kissed the other
on the shores of the sea;
the orange blossom moon
was gliding over the waters.
And my blood did not anoint
the sea's expanse!

He will go away with the other
for all eternity.
There will be fair skies
(God wishes to keep still.)
And he will go with the other
for all eternity!

— MURIEL KITTEL

To the Children

Many years from now, when I am a little heap of silenced dust, play
with me, with the earth of my heart and my bones. If a mason were to
gather me up, he would make me into a brick, and I should remain
locked forever into a wall; and I hate quiet crevices. If they made me
into a brick for a prison, I should redden with shame to have to hear
the men sob; and if I became a brick in a schoolhouse, it would pain
me, too, not to be able to sing with you in the mornings.

Mejor quiero ser el polvo con que jugáis en los caminos del campo. Oprimidme: he sido vuestra; deshacedme, porque os hice; pisadme, porque no os di toda la verdad y toda la belleza. O, simplemente, cantad y corred sobre mí, para besaros las plantas amadas. . . . Decid, cuando me tengáis en las manos, un verso hermoso y crepitaré de placer entre vuestros dedos. Me empinaré para miraros, buscando entre vosotros los ojos, los cabellos de los que enseñé.

Y cuando hagáis conmigo cualquier imagen, rompedla a cada instante, que a cada instante me rompieron los niños de ternura y de dolor!

Palabras serenas

Ya en la mitad de mis días espigo
esta verdad con frescura de flor:
la vida es oro y dulzura de trigo,
es breve el odio e inmenso el amor.

Mudemos ya por el verso sonriente
aquel listado de sangre con hiel.
Abren violetas divinas, y el viento,
desprende al valle un aliento de miel.

Ahora no sólo comprendo al que reza;
ahora comprendo al que rompe a cantar.
La sed es larga, la cuesta es aviesa;
pero en un lirio se enreda el mirar.

Grávidos van nuestros ojos de llanto
y un arroyuelo nos hace sonreír;
por una alondra que erige su canto
nos olvidamos que es duro morir.

No hay nada ya que mis carnes taladre.
Con el amor acabóse el hervir.
Aún me apacienta el mirar de mi madre.
¡Siento que Dios me va haciendo dormir!

Rather, I should like to be the dust you play with along the country roads. Squeeze me: I shall have been yours; crumble me, for having been the one who made you; trample upon me, for not having given you all truth and all beauty. Or simply sing and run upon me, that I may kiss your dear soles.

Recite a pretty verse when you have me in your hands, and I will throb with joy between your fingers. I will stand up tall to watch you, seeking among you the eyes, the hair of those I taught.

And when you shape me into some figure, keep shattering it, as you in your tenderness and sorrow shattered me. —KATE FLORES

Serene Words

Now in my middle years I glean
This truth of flowerlike innocence:
Life, like wheat, is sweet and golden,
Hate is brief and love immense.

So let us exchange for laughing verse
Those lines where blood and gall are paired;
Heavenly violets open, and the wind
Spreads through the valley a honeyed air.

I understand now those who burst with song,
As I understand him who prays.
The hillside twists and thirst lasts long,
But a lily can ensnare our gaze.

Our eyes are growing heavy with tears,
But a little brook can make us smile;
Because of a lark and its song ascending
We forget that it is hard to die.

Nothing more can pierce my flesh,
Love has made all turmoil cease.
My mother's eyes still bring peace to me.
I feel that God is putting me to sleep. —MURIEL KITTEL

Otoño

A esta alameda muriente
he traído mi cansancio,
y estoy ya no sé qué tiempo
tendida bajo los álamos,
que van cubriendo mi pecho
de su oro divino y tardo.

Sin un ímpetu la tarde
se apagó tras de los álamos.
Por mi corazón mendigo
ella no se ha ensangrentado.
Y el amor al que tendí,
para salvarme, los brazos,
se está muriendo en mi alma
como arrebol desflocado.

Y no llevaba más que este
manojito atribulado
de ternura, entre mis carnes
como un infante, temblando.
¡Ahora se me va perdiendo
como un agua entre los álamos;
pero es otoño, y no agito,
para salvarlo, mis brazos!

En mis sienes la hojarasca
exhala un perfume manso.
Tal vez morir sólo sea
ir con asombro marchando
entre un rumor de hojas secas
y por un parque extasiado.

Aunque va a llegar la noche,
y estoy sola, y ha blanqueado
el suelo un azahar de escarcha,
para regresar no me alzo,
ni hago lecho, entre las hojas,
ni acierto a dar, sollozando,
un inmenso Padre Nuestro
por mi inmenso desamparo.

Autumn

To this grove of dying poplars
I have brought my weariness,
and I have been I know not how long
lying beneath the poplars
that are covering my breast
with their heavenly gold, slow falling.

Without shock the evening
fades between the poplars.
By my beggar heart
it goes unreddened.
And the love to which I stretched
my arms to save me,
is dying in my soul,
its own ragged sunset.

I bore nothing but this
small despondent handful
of tenderness within me
like a child, tremblingly.
Now it is slipping from me
like water among the poplars;
yet it is autumn, and I cannot
move my arms to save it!

On my temples the dead leaves
give off a faint fragrance.
Perhaps dying will only be
moving with astonished step
among a murmur of dry leaves
through a park enraptured.

Although the night advances,
and I am alone, and the flowers
of frost have whitened the earth,
I do not rise and go home,
nor make a bed among the leaves,
nor sobbing, manage to offer
an immense paternoster
for my immense despair.

—MURIEL KITTEL

Vasos

—Todos somos vasos —me dijo el alfarero, y como yo sonriera,
añadió— Tú eres un vaso vaciado. Te volcó un grande amor y ya no te
vuelves a colmar más. No eres humilde, y rehusas bajar como otros vasos
a las cisternas, a llenarte de agua impura. Tampoco te abres para alimen-
tarte de las pequeñas ternuras, como algunas de mis ánforas que reciben
las lentas gotas que les vierte la noche y viven de esa breve frescura.
Y no estás roja, sino blanca de sed, porque el sumo ardor tiene esa
tremenda blancura.

Meciendo

El mar sus millares de olas
   mece, divino.
Oyendo a los mares amantes,
   mezo a mi niño.

El viento errabundo en la noche
   mece a los trigos.
Oyendo a los vientos amantes,
   mezo a mi niño.

Dios Padre sus miles de mundos
   mece sin ruido.
Sintiendo su mano en la sombra,
   mezo a mi niño.

La rosa

La riqueza del centro de la rosa
es la riqueza de tu corazón.
Desátala como ella:
su ceñidura es toda tu aflicción.

Desátala en un canto
o en un tremendo amor.
No defiendas la rosa:
¡te quemaría con el resplandor!

Earthen Jugs

"We are all jugs," the potter said; and, when I smiled, he added: "You are an emptied jug. You were overturned by a great love and now can be filled no more. You are not humble, and you refuse to go down to the wells, like the other jugs, to fill yourself with impure water. Nor do you even open a little to nurture yourself on small tendernesses, like some of my jugs, which garner the slow drops shed by the night and subsist on that brief coolness. And you are not red, but white with thirst, for the fiercest heat has that tremendous whiteness."

—KATE FLORES

Rocking

With divine rhythm the ocean
　　rocks its myriad waves.
Listening to the waters' love,
　　I rock this child of mine.

The night-wandering wind
　　rocks the fields of wheat.
Listening to the winds' love,
　　I rock this child of mine.

Silently God the Father
　　rocks his numerous worlds.
Feeling his hands in the darkness,
　　I rock this child of mine.

—MURIEL KITTEL

The Rose

The wealth in the deep of the rose
Is the wealth within your heart.
Lavish it as she does:
In restraint is all your sorrow.

Lavish it in a song
Or in a love uncontained.
Do not keep back the rose:
She will sear you with her flame!

—KATE FLORES

La extranjera

—"Habla con dejo de sus mares bárbaros,
con no sé qué algas y no sé qué arenas;
reza oración a dios sin bulto y peso,
envejecida como si muriera.
Ese huerto nuestro que nos hizo extraño,
ha puesto cactus y zarpadas hierbas.
Alienta del resuello del desierto
y ha amado con pasión de que blanquea,
que nunca cuenta y que si nos contase
sería como el mapa de otra estrella.
Vivirá entre nosotros ochenta años,
pero siempre será como si llega,
hablando lengua que jadea y gime
y que le entienden sólo bestezuelas.
Y va a morirse en medio de nosotros,
en una noche en la que más padezca,
con sólo su destino por almohada,
de una muerte callada y *extranjera*".

Ausencia

Se va de ti mi cuerpo gota a gota.
Se va mi cara en un óleo sordo;
se van mis manos en azogue suelto;
se van mis pies en dos tiempos de polvo.

¡Se te va todo, se nos va todo!

Se va mi voz, que te hacía campana
cerrada a cuanto no somos nosotros.
Se van mis gestos que se devanaban,
en lanzaderas, debajo tus ojos.
Y se te va la mirada que entrega,
cuando te mira, el enebro y el olmo.

Me voy de ti con tus mismos alientos:
como humedad de tu cuerpo evaporo.
Me voy de ti con vigilia y con sueño,

The Stranger

—"She speaks with the accent of her wild seas
Of I know not what seaweeds, I know not what sands;
She worships a god without bulk or weight,
Old as if she would die.
This garden of ours which she estranged from us
She sowed with cactus and thorn.
She exhales the breath of the desert,
And she loved with a parching passion
She never tells us of, and which, if she told,
Would be like the map of another star.
She will live among us for eighty years
But always seem newly come,
With that language of hers that moans and pants
And only creatures of the field understand.
And she is going to die in our midst
Some night of her worst affliction,
With only her fate for a pillow,
Of a death unspoken and *strange*."

—KATE FLORES

Absence

My body leaves you drop by drop.
My face leaves in a deaf anointment;
My hands are leaving in loosed mercury;
My feet leave in two tides of dust.

Everything leaves you, everything leaves us!

My voice is leaving, that made you a bell
Closed to all except ourselves.
My gestures leave, that before your eyes
Round on spindles wound themselves,
And the gaze is leaving that fixed on you
Gave forth juniper and elm.

With your very breathing I am leaving you:
I am exuded like your body's mist.
Asleep and waking I am leaving you,

y en tu recuerdo más fiel ya me borro.
Y en tu memoria me vuelvo como esos
que no nacieron en llanos ni en sotos.

Sangre sería y me fuese en las palmas
de tu labor, y en tu boca de mosto.
Tu entraña fuese, y sería quemada
en marchas tuyas que nunca más oigo,
¡y en tu pasión que retumba en la noche
como demencia de mares solos!

¡Se nos va todo, se nos va todo!

And in your most faithful recollection I am already blurred,
And in your memory faded with those
Born in neither field nor wood.

Would I were blood, and leaving in the palms
Of your labor, and in your mouth of attar of grape.
In your sinews I should leave, and be burned
In your motions I could never hear again,
And in your passion pounding in the night
Like the dementia of lonely seas!

Everything leaves us, everything leaves us!
                                        — KATE FLORES

FEDERICO GARCÍA LORCA
(1898–1936)

In Lorca three strains merge: Spanish folklore, especially the gypsy; the modernism of Darío and Jiménez; and the European "isms" of post-World War I. Born in Fuente Vaqueros (near Granada) of a well-to-do family, Lorca studied at home and in local schools and later at the Institute and the University of Granada. On his arrival in Madrid (1919), where he planned to continue his studies, he soon found himself drawn to the capital's effervescent literary life. His first play, *El maleficio de la mariposa*, was produced by Martínez Sierra in 1920 and the following year his first collection of poems, *Libro de poemas*, was published. Both passed unnoticed, but Juan Ramón Jiménez invited him to collaborate in his literary magazine, *Indice*. In 1922 Lorca helped Manuel de Falla organize in Granada the *Fiesta del Cante Jondo*, calculated to attract attention to Spain's rich heritage of folk poetry and folk music. Seven years later Lorca was deeply involved in the celebrations of the 300th anniversary of Góngora's death and delivered a lecture on Góngora's imagery. Góngora's revival strengthened Ortega y Gasset's thesis of the dehumanization of art and stressed the literary and artistic trends rampant throughout Europe: cubism, futurism, surrealism, which in their Spanish garb became known as ultraism and creationism. Lorca most effectively blended the old roots of Spain (a folk poetry which oftentimes was—surrealist) with Golden Age Gongorism and twentieth-century surrealism. This is clearly shown in his *Romancero gitano* (1928), his outstanding book of verse.

After a brief sojourn in America (1929), surrealistically reflected in *Poeta en Nueva York* (1940), Lorca returned to Spain and there organized a traveling theater group, "La Barraca." Thereafter, he devoted his talent to playwriting, crowning it in 1933 with his masterpiece, *Bodas de sangre (Blood Wedding)*.

378

At the outbreak of the Civil War, Lorca was at the height of his creativity: he had just finished the play *La casa de Bernarda Alba* and was planning *Sodom's Destruction,* which, with *Yerma* (1935), was to constitute a trilogy on barren love. But during the autumn of 1936, García Lorca was arrested and shot to death while visiting in Granada with his friend, the poet Luis Rosales.

BEST EDITIONS: *Obras completas,* Buenos Aires, 1938, 6 volumes; Arturo de Hoyo (ed.): *Obras completas,* Madrid, 1955.

ABOUT FEDERICO GARCÍA LORCA: A. Barea: *The Poet and His People,* London, 1944; C. M. Bowra: *The Creative Experiment,* London and New York, 1949, pp. 189–219; R. Campbell: *Lorca,* Cambridge, 1952; J. Crow: *Federico García Lorca,* Los Angeles, 1945; E. Honig: *García Lorca,* New York, 1944; J. B. Trend: *F. García Lorca and the Spanish Poetic Tradition,* Oxford, 1945. *Also:* D. V. Baker (ed.): *Writers of Today,* London, 1946; W. Carrier: "Meaning in the Poetry of Lorca," *Accent* 10 (1950), pp. 159–70; H. H. Chapman: "Two Poetical Techniques: Lorca's *Romance de la luna* and Goethe's *Erlkönig,*" *Hispania* 39 (1956), pp. 450–55; P. Salinas: "Lorca and the Poetry of Death," *Hopkins Review* 5 (1951), pp. 5–12; E. Vivas: *Creation and Discipline,* New York, 1955; W. C. Williams: "F. García Lorca," *Kenyon Review* 1 (1939), pp. 148–58.

SOME COLLECTIONS AND CRITICISM PUBLISHED SINCE 1958. Felicia Hardison Londre: *Federico García Lorca,* New York, F. Ungar, 1984.

Canción primaveral

I

Salen los niños alegres
De la escuela,
Poniendo en el aire tibio
Del Abril, canciones tiernas.
¡Qué alegría tiene el hondo
Silencio de la calleja!
Un silencio hecho pedazos
Por risas de plata nueva.

II

Voy camino de la tarde,
Entre flores de la huerta,
Dejando sobre el camino
El agua de mi tristeza.
En el monte solitario,
Un cementerio de aldea
Parece un campo sembrado
Con granos de calaveras.
Y han florecido cipreses
Como gigantes cabezas
Que con órbitas vacías
Y verdosas cabelleras
Pensativos y dolientes
El horizonte contemplan.

¡Abril divino, que vienes
Cargado de sol y esencias,
Llena con nidos de oro
Las floridas calaveras!

La guitarra

Empieza el llanto
de la guitarra.
Se rompen las copas
de la madrugada.

Spring Song

I

The laughing youngsters
erupt from school,
planting the tepid April air
with tender songs.
Such joy in the deep
silence of the alleys!
A silence made of pieces
of new silver laughter.

II

I follow the road of afternoon
among the garden flowers,
leaving the water of my sadness
along the way.
On the solitary mountain
a village cemetery
seems to be a field
sown with seeds of skulls.
And cypresses have flowered
like enormous heads
which, with hollow eyes
and long green hair,
sorrowful and pensive,
contemplate the horizon.

Divine April, coming
laden with sun and perfumes,
fill with golden nests
the flowering skulls!

—RACHEL BENSON & ROBERT O'BRIEN

The Guitar

The cry of the guitar
begins.
The crystals of dawn are
breaking.

Empieza el llanto
de la guitarra.
Es inútil
callarla.
Es imposible
callarla.
Llora monótona
como llora el agua,
como llora el viento
sobre la nevada.
Es imposible
callarla.
Llora por cosas
lejanas.
Arena del Sur caliente
que pide camelias blancas.
Llora flecha sin blanco,
la tarde sin mañana,
y el primer pájaro muerto
sobre la rama.
¡Oh, guitarra!
Corazón malherido
por cinco espadas.

Amparo

Amparo,
¡qué sola estás en tu casa
vestida de blanco!
(Ecuador entre el jazmín
y el nardo.)

Oyes los maravillosos
surtidores de tu patio,
y el débil trino amarillo
del canario.

Por la tarde ves temblar
los cipreses con los pájaros,
mientras bordas lentamente
letras sobre el cañamazo.

The cry of the guitar
begins.
It's useless to stop it.
It's impossible to
stop it.
Its cry monotonous
as the weeping of water,
as the weeping of wind
over the snowfall.
It's impossible to
stop it.
It cries for
distant things.
Sand of the scalding South
seeking white camellias.
It mourns the arrow without target,
evening without morning,
and the first bird dead
upon the branch.
Oh, guitar!
Heart wounded
by five swords.

                     —RACHEL BENSON & ROBERT O'BRIEN

Amparo

Amparo,
sitting alone at home,
dressed in white!
(Halfway between the jasmine
and the spikenard.)

You hear the wonderful water
gushing in the garden,
and the feeble yellow trill
of the canary.

You see the cypresses, in the afternoon,
trembling with birds,
while slowly embroidering
letters upon the cloth.

Amparo,
¡qué sola estás en tu casa,
vestida de blanco!
Amparo,
¡y qué difícil decirte:
yo te amo!

Retrato de Silverio Franconetti

Entre italiano
y flamenco,
¿cómo cantaría
aquel Silverio?
La densa miel de Italia,
con el limón nuestro,
iba en el hondo llanto
del siguiriyero.
Su grito fue terrible.
Los viejos
dicen que se erizaban
los cabellos
y se abría el azogue
de los espejos.
Pasaba por los tonos
sin romperlos.
Y fue un creador
y un jardinero.
Un creador de glorietas
para el silencio.
Ahora su melodía
duerme con los ecos.
Definitiva y pura.
¡Con los últimos ecos!

El canto quiere ser luz . . .

El canto quiere ser luz.
En lo oscuro el canto tiene,
hilos de fósforo y luna.

Amparo,
sitting alone at home,
dressed in white!
Amparo,
how difficult to say:
I love you!   —RACHEL BENSON & ROBERT O'BRIEN

Portrait of Silverio Franconetti

What with the Italian
and the flamenco,
how would he sing,
this Silverio?
The thick honey of Italy
flowed with our lemon
in the deep lament
of the *siguiriyero*.
His cry was terrible.
The old people say
he used to make your hair
stand on end
and split the quicksilver
from mirrors.
He passed through the notes
without breaking them.
And he was a creator
and a gardener.
A creator of bowers
for silence.
Now his melody
sleeps with the echoes.
Final and pure.
With the last echoes!   —RACHEL BENSON & ROBERT O'BRIEN

The Song Wants to Be Light . . .

The song wants to be light.
In the darkness the song holds
threads of phosphorus and moonlight.

La luz no sabe qué quiere.
En sus límites de ópalo,
se encuentra ella misma,
y vuelve.

Mi niña se fue a la mar . . .

Mi niña se fue a la mar,
a contar olas y chinas,
pero se encontró, de pronto,
con el río de Sevilla.

    Entre adelfas y campanas
cinco barcos se mecían,
con los remos en el agua
y las velas en la brisa.

    ¿Quién mira dentro la torre
enjaezada, de Sevilla?
Cinco voces contestaban
redondas como sortijas.

    El cielo monta gallardo
al río, de orilla a orilla.
En el aire sonrosado,
cinco anillos se mecían.

Segundo aniversario

La luna clava en el mar
un largo cuerno de luz.

    Unicornio gris y verde,
estremecido, pero extático.
El cielo flota sobre el aire
como una inmensa flor de loto.

The light does not know what it wants.
Within its opal limits
it meets itself
and turns.

—RACHEL BENSON & ROBERT O'BRIEN

My Little Girl Went to the Sea . . .

My little girl went to the sea
to count waves and pebbles,
but suddenly she met
the river of Seville.

   Among bells and oleanders
five boats were rocking,
with oars in the water
and sails to the wind.

   What does she see in
the caparisoned tower of Seville?
Five voices answer
round as rings.

   The sky gracefully mounts
the river, from bank to bank.
In the blushing air,
five rings were rocking.

—RACHEL BENSON & ROBERT O'BRIEN

Second Anniversary

The moon nails a long horn
of light to the sea.

   Gray and green unicorn,
shivering, yet ecstatic.
The sky floats upon the air
like an immense lotus flower.

(¡Oh, tú sola paseando
la última estancia de la noche!)

Romance sonámbulo

Verde que te quiero verde.
Verde viento. Verdes ramas.
El barco sobre la mar
y el caballo en la montaña.
Con la sombra en la cintura
ella sueña en su baranda,
verde carne, pelo verde,
con ojos de fría plata.
Verde que te quiero verde.
Bajo la luna gitana,
las cosas la están mirando
y ella no puede mirarlas.

    Verde que te quiero verde.
Grandes estrellas de escarcha
vienen con el pez de sombra
que abre el camino del alba.
La higuera frota su viento
con la lija de sus ramas,
y el monte, gato garduño,
eriza sus pitas agrias.
Pero, ¿quién vendrá? ¿Y por dónde . . . ?
Ella sigue en su baranda,
verde carne, pelo verde,
soñando en la mar amarga.

    —Compadre, quiero cambiar
mi caballo por su casa,
mi montura por su espejo,
mi cuchillo por su manta.
Compadre, vengo sangrando,
desde los puertos de Cabra.

(Oh, you who walk alone
through the last mansion of the night!)
—RACHEL BENSON & ROBERT O'BRIEN

Somnambulist Ballad

Green. I want you green.
Green wind. Green branches.
The boat on the sea
and the horse in the mountains.
With a shadow round her waist
she dreams upon her railing,
green flesh, green hair,
with eyes of frozen silver.
Green. I want you green.
Beneath the gypsy moon,
things are watching her
and she cannot look back.

　　Green. I want you green.
Great rime-frost stars
come with the fish of the shadow
that opens the road of dawn.
The fig tree rubs the wind
with sandpaper branches,
while the wildcat mountain
bristles its acid fibers.
But who's coming? And where . . . ?
She lingers on her railing,
green flesh, green hair,
dreaming of the bitter sea.

　　Friend, let me exchange
my horse for your house,
my saddle for your mirror,
my dagger for your blanket.
Friend, I come here bleeding
from Cabra's mountain passes.

—Si yo pudiera, mocito,
este trato se cerraba.
Pero yo ya no soy yo,
ni mi casa es ya mi casa.

—Compadre, quiero morir
decentemente en mi cama.
De acero, si puede ser,
con las sábanas de holanda.
¿No ves la herida que tengo
desde el pecho a la garganta?

—Trescientas rosas morenas
lleva tu pechera blanca.
Tu sangre rezuma y huele
alrededor de tu faja.
Pero yo ya no soy yo,
ni mi casa es ya mi casa.

—Dejadme subir al menos
hasta las altas barandas;
¡dejadme subir!, dejadme
hasta las verdes barandas.
Barandales de la luna
por donde retumba el agua.

Ya suben los dos compadres
hacia las altas barandas.
Dejando un rastro de sangre.
Dejando un rastro de lágrimas.
Temblaban en los tejados
farolillos de hojalata.
Mil panderos de cristal
herían la madrugada.

Verde que te quiero verde,
verde viento, verdes ramas.
Los dos compadres subieron.
El largo viento dejaba
en la boca un raro gusto
de hiel, de menta y de albahaca.

If I were able, youngster,
we might strike a bargain.
But I'm no longer I,
my house is not my house.

Friend, I want to die
decently in my bed.
Of steel, if that could be,
on sheets of Holland linen.
Don't you see the wound I have
from my breast up to my throat?

Your white shirt front wears
three hundred dark roses.
Your blood breathes and oozes
all around your sash.
But I'm no longer I,
my house is not my house.

Let me climb at least
as far as the upper railings.
Let me climb! Let me!
To the green balustrade.
Railings of the moon
where the water sounds.

The two friends now go up
toward the upper railings.
Leaving a trail of blood.
Leaving a trail of tears.
Little lanterns made of tin
trembled on the rooftops.
A thousand crystal tambourines
pierced the early dawn.

Green. I want you green.
Green wind. Green branches.
The two friends went up.
The long wind was leaving
a strange taste in the mouth,
of gall, of mint and of sweet basil.

—¡Compadre! ¿Dónde está, dime,
dónde está tu niña amarga?
¡Cuántas veces te esperó!
¡Cuántas veces te esperara,
cara fresca, negro pelo,
en esta verde baranda!

Sobre el rostro del aljibe
se mecía la gitana.
Verde carne, pelo verde,
con ojos de fría plata.
Un carámbano de luna
la sostiene sobre el agua.

La noche se puso íntima
como una pequeña plaza.
Guardias civiles borrachos
en la puerta golpeaban.
Verde que te quiero verde.
Verde viento. Verdes ramas.
El barco sobre la mar.
Y el caballo en la montaña.

La casada infiel

Y que yo me la llevé al río
creyendo que era mozuela,
pero tenía marido.
Fue la noche de Santiago
y casi por compromiso.
Se apagaron los faroles
y se encendieron los grillos.
En las últimas esquinas
toqué sus pechos dormidos,
y se me abrieron de pronto
como ramos de jacintos.
El almidón de su enagua
me sonaba en el oído
como una pieza de seda
rasgada por diez cuchillos.

Friend, where is she? Tell me!
Where is your bitter girl?
How often she waited for you!
How many times she waited,
cool face, black hair,
at this same green railing.

On the face of the cistern
sways the gypsy girl.
Green flesh, green hair,
with eyes of frozen silver.
An icicle of the moon
supports her upon the water.

The night grew intimate
like a little square.
Drunken Civil Guards
were pounding on the door.
Green. I want you green.
Green wind. Green branches.
The boat on the sea
and the horse in the mountains.

— ROBERT O'BRIEN

The Faithless Wife

And I took her down by the river,
thinking that she was a virgin,
but she was already married.
It was the evening of Santiago
and almost as if by commitment
the street lamps were extinguished
and crickets were starting to glow.
Beyond the farthest corners
I touched her sleeping breasts;
immediately they opened
like branches of hyacinths.
The starch of her petticoats
rustled in my ears
like a piece of silk
slivered by ten knives.

Sin luz de plata en sus copas
los árboles han crecido,
y un horizonte de perros
ladra muy lejos del río.

　　Pasadas las zarzamoras,
los juncos y los espinos,
bajo su mata de pelo
hice un hoyo sobre el limo.
Yo me quité la corbata.
Ella se quitó el vestido.
Yo el cinturón con revólver.
Ella sus cuatro corpiños.
Ni nardos ni caracolas
tienen el cutis tan fino,
ni los cristales con luna
relumbran con ese brillo.
Sus muslos se me escapaban
como peces sorprendidos,
la mitad llenos de lumbre,
la mitad llenos de frío.
Aquella noche corrí
el mejor de los caminos,
montado en potra de nácar
sin bridas y sin estribos.
No quiero decir, por hombre,
las cosas que ella me dijo.
La luz del entendimiento
me hace ser muy comedido.
Sucia de besos y arena,
yo me la llevé del río.
Con el aire se batían
las espadas de los lirios.

　　Me porté como quien soy.
Como un gitano legítimo.
La regalé un costurero
grande, de raso pajizo,
y no quise enamorarme
porque teniendo marido
me dijo que era mozuela
cuando la llevaba al río.

With no silver light in their branches
the trees were gowing larger,
while a horizon of dogs
barked far away from the river.

Beyond the berry bushes,
the rushes and the hawthorns,
beneath her mass of hair
I hollowed out the mud.
I took off my tie.
She took off her dress.
I my belt with the pistol.
She the four parts of her bodice.
Neither pearl nor spikenard
has a skin so fine,
nor crystals of the moon
so brilliantly illumine.
Her thighs slipped from me
like sudden startled fish,
half bathed in fire,
half bathed in frost.
That night I rode upon
the best of all highways,
astride a pearly mare
with no bridles and no stirrups.
As a man I won't repeat
all the things she told me.
The light of understanding
makes me more discreet.
Stained with sand and kisses,
I led her from the river.
While the swords of the lilies
thrashed about the air.

I behaved as what I am,
like a true-born gypsy.
I gave her a sewing basket,
large, of straw-colored satin,
but I refused to fall in love
for, although she was married,
she told me she was a virgin
when I took her to the river.

—ROBERT O'BRIEN

Prendimiento de Antoñito el Camborio

Antonio Torres Heredia,
hijo y nieto de Camborios,
con una vara de mimbre
va a Sevilla a ver los toros.
Moreno de verde luna
anda despacio y garboso.
Sus empavonados bucles
le brillan entre los ojos.
A la mitad del camino
cortó limones redondos,
y los fue tirando al agua
hasta que la puso de oro.
Y a la mitad del camino,
bajo las ramas de un olmo,
guardia civil caminera
lo llevó codo con codo.

El día se va despacio,
la tarde colgada a un hombro,
dando una larga torera
sobre el mar y los arroyos.
Las aceitunas aguardan
la noche de Capricornio,
y una corta brisa, ecuestre,
salta los montes de plomo.
Antonio Torres Heredia,
hijo y nieto de Camborios,
viene sin vara de mimbre
entre los cinco tricornios.

—Antonio, ¿quién eres tú?
Si te llamaras Camborio,
hubieras hecho una fuente
de sangre con cinco chorros.
Ni tú eres hijo de nadie,
ni legítimo Camborio.
¡Se acabaron los gitanos
que iban por el monte solos!
Están los viejos cuchillos,
tiritando bajo el polvo.

Arrest of Antoñito el Camborio

Antonio Torres Heredia,
son and grandson of Camborios,
with a staff of willow
goes to Seville to see the bulls.
Dark as the green moon
he wanders slow and graceful.
His oily blue-black curls
glisten between his eyes.
Halfway down the road
he cut some round lemons
and tossed them in the water
until it turned to gold.
And halfway down the road,
under the branches of an elm,
the Civil Guard came marching
and took him by the elbows.

The day goes slowly by.
The afternoon hangs by a shoulder,
casting a large bull-cape
over the sea and the streams.
The olive trees are waiting for
the night of Capricorn,
and a sharp breeze on horseback
leaps over the leaden mountains.
Antonio Torres Heredia,
son and grandson of Camborios,
without his staff of willow, comes
between five three-cornered hats.

Antonio, just who are you?
If you were really Camborio
you would have made a fountain
of blood, with five sources.
No, you are the son of no one,
no legitimate Camborio.
For the gypsies have all departed
that walked on the mountains alone!
Now their old knives lie
shivering under the dust.

A las nueve de la noche
lo llevan al calabozo,
mientras los guardias civiles
beben limonada todos.
Y a las nueve de la noche
le cierran el calabozo,
mientras el cielo reluce
como la grupa de un potro.

Muerte de Antoñito el Camborio

Voces de muerte sonaron
cerca del Guadalquivir.
Voces antiguas que cercan
voz de clavel varonil.
Les clavó sobre las botas
mordiscos de jabalí.
En la lucha daba saltos
jabonados de delfín.
Bañó con sangre enemiga
su corbata carmesí,
pero eran cuatro puñales
y tuvo que sucumbir.
Cuando las estrellas clavan
rejones al agua gris,
cuando los erales sueñan
verónicas de alhelí,
voces de muerte sonaron
cerca del Guadalquivir.

—Antonio Torres Heredia,
Camborio de dura crin,
moreno de verde luna,
voz de clavel varonil:
¿Quién te ha quitado la vida
cerca del Guadalquivir?
—Mis cuatro primos Heredias
hijos de Benamejí.
Lo que en otros no envidiaban,
ya lo envidiaban en mí.

At nine o'clock at night
they take him to the jailhouse,
while all the Civil Guards
are drinking lemonade.
And at nine o'clock at night
they lock him in the jailhouse
while the sky above is shining
like the haunches of a colt.

—ROBERT O'BRIEN

Death of Antoñito el Camborio

Voices of death are sounding
near the Guadalquivir.
Ancient voices surrounding
the voice of the male carnation.
He stabbed them through the boots
with the bite of a wild boar.
In the fight he made leaps
as soap-slick as a dolphin.
He bathed his crimson tie
in enemy blood,
but there were four daggers
and he had to succumb.
While the stars are driving
spears into gray water,
while young bulls are dreaming
veronicas of violets,
voices of death are sounding
near the Guadalquivir.

Antonio Torres Heredia,
Camborio of the tough mane,
dark as the green moon,
voice of the male carnation:
Who has taken your life
near the Guadalquivir?
My four cousins Heredia,
sons of Benamejí.
What they didn't envy in others
they always envied in me:

Zapatos color corinto,
medallones de marfil,
y este cutis amasado
con aceituna y jazmín.
—¡Ay, Antoñito el Camborio,
digno de una Emperatriz!
Acuérdate de la Virgen
porque te vas a morir.
—¡Ay, Federico García,
llama a la Guardia Civil!
Ya mi talle se ha quebrado
como caña de maíz.

Tres golpes de sangre tuvo
y se murió de perfil.
Viva moneda que nunca
se volverá a repetir.
Un ángel marchoso pone
su cabeza en un cojín.
Otros de rubor cansado
encendieron un candil.
Y cuando los cuatro primos
llegan a Benamejí,
voces de muerte cesaron
cerca del Guadalquivir.

Shoes the color of raisins,
ivory medallions,
and this skin that's kneaded
with olive oil and jasmine.
Ay, Antoñito el Camborio,
worthy of an Empress!
Think upon the Virgin
for you're about to die.
Ay, Federico García,
call the Civil Guard!
For my waist has split
like a stalk of corn.

He gave three spurts of blood
and died in profile.
Living coin which never
can be repeated.
A jaunty angel places
his head upon a cushion.
Others, flushed and weary,
light an oil lantern.
And when the four cousins
arrive at Benamejí,
voices of death have ceased
near the Guadalquivir.

—ROBERT O'BRIEN

A CATALOG OF SELECTED
DOVER BOOKS
IN ALL FIELDS OF INTEREST

A CATALOG OF SELECTED DOVER
BOOKS IN ALL FIELDS OF INTEREST

CONCERNING THE SPIRITUAL IN ART, Wassily Kandinsky. Pioneering work by father of abstract art. Thoughts on color theory, nature of art. Analysis of earlier masters. 12 illustrations. 80pp. of text. 5⅜ x 8½. 23411-8 Pa. $3.95

ANIMALS: 1,419 Copyright-Free Illustrations of Mammals, Birds, Fish, Insects, etc., Jim Harter (ed.). Clear wood engravings present, in extremely lifelike poses, over 1,000 species of animals. One of the most extensive pictorial sourcebooks of its kind. Captions. Index. 284pp. 9 x 12. 23766-4 Pa. $12.95

CELTIC ART: The Methods of Construction, George Bain. Simple geometric techniques for making Celtic interlacements, spirals, Kells-type initials, animals, humans, etc. Over 500 illustrations. 160pp. 9 x 12. (USO) 22923-8 Pa. $9.95

AN ATLAS OF ANATOMY FOR ARTISTS, Fritz Schider. Most thorough reference work on art anatomy in the world. Hundreds of illustrations, including selections from works by Vesalius, Leonardo, Goya, Ingres, Michelangelo, others. 593 illustrations. 192pp. 7⅛ x 10¼. 20241-0 Pa. $9.95

CELTIC HAND STROKE-BY-STROKE (Irish Half-Uncial from "The Book of Kells"): An Arthur Baker Calligraphy Manual, Arthur Baker. Complete guide to creating each letter of the alphabet in distinctive Celtic manner. Covers hand position, strokes, pens, inks, paper, more. Illustrated. 48pp. 8¼ x 11. 24336-2 Pa. $3.95

EASY ORIGAMI, John Montroll. Charming collection of 32 projects (hat, cup, pelican, piano, swan, many more) specially designed for the novice origami hobbyist. Clearly illustrated easy-to-follow instructions insure that even beginning papercrafters will achieve successful results. 48pp. 8¼ x 11. 27298-2 Pa. $3.50

THE COMPLETE BOOK OF BIRDHOUSE CONSTRUCTION FOR WOODWORKERS, Scott D. Campbell. Detailed instructions, illustrations, tables. Also data on bird habitat and instinct patterns. Bibliography. 3 tables. 63 illustrations in 15 figures. 48pp. 5¼ x 8½. 24407-5 Pa. $2.50

BLOOMINGDALE'S ILLUSTRATED 1886 CATALOG: Fashions, Dry Goods and Housewares, Bloomingdale Brothers. Famed merchants' extremely rare catalog depicting about 1,700 products: clothing, housewares, firearms, dry goods, jewelry, more. Invaluable for dating, identifying vintage items. Also, copyright-free graphics for artists, designers. Co-published with Henry Ford Museum & Greenfield Village. 160pp. 8¼ x 11. 25780-0 Pa. $10.95

HISTORIC COSTUME IN PICTURES, Braun & Schneider. Over 1,450 costumed figures in clearly detailed engravings—from dawn of civilization to end of 19th century. Captions. Many folk costumes. 256pp. 8⅜ x 11¾. 23150-X Pa. $12.95

STICKLEY CRAFTSMAN FURNITURE CATALOGS, Gustav Stickley and L. & J. G. Stickley. Beautiful, functional furniture in two authentic catalogs from 1910. 594 illustrations, including 277 photos, show settles, rockers, armchairs, reclining chairs, bookcases, desks, tables. 183pp. 6½ x 9¼. 23838-5 Pa. $9.95

AMERICAN LOCOMOTIVES IN HISTORIC PHOTOGRAPHS: 1858 to 1949, Ron Ziel (ed.). A rare collection of 126 meticulously detailed official photographs, called "builder portraits," of American locomotives that majestically chronicle the rise of steam locomotive power in America. Introduction. Detailed captions. xi + 129pp. 9 x 12. 27393-8 Pa. $12.95

AMERICA'S LIGHTHOUSES: An Illustrated History, Francis Ross Holland, Jr. Delightfully written, profusely illustrated fact-filled survey of over 200 American lighthouses since 1716. History, anecdotes, technological advances, more. 240pp. 8 x 10¾. 25576-X Pa. $12.95

TOWARDS A NEW ARCHITECTURE, Le Corbusier. Pioneering manifesto by founder of "International School." Technical and aesthetic theories, views of industry, economics, relation of form to function, "mass-production split" and much more. Profusely illustrated. 320pp. 6⅛ x 9¼. (USO) 25023-7 Pa. $9.95

HOW THE OTHER HALF LIVES, Jacob Riis. Famous journalistic record, exposing poverty and degradation of New York slums around 1900, by major social reformer. 100 striking and influential photographs. 233pp. 10 x 7⅞. 22012-5 Pa. $10.95

FRUIT KEY AND TWIG KEY TO TREES AND SHRUBS, William M. Harlow. One of the handiest and most widely used identification aids. Fruit key covers 120 deciduous and evergreen species; twig key 160 deciduous species. Easily used. Over 300 photographs. 126pp. 5⅜ x 8½. 20511-8 Pa. $3.95

COMMON BIRD SONGS, Dr. Donald J. Borror. Songs of 60 most common U.S. birds: robins, sparrows, cardinals, bluejays, finches, more—arranged in order of increasing complexity. Up to 9 variations of songs of each species. Cassette and manual 99911-4 $8.95

ORCHIDS AS HOUSE PLANTS, Rebecca Tyson Northen. Grow cattleyas and many other kinds of orchids—in a window, in a case, or under artificial light. 63 illustrations. 148pp. 5⅜ x 8½. 23261-1 Pa. $4.95

MONSTER MAZES, Dave Phillips. Masterful mazes at four levels of difficulty. Avoid deadly perils and evil creatures to find magical treasures. Solutions for all 32 exciting illustrated puzzles. 48pp. 8¼ x 11. 26005-4 Pa. $2.95

MOZART'S DON GIOVANNI (DOVER OPERA LIBRETTO SERIES), Wolfgang Amadeus Mozart. Introduced and translated by Ellen H. Bleiler. Standard Italian libretto, with complete English translation. Convenient and thoroughly portable—an ideal companion for reading along with a recording or the performance itself. Introduction. List of characters. Plot summary. 121pp. 5¼ x 8½. 24944-1 Pa. $2.95

TECHNICAL MANUAL AND DICTIONARY OF CLASSICAL BALLET, Gail Grant. Defines, explains, comments on steps, movements, poses and concepts. 15-page pictorial section. Basic book for student, viewer. 127pp. 5⅜ x 8½. 21843-0 Pa. $4.95

BRASS INSTRUMENTS: Their History and Development, Anthony Baines. Authoritative, updated survey of the evolution of trumpets, trombones, bugles, cornets, French horns, tubas and other brass wind instruments. Over 140 illustrations and 48 music examples. Corrected and updated by author. New preface. Bibliography. 320pp. 5⅜ x 8½. 27574-4 Pa. $9.95

HOLLYWOOD GLAMOR PORTRAITS, John Kobal (ed.). 145 photos from 1926-49. Harlow, Gable, Bogart, Bacall; 94 stars in all. Full background on photographers, technical aspects. 160pp. 8⅜ x 11¼. 23352-9 Pa. $12.95

MAX AND MORITZ, Wilhelm Busch. Great humor classic in both German and English. Also 10 other works: "Cat and Mouse," "Plisch and Plumm," etc. 216pp. 5⅜ x 8½. 20181-3 Pa. $6.95

THE RAVEN AND OTHER FAVORITE POEMS, Edgar Allan Poe. Over 40 of the author's most memorable poems: "The Bells," "Ulalume," "Israfel," "To Helen," "The Conqueror Worm," "Eldorado," "Annabel Lee," many more. Alphabetic lists of titles and first lines. 64pp. 5³⁄₁₆ x 8¼. 26685-0 Pa. $1.00

PERSONAL MEMOIRS OF U. S. GRANT, Ulysses Simpson Grant. Intelligent, deeply moving firsthand account of Civil War campaigns, considered by many the finest military memoirs ever written. Includes letters, historic photographs, maps and more. 528pp. 6⅛ x 9¼. 28587-1 Pa. $11.95

AMULETS AND SUPERSTITIONS, E. A. Wallis Budge. Comprehensive discourse on origin, powers of amulets in many ancient cultures: Arab, Persian Babylonian, Assyrian, Egyptian, Gnostic, Hebrew, Phoenician, Syriac, etc. Covers cross, swastika, crucifix, seals, rings, stones, etc. 584pp. 5⅜ x 8½. 23573-4 Pa. $12.95

RUSSIAN STORIES/PYCCKNE PACCKA3bl: A Dual-Language Book, edited by Gleb Struve. Twelve tales by such masters as Chekhov, Tolstoy, Dostoevsky, Pushkin, others. Excellent word-for-word English translations on facing pages, plus teaching and study aids, Russian/English vocabulary, biographical/critical introductions, more. 416pp. 5⅜ x 8½. 26244-8 Pa. $8.95

PHILADELPHIA THEN AND NOW: 60 Sites Photographed in the Past and Present, Kenneth Finkel and Susan Oyama. Rare photographs of City Hall, Logan Square, Independence Hall, Betsy Ross House, other landmarks juxtaposed with contemporary views. Captures changing face of historic city. Introduction. Captions. 128pp. 8¼ x 11. 25790-8 Pa. $9.95

AIA ARCHITECTURAL GUIDE TO NASSAU AND SUFFOLK COUNTIES, LONG ISLAND, The American Institute of Architects, Long Island Chapter, and the Society for the Preservation of Long Island Antiquities. Comprehensive, well-researched and generously illustrated volume brings to life over three centuries of Long Island's great architectural heritage. More than 240 photographs with authoritative, extensively detailed captions. 176pp. 8¼ x 11. 26946-9 Pa. $14.95

NORTH AMERICAN INDIAN LIFE: Customs and Traditions of 23 Tribes, Elsie Clews Parsons (ed.). 27 fictionalized essays by noted anthropologists examine religion, customs, government, additional facets of life among the Winnebago, Crow, Zuni, Eskimo, other tribes. 480pp. 6⅛ x 9¼. 27377-6 Pa. $10.95

FRANK LLOYD WRIGHT'S HOLLYHOCK HOUSE, Donald Hoffmann. Lavishly illustrated, carefully documented study of one of Wright's most controversial residential designs. Over 120 photographs, floor plans, elevations, etc. Detailed perceptive text by noted Wright scholar. Index. 128pp. 9¼ x 10¾. 27133-1 Pa. $11.95

THE MALE AND FEMALE FIGURE IN MOTION: 60 Classic Photographic Sequences, Eadweard Muybridge. 60 true-action photographs of men and women walking, running, climbing, bending, turning, etc., reproduced from rare 19th-century masterpiece. vi + 121pp. 9 x 12. 24745-7 Pa. $10.95

1001 QUESTIONS ANSWERED ABOUT THE SEASHORE, N. J. Berrill and Jacquelyn Berrill. Queries answered about dolphins, sea snails, sponges, starfish, fishes, shore birds, many others. Covers appearance, breeding, growth, feeding, much more. 305pp. 5¼ x 8¼. 23366-9 Pa. $8.95

GUIDE TO OWL WATCHING IN NORTH AMERICA, Donald S. Heintzelman. Superb guide offers complete data and descriptions of 19 species: barn owl, screech owl, snowy owl, many more. Expert coverage of owl-watching equipment, conservation, migrations and invasions, etc. Guide to observing sites. 84 illustrations. xiii + 193pp. 5⅜ x 8½. 27344-X Pa. $8.95

MEDICINAL AND OTHER USES OF NORTH AMERICAN PLANTS: A Historical Survey with Special Reference to the Eastern Indian Tribes, Charlotte Erichsen-Brown. Chronological historical citations document 500 years of usage of plants, trees, shrubs native to eastern Canada, northeastern U.S. Also complete identifying information. 343 illustrations. 544pp. 6½ x 9¼. 25951-X Pa. $12.95

STORYBOOK MAZES, Dave Phillips. 23 stories and mazes on two-page spreads: Wizard of Oz, Treasure Island, Robin Hood, etc. Solutions. 64pp. 8¼ x 11. 23628-5 Pa. $2.95

NEGRO FOLK MUSIC, U.S.A., Harold Courlander. Noted folklorist's scholarly yet readable analysis of rich and varied musical tradition. Includes authentic versions of over 40 folk songs. Valuable bibliography and discography. xi + 324pp. 5⅜ x 8½. 27350-4 Pa. $9.95

MOVIE-STAR PORTRAITS OF THE FORTIES, John Kobal (ed.). 163 glamor, studio photos of 106 stars of the 1940s: Rita Hayworth, Ava Gardner, Marlon Brando, Clark Gable, many more. 176pp. 8⅝ x 11¼. 23546-7 Pa. $12.95

BENCHLEY LOST AND FOUND, Robert Benchley. Finest humor from early 30s, about pet peeves, child psychologists, post office and others. Mostly unavailable elsewhere. 73 illustrations by Peter Arno and others. 183pp. 5⅜ x 8½. 22410-4 Pa. $6.95

YEKL and THE IMPORTED BRIDEGROOM AND OTHER STORIES OF YIDDISH NEW YORK, Abraham Cahan. Film Hester Street based on Yekl (1896). Novel, other stories among first about Jewish immigrants on N.Y.'s East Side. 240pp. 5⅜ x 8½. 22427-9 Pa. $6.95

SELECTED POEMS, Walt Whitman. Generous sampling from *Leaves of Grass*. Twenty-four poems include "I Hear America Singing," "Song of the Open Road," "I Sing the Body Electric," "When Lilacs Last in the Dooryard Bloom'd," "O Captain! My Captain!"—all reprinted from an authoritative edition. Lists of titles and first lines. 128pp. 5³⁄₁₆ x 8¼. 26878-0 Pa. $1.00

THE BEST TALES OF HOFFMANN, E. T. A. Hoffmann. 10 of Hoffmann's most important stories: "Nutcracker and the King of Mice," "The Golden Flowerpot," etc. 458pp. 5⅜ x 8½. 21793-0 Pa. $9.95

FROM FETISH TO GOD IN ANCIENT EGYPT, E. A. Wallis Budge. Rich detailed survey of Egyptian conception of "God" and gods, magic, cult of animals, Osiris, more. Also, superb English translations of hymns and legends. 240 illustrations. 545pp. 5⅜ x 8½. 25803-3 Pa. $13.95

FRENCH STORIES/CONTES FRANÇAIS: A Dual-Language Book, Wallace Fowlie. Ten stories by French masters, Voltaire to Camus: "Micromegas" by Voltaire; "The Atheist's Mass" by Balzac; "Minuet" by de Maupassant; "The Guest" by Camus, six more. Excellent English translations on facing pages. Also French-English vocabulary list, exercises, more. 352pp. 5⅜ x 8½. 26443-2 Pa. $8.95

CHICAGO AT THE TURN OF THE CENTURY IN PHOTOGRAPHS: 122 Historic Views from the Collections of the Chicago Historical Society, Larry A. Viskochil. Rare large-format prints offer detailed views of City Hall, State Street, the Loop, Hull House, Union Station, many other landmarks, circa 1904-1913. Introduction. Captions. Maps. 144pp. 9⅜ x 12¼. 24656-6 Pa. $12.95

OLD BROOKLYN IN EARLY PHOTOGRAPHS, 1865-1929, William Lee Younger. Luna Park, Gravesend race track, construction of Grand Army Plaza, moving of Hotel Brighton, etc. 157 previously unpublished photographs. 165pp. 8⅞ x 11¾. 23587-4 Pa. $13.95

THE MYTHS OF THE NORTH AMERICAN INDIANS, Lewis Spence. Rich anthology of the myths and legends of the Algonquins, Iroquois, Pawnees and Sioux, prefaced by an extensive historical and ethnological commentary. 36 illustrations. 480pp. 5⅜ x 8½. 25967-6 Pa. $8.95

AN ENCYCLOPEDIA OF BATTLES: Accounts of Over 1,560 Battles from 1479 B.C. to the Present, David Eggenberger. Essential details of every major battle in recorded history from the first battle of Megiddo in 1479 B.C. to Grenada in 1984. List of Battle Maps. New Appendix covering the years 1967-1984. Index. 99 illustrations. 544pp. 6½ x 9¼. 24913-1 Pa. $14.95

SAILING ALONE AROUND THE WORLD, Captain Joshua Slocum. First man to sail around the world, alone, in small boat. One of great feats of seamanship told in delightful manner. 67 illustrations. 294pp. 5⅜ x 8½. 20326-3 Pa. $5.95

ANARCHISM AND OTHER ESSAYS, Emma Goldman. Powerful, penetrating, prophetic essays on direct action, role of minorities, prison reform, puritan hypocrisy, violence, etc. 271pp. 5⅜ x 8½. 22484-8 Pa. $6.95

MYTHS OF THE HINDUS AND BUDDHISTS, Ananda K. Coomaraswamy and Sister Nivedita. Great stories of the epics; deeds of Krishna, Shiva, taken from puranas, Vedas, folk tales; etc. 32 illustrations. 400pp. 5⅜ x 8½. 21759-0 Pa. $10.95

BEYOND PSYCHOLOGY, Otto Rank. Fear of death, desire of immortality, nature of sexuality, social organization, creativity, according to Rankian system. 291pp. 5⅜ x 8½. 20485-5 Pa. $8.95

A THEOLOGICO-POLITICAL TREATISE, Benedict Spinoza. Also contains unfinished Political Treatise. Great classic on religious liberty, theory of government on common consent. R. Elwes translation. Total of 421pp. 5⅜ x 8½. 20249-6 Pa. $9.95

MY BONDAGE AND MY FREEDOM, Frederick Douglass. Born a slave, Douglass became outspoken force in antislavery movement. The best of Douglass' autobiographies. Graphic description of slave life. 464pp. 5⅜ x 8½. 22457-0 Pa. $8.95

FOLLOWING THE EQUATOR: A Journey Around the World, Mark Twain. Fascinating humorous account of 1897 voyage to Hawaii, Australia, India, New Zealand, etc. Ironic, bemused reports on peoples, customs, climate, flora and fauna, politics, much more. 197 illustrations. 720pp. 5⅜ x 8½. 26113-1 Pa. $15.95

THE PEOPLE CALLED SHAKERS, Edward D. Andrews. Definitive study of Shakers: origins, beliefs, practices, dances, social organization, furniture and crafts, etc. 33 illustrations. 351pp. 5⅜ x 8½. 21081-2 Pa. $8.95

THE MYTHS OF GREECE AND ROME, H. A. Guerber. A classic of mythology, generously illustrated, long prized for its simple, graphic, accurate retelling of the principal myths of Greece and Rome, and for its commentary on their origins and significance. With 64 illustrations by Michelangelo, Raphael, Titian, Rubens, Canova, Bernini and others. 480pp. 5⅜ x 8½. 27584-1 Pa. $9.95

PSYCHOLOGY OF MUSIC, Carl E. Seashore. Classic work discusses music as a medium from psychological viewpoint. Clear treatment of physical acoustics, auditory apparatus, sound perception, development of musical skills, nature of musical feeling, host of other topics. 88 figures. 408pp. 5⅜ x 8½. 21851-1 Pa. $10.95

THE PHILOSOPHY OF HISTORY, Georg W. Hegel. Great classic of Western thought develops concept that history is not chance but rational process, the evolution of freedom. 457pp. 5⅜ x 8½. 20112-0 Pa. $9.95

THE BOOK OF TEA, Kakuzo Okakura. Minor classic of the Orient: entertaining, charming explanation, interpretation of traditional Japanese culture in terms of tea ceremony. 94pp. 5⅜ x 8½. 20070-1 Pa. $3.95

LIFE IN ANCIENT EGYPT, Adolf Erman. Fullest, most thorough, detailed older account with much not in more recent books, domestic life, religion, magic, medicine, commerce, much more. Many illustrations reproduce tomb paintings, carvings, hieroglyphs, etc. 597pp. 5⅜ x 8½. 22632-8 Pa. $11.95

SUNDIALS, Their Theory and Construction, Albert Waugh. Far and away the best, most thorough coverage of ideas, mathematics concerned, types, construction, adjusting anywhere. Simple, nontechnical treatment allows even children to build several of these dials. Over 100 illustrations. 230pp. 5⅜ x 8½. 22947-5 Pa. $7.95

DYNAMICS OF FLUIDS IN POROUS MEDIA, Jacob Bear. For advanced students of ground water hydrology, soil mechanics and physics, drainage and irrigation engineering, and more. 335 illustrations. Exercises, with answers. 784pp. 6⅛ x 9¼. 65675-6 Pa. $19.95

SONGS OF EXPERIENCE: Facsimile Reproduction with 26 Plates in Full Color, William Blake. 26 full-color plates from a rare 1826 edition. Includes "The Tyger," "London," "Holy Thursday," and other poems. Printed text of poems. 48pp. 5¼ x 7. 24636-1 Pa. $4.95

OLD-TIME VIGNETTES IN FULL COLOR, Carol Belanger Grafton (ed.). Over 390 charming, often sentimental illustrations, selected from archives of Victorian graphics—pretty women posing, children playing, food, flowers, kittens and puppies, smiling cherubs, birds and butterflies, much more. All copyright-free. 48pp. 9¼ x 12¼. 27269-9 Pa. $7.95

PERSPECTIVE FOR ARTISTS, Rex Vicat Cole. Depth, perspective of sky and sea, shadows, much more, not usually covered. 391 diagrams, 81 reproductions of drawings and paintings. 279pp. 5⅜ x 8½. 22487-2 Pa. $7.95

DRAWING THE LIVING FIGURE, Joseph Sheppard. Innovative approach to artistic anatomy focuses on specifics of surface anatomy, rather than muscles and bones. Over 170 drawings of live models in front, back and side views, and in widely varying poses. Accompanying diagrams. 177 illustrations. Introduction. Index. 144pp. 8⅜ x11¼. 26723-7 Pa. $8.95

GOTHIC AND OLD ENGLISH ALPHABETS: 100 Complete Fonts, Dan X. Solo. Add power, elegance to posters, signs, other graphics with 100 stunning copyright-free alphabets: Blackstone, Dolbey, Germania, 97 more–including many lower-case, numerals, punctuation marks. 104pp. 8⅛ x 11. 24695-7 Pa. $8.95

HOW TO DO BEADWORK, Mary White. Fundamental book on craft from simple projects to five-bead chains and woven works. 106 illustrations. 142pp. 5⅜ x 8. 20697-1 Pa. $4.95

THE BOOK OF WOOD CARVING, Charles Marshall Sayers. Finest book for beginners discusses fundamentals and offers 34 designs. "Absolutely first rate . . . well thought out and well executed."–E. J. Tangerman. 118pp. 7¾ x 10⅝. 23654-4 Pa. $6.95

ILLUSTRATED CATALOG OF CIVIL WAR MILITARY GOODS: Union Army Weapons, Insignia, Uniform Accessories, and Other Equipment, Schuyler, Hartley, and Graham. Rare, profusely illustrated 1846 catalog includes Union Army uniform and dress regulations, arms and ammunition, coats, insignia, flags, swords, rifles, etc. 226 illustrations. 160pp. 9 x 12. 24939-5 Pa. $10.95

WOMEN'S FASHIONS OF THE EARLY 1900s: An Unabridged Republication of "New York Fashions, 1909," National Cloak & Suit Co. Rare catalog of mail-order fashions documents women's and children's clothing styles shortly after the turn of the century. Captions offer full descriptions, prices. Invaluable resource for fashion, costume historians. Approximately 725 illustrations. 128pp. 8⅜ x 11¼. 27276-1 Pa. $11.95

THE 1912 AND 1915 GUSTAV STICKLEY FURNITURE CATALOGS, Gustav Stickley. With over 200 detailed illustrations and descriptions, these two catalogs are essential reading and reference materials and identification guides for Stickley furniture. Captions cite materials, dimensions and prices. 112pp. 6½ x 9¼. 26676-1 Pa. $9.95

EARLY AMERICAN LOCOMOTIVES, John H. White, Jr. Finest locomotive engravings from early 19th century: historical (1804–74), main-line (after 1870), special, foreign, etc. 147 plates. 142pp. 11⅜ x 8¼. 22772-3 Pa. $10.95

THE TALL SHIPS OF TODAY IN PHOTOGRAPHS, Frank O. Braynard. Lavishly illustrated tribute to nearly 100 majestic contemporary sailing vessels: Amerigo Vespucci, Clearwater, Constitution, Eagle, Mayflower, Sea Cloud, Victory, many more. Authoritative captions provide statistics, background on each ship. 190 black-and-white photographs and illustrations. Introduction. 128pp. 8⅞ x 11¾. 27163-3 Pa. $13.95

EARLY NINETEENTH-CENTURY CRAFTS AND TRADES, Peter Stockham (ed.). Extremely rare 1807 volume describes to youngsters the crafts and trades of the day: brickmaker, weaver, dressmaker, bookbinder, ropemaker, saddler, many more. Quaint prose, charming illustrations for each craft. 20 black-and-white line illustrations. 192pp. 4⅝ x 6. 27293-1 Pa. $4.95

VICTORIAN FASHIONS AND COSTUMES FROM HARPER'S BAZAR, 1867–1898, Stella Blum (ed.). Day costumes, evening wear, sports clothes, shoes, hats, other accessories in over 1,000 detailed engravings. 320pp. 9⅜ x 12¼. 22990-4 Pa. $14.95

GUSTAV STICKLEY, THE CRAFTSMAN, Mary Ann Smith. Superb study surveys broad scope of Stickley's achievement, especially in architecture. Design philosophy, rise and fall of the Craftsman empire, descriptions and floor plans for many Craftsman houses, more. 86 black-and-white halftones. 31 line illustrations. Introduction 208pp. 6½ x 9¼. 27210-9 Pa. $9.95

THE LONG ISLAND RAIL ROAD IN EARLY PHOTOGRAPHS, Ron Ziel. Over 220 rare photos, informative text document origin (1844) and development of rail service on Long Island. Vintage views of early trains, locomotives, stations, passengers, crews, much more. Captions. 8⅞ x 11¾. 26301-0 Pa. $13.95

THE BOOK OF OLD SHIPS: From Egyptian Galleys to Clipper Ships, Henry B. Culver. Superb, authoritative history of sailing vessels, with 80 magnificent line illustrations. Galley, bark, caravel, longship, whaler, many more. Detailed, informative text on each vessel by noted naval historian. Introduction. 256pp. 5⅜ x 8½. 27332-6 Pa. $7.95

TEN BOOKS ON ARCHITECTURE, Vitruvius. The most important book ever written on architecture. Early Roman aesthetics, technology, classical orders, site selection, all other aspects. Morgan translation. 331pp. 5⅜ x 8½. 20645-9 Pa. $8.95

THE HUMAN FIGURE IN MOTION, Eadweard Muybridge. More than 4,500 stopped-action photos, in action series, showing undraped men, women, children jumping, lying down, throwing, sitting, wrestling, carrying, etc. 390pp. 7⅞ x 10⅝. 20204-6 Clothbd. $25.95

TREES OF THE EASTERN AND CENTRAL UNITED STATES AND CANADA, William M. Harlow. Best one-volume guide to 140 trees. Full descriptions, woodlore, range, etc. Over 600 illustrations. Handy size. 288pp. 4½ x 6⅜. 20395-6 Pa. $6.95

SONGS OF WESTERN BIRDS, Dr. Donald J. Borror. Complete song and call repertoire of 60 western species, including flycatchers, juncoes, cactus wrens, many more–includes fully illustrated booklet. Cassette and manual 99913-0 $8.95

GROWING AND USING HERBS AND SPICES, Milo Miloradovich. Versatile handbook provides all the information needed for cultivation and use of all the herbs and spices available in North America. 4 illustrations. Index. Glossary. 236pp. 5⅜ x 8½. 25058-X Pa. $6.95

BIG BOOK OF MAZES AND LABYRINTHS, Walter Shepherd. 50 mazes and labyrinths in all–classical, solid, ripple, and more–in one great volume. Perfect inexpensive puzzler for clever youngsters. Full solutions. 112pp. 8⅛ x 11. 22951-3 Pa. $4.95

PIANO TUNING, J. Cree Fischer. Clearest, best book for beginner, amateur. Simple repairs, raising dropped notes, tuning by easy method of flattened fifths. No previous skills needed. 4 illustrations. 201pp. 5⅜ x 8½. 23267-0 Pa. $6.95

A SOURCE BOOK IN THEATRICAL HISTORY, A. M. Nagler. Contemporary observers on acting, directing, make-up, costuming, stage props, machinery, scene design, from Ancient Greece to Chekhov. 611pp. 5⅜ x 8½. 20515-0 Pa. $12.95

THE COMPLETE NONSENSE OF EDWARD LEAR, Edward Lear. All nonsense limericks, zany alphabets, Owl and Pussycat, songs, nonsense botany, etc., illustrated by Lear. Total of 320pp. 5⅜ x 8½. (USO) 20167-8 Pa. $6.95

VICTORIAN PARLOUR POETRY: An Annotated Anthology, Michael R. Turner. 117 gems by Longfellow, Tennyson, Browning, many lesser-known poets. "The Village Blacksmith," "Curfew Must Not Ring Tonight," "Only a Baby Small," dozens more, often difficult to find elsewhere. Index of poets, titles, first lines. xxiii + 325pp. 5⅝ x 8¼. 27044-0 Pa. $8.95

DUBLINERS, James Joyce. Fifteen stories offer vivid, tightly focused observations of the lives of Dublin's poorer classes. At least one, "The Dead," is considered a masterpiece. Reprinted complete and unabridged from standard edition. 160pp. 5$\frac{3}{16}$ x 8¼. 26870-5 Pa. $1.00

THE HAUNTED MONASTERY and THE CHINESE MAZE MURDERS, Robert van Gulik. Two full novels by van Gulik, set in 7th-century China, continue adventures of Judge Dee and his companions. An evil Taoist monastery, seemingly supernatural events; overgrown topiary maze hides strange crimes. 27 illustrations. 328pp. 5⅜ x 8½. 23502-5 Pa. $8.95

THE BOOK OF THE SACRED MAGIC OF ABRAMELIN THE MAGE, translated by S. MacGregor Mathers. Medieval manuscript of ceremonial magic. Basic document in Aleister Crowley, Golden Dawn groups. 268pp. 5⅜ x 8½. 23211-5 Pa. $8.95

NEW RUSSIAN-ENGLISH AND ENGLISH-RUSSIAN DICTIONARY, M. A. O'Brien. This is a remarkably handy Russian dictionary, containing a surprising amount of information, including over 70,000 entries. 366pp. 4½ x 6⅛. 20208-9 Pa. $9.95

HISTORIC HOMES OF THE AMERICAN PRESIDENTS, Second, Revised Edition, Irvin Haas. A traveler's guide to American Presidential homes, most open to the public, depicting and describing homes occupied by every American President from George Washington to George Bush. With visiting hours, admission charges, travel routes. 175 photographs. Index. 160pp. 8¼ x 11. 26751-2 Pa. $11.95

NEW YORK IN THE FORTIES, Andreas Feininger. 162 brilliant photographs by the well-known photographer, formerly with *Life* magazine. Commuters, shoppers, Times Square at night, much else from city at its peak. Captions by John von Hartz. 181pp. 9¼ x 10¾. 23585-8 Pa. $12.95

INDIAN SIGN LANGUAGE, William Tomkins. Over 525 signs developed by Sioux and other tribes. Written instructions and diagrams. Also 290 pictographs. 111pp. 6⅛ x 9¼. 22029-X Pa. $3.95

CATALOG OF DOVER BOOKS

ANATOMY: A Complete Guide for Artists, Joseph Sheppard. A master of figure drawing shows artists how to render human anatomy convincingly. Over 460 illustrations. 224pp. 8⅜ x 11¼. 27279-6 Pa. $10.95

MEDIEVAL CALLIGRAPHY: Its History and Technique, Marc Drogin. Spirited history, comprehensive instruction manual covers 13 styles (ca. 4th century thru 15th). Excellent photographs; directions for duplicating medieval techniques with modern tools. 224pp. 8⅜ x 11¼. 26142-5 Pa. $12.95

DRIED FLOWERS: How to Prepare Them, Sarah Whitlock and Martha Rankin. Complete instructions on how to use silica gel, meal and borax, perlite aggregate, sand and borax, glycerine and water to create attractive permanent flower arrangements. 12 illustrations. 32pp. 5⅜ x 8½. 21802-3 Pa. $1.00

EASY-TO-MAKE BIRD FEEDERS FOR WOODWORKERS, Scott D. Campbell. Detailed, simple-to-use guide for designing, constructing, caring for and using feeders. Text, illustrations for 12 classic and contemporary designs. 96pp. 5⅜ x 8½. 25847-5 Pa. $2.95

SCOTTISH WONDER TALES FROM MYTH AND LEGEND, Donald A. Mackenzie. 16 lively tales tell of giants rumbling down mountainsides, of a magic wand that turns stone pillars into warriors, of gods and goddesses, evil hags, powerful forces and more. 240pp. 5⅜ x 8½. 29677-6 Pa. $6.95

THE HISTORY OF UNDERCLOTHES, C. Willett Cunnington and Phyllis Cunnington. Fascinating, well-documented survey covering six centuries of English undergarments, enhanced with over 100 illustrations: 12th-century laced-up bodice, footed long drawers (1795), 19th-century bustles, 19th-century corsets for men, Victorian "bust improvers," much more. 272pp. 5⅝ x 8¼. 27124-2 Pa. $9.95

ARTS AND CRAFTS FURNITURE: The Complete Brooks Catalog of 1912, Brooks Manufacturing Co. Photos and detailed descriptions of more than 150 now very collectible furniture designs from the Arts and Crafts movement depict davenports, settees, buffets, desks, tables, chairs, bedsteads, dressers and more, all built of solid, quarter-sawed oak. Invaluable for students and enthusiasts of antiques, Americana and the decorative arts. 80pp. 6½ x 9¼. 27471-3 Pa. $8.95

HOW WE INVENTED THE AIRPLANE: An Illustrated History, Orville Wright. Fascinating firsthand account covers early experiments, construction of planes and motors, first flights, much more. Introduction and commentary by Fred C. Kelly. 76 photographs. 96pp. 8¼ x 11. 25662-6 Pa. $8.95

THE ARTS OF THE SAILOR: Knotting, Splicing and Ropework, Hervey Garrett Smith. Indispensable shipboard reference covers tools, basic knots and useful hitches; handsewing and canvas work, more. Over 100 illustrations. Delightful reading for sea lovers. 256pp. 5⅜ x 8½. 26440-8 Pa. $7.95

FRANK LLOYD WRIGHT'S FALLINGWATER: The House and Its History, Second, Revised Edition, Donald Hoffmann. A total revision–both in text and illustrations–of the standard document on Fallingwater, the boldest, most personal architectural statement of Wright's mature years, updated with valuable new material from the recently opened Frank Lloyd Wright Archives. "Fascinating"–*The New York Times*. 116 illustrations. 128pp. 9¼ x 10¾. 27430-6 Pa. $11.95

PHOTOGRAPHIC SKETCHBOOK OF THE CIVIL WAR, Alexander Gardner. 100 photos taken on field during the Civil War. Famous shots of Manassas Harper's Ferry, Lincoln, Richmond, slave pens, etc. 244pp. 10⅝ x 8¼. 22731-6 Pa. $9.95

FIVE ACRES AND INDEPENDENCE, Maurice G. Kains. Great back-to-the-land classic explains basics of self-sufficient farming. The one book to get. 95 illustrations. 397pp. 5⅜ x 8½. 20974-1 Pa. $7.95

SONGS OF EASTERN BIRDS, Dr. Donald J. Borror. Songs and calls of 60 species most common to eastern U.S.: warblers, woodpeckers, flycatchers, thrushes, larks, many more in high-quality recording. Cassette and manual 99912-2 $9.95

A MODERN HERBAL, Margaret Grieve. Much the fullest, most exact, most useful compilation of herbal material. Gigantic alphabetical encyclopedia, from aconite to zedoary, gives botanical information, medical properties, folklore, economic uses, much else. Indispensable to serious reader. 161 illustrations. 888pp. 6½ x 9¼. 2-vol. set. (USO) Vol. I: 22798-7 Pa. $9.95
Vol. II: 22799-5 Pa. $9.95

HIDDEN TREASURE MAZE BOOK, Dave Phillips. Solve 34 challenging mazes accompanied by heroic tales of adventure. Evil dragons, people-eating plants, blood-thirsty giants, many more dangerous adversaries lurk at every twist and turn. 34 mazes, stories, solutions. 48pp. 8¼ x 11. 24566-7 Pa. $2.95

LETTERS OF W. A. MOZART, Wolfgang A. Mozart. Remarkable letters show bawdy wit, humor, imagination, musical insights, contemporary musical world; includes some letters from Leopold Mozart. 276pp. 5⅜ x 8½. 22859-2 Pa. $7.95

BASIC PRINCIPLES OF CLASSICAL BALLET, Agrippina Vaganova. Great Russian theoretician, teacher explains methods for teaching classical ballet. 118 illustrations. 175pp. 5⅜ x 8½. 22036-2 Pa. $5.95

THE JUMPING FROG, Mark Twain. Revenge edition. The original story of The Celebrated Jumping Frog of Calaveras County, a hapless French translation, and Twain's hilarious "retranslation" from the French. 12 illustrations. 66pp. 5⅜ x 8½. 22686-7 Pa. $3.95

BEST REMEMBERED POEMS, Martin Gardner (ed.). The 126 poems in this superb collection of 19th- and 20th-century British and American verse range from Shelley's "To a Skylark" to the impassioned "Renascence" of Edna St. Vincent Millay and to Edward Lear's whimsical "The Owl and the Pussycat." 224pp. 5⅜ x 8½. 27165-X Pa. $4.95

COMPLETE SONNETS, William Shakespeare. Over 150 exquisite poems deal with love, friendship, the tyranny of time, beauty's evanescence, death and other themes in language of remarkable power, precision and beauty. Glossary of archaic terms. 80pp. 5³⁄₁₆ x 8¼. 26686-9 Pa. $1.00

BODIES IN A BOOKSHOP, R. T. Campbell. Challenging mystery of blackmail and murder with ingenious plot and superbly drawn characters. In the best tradition of British suspense fiction. 192pp. 5⅜ x 8½. 24720-1 Pa. $6.95

THE WIT AND HUMOR OF OSCAR WILDE, Alvin Redman (ed.). More than 1,000 ripostes, paradoxes, wisecracks: Work is the curse of the drinking classes; I can resist everything except temptation; etc. 258pp. 5⅜ x 8½. 20602-5 Pa. $5.95

SHAKESPEARE LEXICON AND QUOTATION DICTIONARY, Alexander Schmidt. Full definitions, locations, shades of meaning in every word in plays and poems. More than 50,000 exact quotations. 1,485pp. 6½ x 9¼. 2-vol. set.
Vol. 1: 22726-X Pa. $16.95
Vol. 2: 22727-8 Pa. $16.95

SELECTED POEMS, Emily Dickinson. Over 100 best-known, best-loved poems by one of America's foremost poets, reprinted from authoritative early editions. No comparable edition at this price. Index of first lines. 64pp. 5³⁄₁₆ x 8¼. 26466-1 Pa. $1.00

CELEBRATED CASES OF JUDGE DEE (DEE GOONG AN), translated by Robert van Gulik. Authentic 18th-century Chinese detective novel; Dee and associates solve three interlocked cases. Led to van Gulik's own stories with same characters. Extensive introduction. 9 illustrations. 237pp. 5⅜ x 8½. 23337-5 Pa. $6.95

THE MALLEUS MALEFICARUM OF KRAMER AND SPRENGER, translated by Montague Summers. Full text of most important witchhunter's "bible," used by both Catholics and Protestants. 278pp. 6⅝ x 10. 22802-9 Pa. $12.95

SPANISH STORIES/CUENTOS ESPAÑOLES: A Dual-Language Book, Angel Flores (ed.). Unique format offers 13 great stories in Spanish by Cervantes, Borges, others. Faithful English translations on facing pages. 352pp. 5⅜ x 8½. 25399-6 Pa. $8.95

THE CHICAGO WORLD'S FAIR OF 1893: A Photographic Record, Stanley Appelbaum (ed.). 128 rare photos show 200 buildings, Beaux Arts architecture, Midway, original Ferris Wheel, Edison's kinetoscope, more. Architectural emphasis; full text. 116pp. 8¼ x 11. 23990-X Pa. $9.95

OLD QUEENS, N.Y., IN EARLY PHOTOGRAPHS, Vincent F. Seyfried and William Asadorian. Over 160 rare photographs of Maspeth, Jamaica, Jackson Heights, and other areas. Vintage views of DeWitt Clinton mansion, 1939 World's Fair and more. Captions. 192pp. 8⅞ x 11. 26358-4 Pa. $12.95

CAPTURED BY THE INDIANS: 15 Firsthand Accounts, 1750-1870, Frederick Drimmer. Astounding true historical accounts of grisly torture, bloody conflicts, relentless pursuits, miraculous escapes and more, by people who lived to tell the tale. 384pp. 5⅜ x 8½. 24901-8 Pa. $8.95

THE WORLD'S GREAT SPEECHES, Lewis Copeland and Lawrence W. Lamm (eds.). Vast collection of 278 speeches of Greeks to 1970. Powerful and effective models; unique look at history. 842pp. 5⅜ x 8½. 20468-5 Pa. $14.95

THE BOOK OF THE SWORD, Sir Richard F. Burton. Great Victorian scholar/adventurer's eloquent, erudite history of the "queen of weapons"–from prehistory to early Roman Empire. Evolution and development of early swords, variations (sabre, broadsword, cutlass, scimitar, etc.), much more. 336pp. 6⅛ x 9¼. 25434-8 Pa. $9.95

AUTOBIOGRAPHY: The Story of My Experiments with Truth, Mohandas K. Gandhi. Boyhood, legal studies, purification, the growth of the Satyagraha (nonviolent protest) movement. Critical, inspiring work of the man responsible for the freedom of India. 480pp. 5⅜ x 8½. (USO) 24593-4 Pa. $8.95

CELTIC MYTHS AND LEGENDS, T. W. Rolleston. Masterful retelling of Irish and Welsh stories and tales. Cuchulain, King Arthur, Deirdre, the Grail, many more. First paperback edition. 58 full-page illustrations. 512pp. 5⅜ x 8½. 26507-2 Pa. $9.95

THE PRINCIPLES OF PSYCHOLOGY, William James. Famous long course complete, unabridged. Stream of thought, time perception, memory, experimental methods; great work decades ahead of its time. 94 figures. 1,391pp. 5⅜ x 8½. 2-vol. set.
Vol. I: 20381-6 Pa. $12.95
Vol. II: 20382-4 Pa. $12.95

THE WORLD AS WILL AND REPRESENTATION, Arthur Schopenhauer. Definitive English translation of Schopenhauer's life work, correcting more than 1,000 errors, omissions in earlier translations. Translated by E. F. J. Payne. Total of 1,269pp. 5⅜ x 8½. 2-vol. set. Vol. 1: 21761-2 Pa. $11.95
Vol. 2: 21762-0 Pa. $12.95

MAGIC AND MYSTERY IN TIBET, Madame Alexandra David-Neel. Experiences among lamas, magicians, sages, sorcerers, Bonpa wizards. A true psychic discovery. 32 illustrations. 321pp. 5⅜ x 8½. (USO) 22682-4 Pa. $8.95

THE EGYPTIAN BOOK OF THE DEAD, E. A. Wallis Budge. Complete reproduction of Ani's papyrus, finest ever found. Full hieroglyphic text, interlinear transliteration, word-for-word translation, smooth translation. 533pp. 6½ x 9¼.
21866-X Pa. $10.95

MATHEMATICS FOR THE NONMATHEMATICIAN, Morris Kline. Detailed, college-level treatment of mathematics in cultural and historical context, with numerous exercises. Recommended Reading Lists. Tables. Numerous figures. 641pp. 5⅜ x 8½.
24823-2 Pa. $11.95

THEORY OF WING SECTIONS: Including a Summary of Airfoil Data, Ira H. Abbott and A. E. von Doenhoff. Concise compilation of subsonic aerodynamic characteristics of NACA wing sections, plus description of theory. 350pp. of tables. 693pp. 5⅜ x 8½. 60586-8 Pa. $14.95

THE RIME OF THE ANCIENT MARINER, Gustave Doré, S. T. Coleridge. Doré's finest work; 34 plates capture moods, subtleties of poem. Flawless full-size reproductions printed on facing pages with authoritative text of poem. "Beautiful. Simply beautiful."–*Publisher's Weekly*. 77pp. 9¼ x 12. 22305-1 Pa. $6.95

NORTH AMERICAN INDIAN DESIGNS FOR ARTISTS AND CRAFTSPEOPLE, Eva Wilson. Over 360 authentic copyright-free designs adapted from Navajo blankets, Hopi pottery, Sioux buffalo hides, more. Geometrics, symbolic figures, plant and animal motifs, etc. 128pp. 8⅜ x 11. (EUK) 25341-4 Pa. $8.95

SCULPTURE: Principles and Practice, Louis Slobodkin. Step-by-step approach to clay, plaster, metals, stone; classical and modern. 253 drawings, photos. 255pp. 8⅛ x 11.
22960-2 Pa. $11.95

CATALOG OF DOVER BOOKS

THE INFLUENCE OF SEA POWER UPON HISTORY, 1660–1783, A. T. Mahan. Influential classic of naval history and tactics still used as text in war colleges. First paperback edition. 4 maps. 24 battle plans. 640pp. 5⅜ x 8½. 25509-3 Pa. $12.95

THE STORY OF THE TITANIC AS TOLD BY ITS SURVIVORS, Jack Winocour (ed.). What it was really like. Panic, despair, shocking inefficiency, and a little heroism. More thrilling than any fictional account. 26 illustrations. 320pp. 5⅜ x 8½. 20610-6 Pa. $8.95

FAIRY AND FOLK TALES OF THE IRISH PEASANTRY, William Butler Yeats (ed.). Treasury of 64 tales from the twilight world of Celtic myth and legend: "The Soul Cages," "The Kildare Pooka," "King O'Toole and his Goose," many more. Introduction and Notes by W. B. Yeats. 352pp. 5⅜ x 8½. 26941-8 Pa. $8.95

BUDDHIST MAHAYANA TEXTS, E. B. Cowell and Others (eds.). Superb, accurate translations of basic documents in Mahayana Buddhism, highly important in history of religions. The Buddha-karita of Asvaghosha, Larger Sukhavativyuha, more. 448pp. 5⅜ x 8½. 25552-2 Pa. $12.95

ONE TWO THREE . . . INFINITY: Facts and Speculations of Science, George Gamow. Great physicist's fascinating, readable overview of contemporary science: number theory, relativity, fourth dimension, entropy, genes, atomic structure, much more. 128 illustrations. Index. 352pp. 5⅜ x 8½. 25664-2 Pa. $8.95

ENGINEERING IN HISTORY, Richard Shelton Kirby, et al. Broad, nontechnical survey of history's major technological advances: birth of Greek science, industrial revolution, electricity and applied science, 20th-century automation, much more. 181 illustrations. ". . . excellent . . ."–*Isis.* Bibliography. vii + 530pp. 5⅜ x 8¼. 26412-2 Pa. $14.95

DALÍ ON MODERN ART: The Cuckolds of Antiquated Modern Art, Salvador Dalí. Influential painter skewers modern art and its practitioners. Outrageous evaluations of Picasso, Cézanne, Turner, more. 15 renderings of paintings discussed. 44 calligraphic decorations by Dalí. 96pp. 5⅜ x 8½. (USO) 29220-7 Pa. $4.95

ANTIQUE PLAYING CARDS: A Pictorial History, Henry René D'Allemagne. Over 900 elaborate, decorative images from rare playing cards (14th–20th centuries). Bacchus, death, dancing dogs, hunting scenes, royal coats of arms, players cheating, much more. 96pp. 9¼ x 12¼. 29265-7 Pa. $11.95

MAKING FURNITURE MASTERPIECES: 30 Projects with Measured Drawings, Franklin H. Gottshall. Step-by-step instructions, illustrations for constructing hand some, useful pieces, among them a Sheraton desk, Chippendale chair, Spanish desk, Queen Anne table and a William and Mary dressing mirror. 224pp. 8⅛ x 11¼. 29338-6 Pa. $13.95

THE FOSSIL BOOK: A Record of Prehistoric Life, Patricia V. Rich et al. Profusely illustrated definitive guide covers everything from single-celled organisms and dinosaurs to birds and mammals and the interplay between climate and man. Over 1,500 illustrations. 760pp. 7½ x 10⅞. 29371-8 Pa. $29.95

Prices subject to change without notice.

Available at your book dealer or write for free catalog to Dept. GI, Dover Publications, Inc., 31 East 2nd St., Mineola, N.Y. 11501. Dover publishes more than 500 books each year on science, elementary and advanced mathematics, biology, music, art, literary history, social sciences and other areas.